Master Therapists

What a wonderful book! It will draw smiles of recognition from advanced practitioners and illuminate the path for those who are training or supervising young practitioners. It is so informative and so readable that I found myself compulsively turning the pages to find out more about the carefully researched path to expertise.

SUSAN NEUFELDT, Ph.D.
UNIVERSITY OF CALIFORNIA
SANTA BARBARA

Here in Master Therapists *there is a rich and detailed account of how everyday, respected, and effective therapists view learning, the clinical process, the human condition, self-awareness and self-care, and the therapeutic alliance. This moving, inspirational, and scholarly book will appeal to all educators, novice counselors, and veteran practitioners who share a vision that becoming a master therapist is a desirable and achievable objective.*

MARK KISELICA, Ph.D.
THE COLLEGE OF NEW JERSEY

This ground-breaking book provides a thoughtful and scholarly discussion of what makes a master therapist. The level of scholarship in this book is exemplary. This work will help generations of therapists to work toward wisdom and mastery in a field that must blend art and science.

CHARLES BENIGHT, Ph.D.
UNIVERSITY OF COLORADO
COLORADO SPRINGS

Skovholt and Jennings and colleagues begin to unravel the mysteries of how master therapists think about and practice psychotherapy. Their interviews with ten master therapists provide the grist for the mill. This book provides trainees as well as practitioners a vision of where they might venture.

BRUCE WAMPOLD, Ph.D.
UNIVERSITY OF WISCONSIN
MADISON

As a teacher and *a clinician, I value the overall motive for the text—to find out who really has expertise, versus academics who just talk about it, and study their work. I really enjoyed reading this book.*

JOHN MILLER, Ph.D.
UNIVERSITY OF OREGON

Master Therapists *is an inspiring study and perceptive guidebook offering wisdom, insight, and challenges for both new and experienced practitioners, and those who train them.*

SALLY HAGE, Ph.D.
COLUMBIA UNIVERSITY

Master Therapists

Exploring Expertise in Therapy and Counseling

Thomas M. Skovholt
University of Minnesota

Len Jennings
University of St. Thomas

Boston   New York   San Francisco
Mexico City   Montreal   Toronto   London   Madrid   Munich   Paris
Hong Kong   Singapore   Tokyo   Cape Town   Sydney

Executive Editor: *Virginia Lanigan*
Series Editorial Assistant: *Robert Champagne*
Marketing Manager: *Taryn Wahlquist*
Production Administrator: *Annette Pagliaro*
Editorial Production: *Walsh & Associates, Inc.*
Composition Buyer: *Linda Cox*
Manufacturing Buyer: *Andrew Turso*
Cover Administrator: *Joel Gendron*
Text Design and Composition: *Publishers' Design and Production Services, Inc.*

For related titles and supported materials, visit our online catalog at www.ablongman.com

Between the time website information is gathered and then published, it is not unusual for some sites to have closed. Also, the transcription of URLs can result in typographical errors. The publisher would appreciate notification where these errors occur so that they may be corrected in subsequent editions.

Library of Congress Cataloging-in-Publication Data

Skovholt, Thomas M.
   Master therapists : exploring expertise in therapy and counseling / Thomas M. Skovholt, Len Jennings.
      p.   cm.
   Includes bibliographical references and index.
   ISBN 0-205-33506-3
   1. Psychotherapy.   2. Counseling.   3. Psychotherapists—Training of.
   4. Counselors—Training of.   I. Jennings, Len.   II. Title.

   RC480.5.S533 2003
   616.89'14—dc21

                                                              2003041814

Printed in the United States of America

10   9   8   7   6   5   4   3   2   08   07   06   05   04   03

To my son, David. A wonderful son who has brought so much joy to me, our family, and many others.
Tom Skovholt

To my family, Karrie, Tristan, and Emma. You are my inspiration. To my parents. Thank you for believing in me and encouraging me to be my best.
Len Jennings

To the ten master therapists who:
—graciously gave of their time for this research project.
—have helped so many suffering from emotional pain.
—inspired other therapists and counselors to reach higher in their professional development.
Tom Skovholt and Len Jennings

CONTENTS

Appendix A

Appendix B

FOREWORD

I am very pleased to write a foreword to this book. I have long been familiar with this group's research on the development of therapists and think it is a very exciting research area. These researchers have provided us with a rich description of these master therapists and how they approach therapy and life. These therapists are an inspiration to us all, if not a source of downright envy when we feel that we don't have our own lives as together as these therapists seem to.

This book is important for all of us who are therapists to read because it provides a standard by which to compare ourselves. How similar are we to the master therapists on a love of learning, self-reflectivity, maturity, interpersonal relationships, self-care, and ethics? These results provide ample opportunity for self-reflection—why am I the same or different from these people?

This book is also important for clients to read because it provides some idea of what to look for in a therapist. It underlines the idea that some therapists are better than others, and it is not always the client's fault when there is not a good match.

In addition, this book is important for those of us who train psychotherapists to read because we need to know what we are aiming for. Finally, this book is important for researchers to read. It provides a great example of a qualitative research paradigm that many will find useful for descriptive studies.

I want to spend the rest of my time in this foreword focusing on the implications of this work for the area of therapist development because this is a topic near and dear to my heart. Much of my career has been spent on issues of therapist skills and training, so these issues are of central interest for me. In my teaching, I have spent most of my energy at the level of teaching basic helping skills to beginning therapists. In my research, I have spent most of my energy trying to understand the effects of therapist interventions. I have a strong belief that therapists contribute a substantial amount to the therapy process, although we haven't been able to demonstrate that so well in our research. I also have a strong belief that our training contributes to making better therapists, although unfortunately we haven't been able to show that too well in our research either.

It is provocative to think about the idea that our training does not make a specific difference. Frank and Frank, in their 1991 book *Persuasion and Healing*, suggested that we provide therapists with a theoretical framework to believe in and build their confidence about their skills, but that it is the belief rather than the skills and the training that are important. In other words, therapists come to have confidence in themselves as therapists and take on a professional identity as therapists, but the specific skills they use are not so important.

Let me step back for a minute and put this research of master therapists into the historical context of the research on the development of therapists. Placing this research in a historical framework might help us understand where this research fits and then think about future directions for research.

The first and largest body of research on the development of therapists involved testing the effects of helping skills programs (such as those developed by Carkhuff, 1969; Ivey, 1994; and Kagan et al., 1965) to beginning therapists. This line of research was popular in the 1960s and 1970s, but there were major methodological problems with the research, and it has since pretty much died out as an area of inquiry. More recently, there has been some research about training experienced therapists to implement manualized therapies.

We also have a burgeoning body of research on therapy supervision (which is typically conceptualized as occurring on an individualized basis after basic skills training). There is research on the developmental models that describe changes in needs of supervisees across different levels of training. In addition, research has been conducted on diverse topics such as the supervisory alliance, supervisory styles, parallel process between supervision and therapy, secrets in supervision, feedback in supervision, and the effects of supervision on therapy process.

Across the years, there has also been a fair amount of research on therapist experience level, with typical results showing no effects of experience on the outcome of therapy (see, for example, Seligman, 1995). Experience level has not typically been well defined and has often been thrown in as an after thought in these studies, but it is provocative to think that the experience level of therapists does not seem to make a difference in terms of outcome. These results certainly throw doubt on our enterprise of training therapists—why bother with the extensive training programs if experience level does not make any difference? Just let beginning enthusiastic therapists do therapy.

Recently, Orlinsky and colleagues (1999) have been engaged in a major research program on the development of therapists. They have asked large numbers of therapists from around the world to take a retrospective view and think about elements of their development that were important. They have provided valuable interdisciplinary and international data about major changes therapists have gone through in their development. Therapists certainly think that their experiences in training, supervision, seeing clients, and in personal therapy influenced their growth as therapists.

And now we have this research program on the development of therapists and on master therapists. The earlier work on the development of therapists provides a framework for understanding changes therapists go through in the lifespan of their careers as therapists. The current research program on master therapists informs us about the end product of training and educates us about what therapists look like when they are experienced and competent.

What is readily apparent in this brief review of the literature is the paucity of studies on therapist development. The most recent editions of the *Handbook of Psychotherapy and Behavior Change* (Lambert, 2003) dropped the chapter on therapist training. The *Handbook of Counseling Psychology* (Brown & Lent, 2000) has always had chapters on therapist training, although the most recent edition focuses primarily on supervision during graduate school.

This leads us to future directions. First of all, I hope that this program of research on master therapists, the burgeoning literature in supervision, and Orlinsky's work on the development of therapists foretell a growing interest in research on therapist development. We need more evidence on what exactly happens in our training and the effects of the training. What methods work best to help therapists become proficient at their craft? Do therapists learn specific skills or do they just gain a sense of confidence in their abilities and learn to play the role of therapists?

We also need to do longitudinal studies of therapists. We need to investigate how input factors prior to training (personality, cognitive and emotional intelligence, early experiences with helping as both a helper and client) interact with different types of training (in basic helping skills, case conceptualization skills, case management skills, diagnostic and assessment skills, manualized treatments) and personal therapy and clinical experience to lead to the development of master therapists.

In conclusion, I urge those of us who are trainers and researchers to read this book and think critically about what it takes to produce master therapists. We keep increasing our demands on students for the number of hours of practicum, predoctoral internship, and now postdoctoral internship, but we do not have evidence that this training is important? Should we just be selecting natural therapists and giving them lots of experience seeing clients or should we be doing systematic training and supervision?

Clara E. Hill, Ph.D.
February 22, 2002

References

Brown, S. D., & Lent, R. W. (2000). *Handbook of counseling psychology*. New York: Wiley.

Carkhuff, R. R. (1969). *Human and helping relations* (Vols. 1 & 2). New York: Holt, Rinehart, & Winston.

Frank, J. D., & Frank, J. B. (1991). *Persuasion and healing: A comparative study of psychotherapy* (3rd ed.). Baltimore: Johns Hopkins University Press.

Ivey, A. E. (1994). *Intentional interviewing and counseling: Facilitating client development in a multicultural society* (3rd ed.). Pacific Grove, CA: Brooks/Cole.

Kagan, N. I., Krathwohl, D. R., Farquhar, W. W., Harvey, S., Ward, R. G., Fuller, B., Hartzell, J., & Woody, R. (1965). *Stimulated recall by videotape in exploratory studies of counseling and teaching-learning* (Research Rep. No. 24). East Lansing, MI: Bureau of Educational Research Services.

Lambert, M. J. (Ed.). (2003). *Handbook of psychotherapy and behavior change*. New York: Wiley.

Orlinsky, D., Ambuehl, H., Rønnestad, M. H., Davis, J., Gerin, P., Davis, M., Willutzki, U., Botermans, J., Dazord, A., Cierpka, M., Aapro, N., Buchheim, P., Sae, S., Davidson, C., Friis-Jorgensen, E., Joo, E., Kalmykova, E., Meyerberg, J., Northcut, T., Parks, B., Scherb, E., Schroder, T., Shefler, G., Stiwne, D., Stuart, S., Tarragona, M., Vasco, A. B., Wiseman, H., SPR Collaborative Network (1999). Development of psychotherapists: Concepts, questions, and methods of a collaborative international study. *Psychotherapy Research, 9*, 127–153.

Seligman, M. E. P. (1995). The effectiveness of psychotherapy: The *Consumer Reports* study. *American Psychologist, 50*, 965–974.

PREFACE

Searching for Mastery

The desire to become better at the elusive art and science of therapy is every new practitioner's wish. Experienced practitioners wish this, too! Unfortunately, mastery involves immersing oneself in the ambiguous complexity of human life, understanding it, and assisting growth. It is an elusive level of competence, like a mirage on the highway where the water spot on the road, seemingly right there, just keeps disappearing.

This book is an attempt to chase down the elusiveness and capture some of it. After all, the therapy process, when it is going well, can transform human life. Great study and great effort are worthy of such a noble endeavor.

The present work consists of four research studies of a group of ten master therapists who were selected for mastery by their professional peers. These are working masters, not famous ones who write and teach more than practice. The expertise research strongly supports the idea that one cannot be an expert in a domain without exhaustive experience in it. Yet, as Himelein and Putnam (2001) note, many therapy academics do not practice. The sample group studied here represent seasoned therapists drawing upon decades of experience engaging in the process of psychotherapy. With great hope, we have studied them and offer insights from them.

The goal with this work is to learn from these masters and try to elevate the general skill level of practice in our field. We are especially interested in providing helpful information for new practitioners and practitioners in training. The goal is not to glamorize the ten master therapists in our sample group; in keeping with this focus, their identity will not be revealed. Guru glamorization has not, in our view, been a fruitful route to increased competence in the therapy and counseling professions.

You may wonder: How did this book begin and evolve? In 1985, Tom Skovholt joined with Helge Rønnestad of the University of Oslo and began a study of therapist/counselor development. A sample of 100 Minnesota-based practitioners who varied by education and experience level were studied in groups of twenty. After a six-year research process, we developed a model of therapist/counselor development. This model and its applications have been published in a variety of places such as Skovholt and Rønnestad (1992, 1995). In addition to his interest in the normative development of therapists, Tom had wanted for a long time to study the extraordinary development of the master therapist. An early attempt to study this group was done by one of Tom's doctoral advisees, Kevin Harrington. In this study, Harrington (1988) utilized quantitative methodology to examine the qualities of master therapists defined as ABPP Diplomates in Psychology. Unfortunately, the method used in this study could not capture the richness of the extremely complex issue of mastery. Yet, the search to study mastery continued.

Then three topics converged. First, the qualitative methods used earlier by Skovholt and Rønnestad were embraced. Second, the use of peer nominations (Anastasi

& Urbina, 1997), and later the addition of the snowball sampling technique (Patton, 1990), ended a long, frustrating search for a valid method to find expert therapists. Finally, Len Jennings showed enthusiasm for this area as a dissertation topic. This occurred in the spring of 1994. Len was excited about the chance to meet with and interview therapists considered to be experts. As a psychologist-in-training at the time, Len wanted to harvest any wisdom he could regarding the developmental pathways of master therapists. Len also joined with Skovholt and Rønnestad to write a preliminary paper on expertise in therapy (Skovholt, Rønnestad, & Jennings, 1997).

It was Len's work that netted the group of ten master therapists identified by their peers as superior in ability and skill. Using the valid selection methods of peer nominations and the snowball sampling technique to find a group of experts took a lot of time. It was, of course, critical to the whole project. We know of only a few studies of experts in therapy where the experts were selected using methods considered to be psychometrically valid.

After Len's dissertation, the interest in studying master therapists fortunately continued with two of Tom's other University of Minnesota doctoral advisees, Mary Mullenbach and Michael Sullivan. Altogether, the ten master therapists were gracious enough to grant a grand total of nearly sixty interviews! A final project, conducted by Len Jennings, Ashley Sovereign, Nancy Bottorff, and Melissa Mussell, used Consensual Qualitative Research methods (Hill, Thompson, & Williams, 1997) to examine transcripts for ethical values embedded in the master therapists' statements.

Searching for Expertise by Chapter

In Chapter 1, Skovholt, Hanson, Jennings, and Grier examine the broad and complicated topic of expertise. In Chapter 2, they attempt to capture the essence of the literature on the prevailing view of expertise in therapy and counseling. In Chapter 3, Jennings and Skovholt's qualitative research on the personal characteristics of the ten master therapists is presented. A highlight of this research is the proposal of a three-domain model of psychotherapy expertise: Expert therapists have highly developed cognitive, emotional, and relational characteristics. In Chapter 4, Sullivan, Skovholt, and Jennings expand on the relational domain by examining the therapeutic alliances these master therapists build and maintain. In Chapter 5, Mullenbach and Skovholt further explore the emotional domain with their study on the self-care practices of these master therapists. In Chapter 6, Jennings, Sovereign, Bottorff, and Mussell present ethical values of these master therapists. In the last chapter, Skovholt, Jennings, and Mullenbach attempt to summarize and integrate all of the data in order to offer pathways to expertise taken by the ten master therapists, culminating with a portrait of the master therapist. Readers wanting to know the specific methodologies utilized in each study can find that information in Appendix A. In Appendix B, three full-length interviews, one from each of the interview studies, are offered for review.

Acknowledgments

We would like to acknowledge those who have contributed so much to this project. First and foremost, we want to offer a heartfelt thank you to the ten master therapists. Without your lifelong journey to expertise, we could not have written this book. We thank you for generously giving of your time and your feedback. For the contributors to this book, Mary Mullenbach, Michael Sullivan, Ashley Sovereign, Matthew Hanson, Nancy Bottorff, Tabitha Grier, and Melissa Mussell, a job well done! We would like to thank our colleagues and friends who supported this project through feedback and encouragement. Tom Skovholt expresses his appreciation to Rhonda. Thank you, Rhonda, for your caring, insights, understanding, and perspective! Len would especially like to recognize his wife, Karrie, for her incredible support during this project. Throughout this long process, you never faltered in your encouragement and enthusiasm. Thank you, Karrie, for your love, support, and patience!

In addition, we extend our thanks and gratitude to Ashley Sovereign for her extraordinary dedication to this project. We would like to thank our department chairs—Mary McEnvoy and Frances Lawrenz at the University of Minnesota and Skip Nolan at the University of St. Thomas—for their support of our work, Alex Dahlquist at the University of Minnesota for valuable help with manuscript preparation, and editor Virginia Lanigan at Allyn and Bacon for her patience and encouragement during the long process of completing this book and Rob Champagne of Allyn and Bacon for responsiveness to many requests. We would also like to extend our thanks to the Allyn and Bacon reviewers who provided us feedback: Carl V. Wyatt, Southwest Texas State University; Nancy Nishimiura, The University of Memphis; and John K. Miller, University of Oregon.

References

Anastasi, A., & Urbina, S. (1997). *Psychological testing* (7th ed.). Englewood Cliffs, NJ: Prentice-Hall.

Harrington, K. M. (1988). *Personal characteristics of diplomates defined as master therapists.* Unpublished doctoral dissertation, University of Minnesota.

Hill, C. E., Thompson, B. J., & Williams, E. N. (1997). A guide to conducting consensual qualitative research. *The Counseling Psychologist, 25*(4), 517–572.

Himelein, M. J., & Putnam, E. A. (2001). Work activities of academic clinical psychologists: Do they practice what they teach? *Professional Psychology: Research and Practice, 32,* 537–542.

Patton, M. Q. (1990). *Qualitative evaluation and research methods* (2nd ed.). Newbury Park, CA: Sage Publications.

Skovholt, T. M., & Rønnestad, M. H. (1992). Themes in therapist and counselor development. *Journal of Counseling and Development, 70,* 505–515.

Skovholt, T. M., & Rønnestad, M. H. (1995). *The evolving professional self: Stages and themes in therapist and counselor development.* New York: John Wiley & Sons.

Skovholt, T. M., Rønnestad, M. H., & Jennings, L. (1997). In search of expertise in counseling, psychotherapy, and professional psychology. *Educational Psychology Review, 9,* 361–369.

Master Therapists

CHAPTER

1

A Brief History of Expertise

THOMAS M. SKOVHOLT

MATTHEW HANSON

LEN JENNINGS

TABITHA GRIER

On the Shoulders of Giants

In 1675, a promising young scientist named Isaac Newton found himself in a bitter argument with the natural philosopher Robert Hooke. It seemed that Hooke, a member of the exclusive scientific Royal Society and by all accounts a man of substantial intellect and social prominence, accused Newton of stealing some of his previously published ideas concerning light and vision. At the time, Newton was already being talked about throughout European scientific circles as somewhat of a budding genius, having made staggering contributions to our understanding of gravity, mathematics (he and Leibniz would independently invent calculus), mechanics (Newton's three laws of motion would "complete" the scientific revolution begun by Copernicus), optics (he had invented the reflecting telescope and demonstrated that sunlight, when passed through a prism, is actually composed of a spectrum of colors). Hooke, however, determined to expose Newton as a charlatan—or at the very least as a plagiarist—maintained his competitive objections to the man who would later be said to have "redesigned the human mind" and "thought and tinkered his way into the mind of God" (Morrow, 1999, p. 173).

Newton was not known for his modesty or humility. Thus, prompted by members of the Royal Society, he sought to resolve the dispute with Hooke and quiet the public argument between two of England's best and brightest scientific minds. To do so, Newton composed a conciliatory letter to his rival explaining how he had happened upon, rather than stolen, his remarkable insights into the mechanics of the natural world. "If I have seen further," Newton famously revealed, "it is by standing on ye shoulders of giants."

Newton spent the better part of his life speculating on the mechanical workings of the natural world. He assembled a miraculously predictable and rational universe that operated on a deceivingly simple set of three laws held together by his universal understanding of gravitation. Mathematically precise, strikingly elegant, and grounded in his experience, Newton's ideas brought order and harmony to a universe that had before seemed chaotic and unpredictable. As Albert Einstein (as cited in Newton, 1931, p. vii) said of him, "The conceptions which he used to reduce the material of experience to order seemed to flow spontaneously from experience itself, from the beautiful experiments which he arranged in order like playthings." To paraphrase Einstein, Newton was—in all senses of the word—an expert of the highest order in his field, understanding complex phenomena with ease, and expressing his ideas about the physical world with a clarity and precision that belied the uniqueness and difficulty of the material.

Based on Experience

The above discussion of Newton and his insights also raises the question, "What is an expert?" The word itself originally comes from the Latin *experiri*, which is a derivative of the word for "experience" and translates literally as "experienced in," or "having experience of." Thus, an expert, as conceived in its original sense, is someone whose fluency of skill in a given domain is grounded in an accumulated set of experiences in that domain. One of the first known written examples of the word "expert" appeared in 1374 in Geoffrey Chaucer's *Troylus II*. In that work, Chaucer described experts as those who acquired mastery through an accumulation of relevant experiences. For example, Chaucer spoke of "experte" in love and science. For Chaucer and others in his era, expertise could be developed in a number of different domains. Though areas of expertise varied, the process of becoming an expert remained the same. One simply had to accumulate enough related experiences through which the necessary skills could be developed and perfected.

Recent biographers such as Gale Christianson have suggested that Newton's phrase "standing on ye shoulders of giants" might actually have been a caustic reference to Hooke's reported diminutive stature. Still, the phrase reflects the notion that Newton's expertise was fundamentally developed through the accumulation of experiences—both his own and his predecessors'. Understandably, this accumulation did not happen overnight or even over several nights. Rather, as Newton, Chaucer, and others throughout history have shown, the development of expertise requires that a person understand related sets of meaningful experiences. This occurs through much time and great perseverance.

Expertise: A Definition Emerges

While it is safe to assume that human history is replete with descriptions and illustrations of experts in a variety of fields, a systematic definition of the term as it is currently used did not begin to emerge until well into the twentieth century during the beginning of the cognitive science revolution. One of the very first attempts to examine what it means to be an expert came in 1966 when famous chess master Adrian de Groot investigated mastery in his field. De Groot wanted to know whether chess masters used qualitatively different mental processes during their matches than their less expert counterparts. To research his question, de Groot asked both expert and novice chess players to talk out loud as they decided their strategies and series of moves. Using recordings of these dialogues, de Groot then began analyzing the content of the players' thought processes. For example, he explored how they searched the playing board as well as the heuristics each player used to make decisions regarding the next move. De Groot strikingly found few if any differences in the actual thought processes employed by novices and experts. He failed to see anything that would indicate why experts chose the "correct" moves most of the time while novices chose the "correct" moves only some of the time (de Groot, 1966).

Undeterred, de Groot decided to explore differences in memory rather than general thinking processes between the masters and novices. For 5 seconds de Groot showed each the twentieth move of a hypothetical chess master. Then he removed the picture from sight and asked the subject to reproduce the board as accurately as possible. De Groot discovered that chess masters could reproduce the content of the board nearly perfectly, while novices struggled to accurately reproduce more than three or four pieces. These findings have served as a cornerstone for future investigations into the cognitive nature of expertise. De Groot concluded that experts were better able to meaningfully "chunk" relevant information in their domain of expertise (e.g., the formation of pieces on a chessboard), and consequently remember more and perform better than novices.

William Chase and Herbert Simon (1973) replicated and extended de Groot's results. These authors found that when chess masters were required to replicate a chessboard with no meaningful configuration, performance was substantially impaired. Using these and de Groot's results, Chase and Simon proposed that the highest levels of mastery were associated with a player's ability to retrieve appropriate moves from a large repertoire of board patterns. Chase and Simon argued that a chess master must have some 10,000 patterns stored in memory from which to draw to enhance performance. While 10,000 may seem astonishingly large, recent estimates of the number of patterns chess grand masters have in memory is larger still, ranging from 100,000 to over a million (Richman, Gobet, Staszewski, & Simon, 1996). Chase and Simon (1973) also examined expertise in several other areas like football, music, and physics. They found that expert performance in different domains requires basically the same thing: vast amounts of knowledge and a pattern-based memory system acquired over many years of experience.

In the 1980s, several studies began to emerge supporting the propositions of de Groot, Simon and Chase, and others. For example, Larkin, McDermott, Simon, and Simon (1980) showed that novice physics students typified the method of "working backward" when solving problems. Take, for instance, an example involving the calculation of velocity, which is unknown. Novices would begin such a task by applying a familiar formula, which in this case requires the calculation of acceleration, which is also unknown. So an equation is then found to solve for acceleration. And so a novice literally "chains backward" (Anderson, 1990) until a set of equations is pieced together that will allow for the solution of the problem.

In contrast, expert physicists will use similar equations but in the direct opposite order. Experts display an ability to "reason forward" (e.g., Larkin, 1981)—identifying a solution plan as part of their initial comprehension of the problem. For the velocity example given above, the expert would start with quantities that are known or can be directly computed and work from there toward the desired solution. With experts, it is as if cues or signposts for potential solutions are imbedded in the problem itself.

In a related study, Chi, Glaser, and Rees (1982) elaborated the concept of expertise. Chi and her associates found that expert physicists have more overall knowledge to help cue them in to solutions. Moreover, expert physicists also have better organized knowledge, allowing them to examine problems through the use of more complex theoretical principles. Thus, for experts knowledge may be like an impressionistic painting where individual brush strokes and colors mean little, but accumulated strokes and colors eventually produce a wonderfully coherent painting. Similarly, the individual bits of information an expert accumulates mean little. In the context of larger, more complex and meaningful patterns, however, this same information allows the expert to solve problems and analyze situations with ever-increasing levels of complexity, facility, and coherence.

So what does all this mean? What can we say distinguishes the very best from those just beginning? We know that experts and novices see the same words in a problem, chess pieces on a board, or notes on a musical score. The difference seems to be that experts see the words, pieces, or notes within a context of accumulated experience, knowledge, and wisdom. This allows the expert to see deeper, faster, further, and better than the novice. Ultimately, experts see differently—as though standing on the shoulders of giants.

The Flow of Expertise

Newton's famous phrase to Hooke neatly, if inadvertently, describes one element of expertise: To be an expert, one must accumulate experiences that deepen, improve, and extend one's vision of a given field or discipline. In Einstein's tribute to his intellectual predecessor Newton, we see another key element of expertise, one that describes what it looks like from the outside and feels like from the inside. Einstein emphasized the effortlessness with which Newton's ideas explained what previously had been unnoticed or misunderstood altogether. He told of the how Newton's wonderful and profound ideas seemed to "flow spontaneously from experience itself" (Morrow, 1999). This "effortlessness" of optimal performance has been observed empirically. It provides yet another insight into the nature of expertise.

Mihaly Csikszentmihalyi, a psychologist who has dedicated the better portion of his professional career to the study of optimal human experience and the phenomenology of enjoyment, has found that individuals can experience effortlessness (and hence happiness) in their everyday endeavors if certain environmental factors and internal conditions are sufficiently controlled or overcome (Csikszentmihalyi, 1990). Csikszentmihalyi calls this experience of spontaneous creativity and enjoyment "flow" and argues that those most experts in their respective fields, such as Newton in physics, are embodiments par excellence of this mental state. Csikszentmihalyi (1990) states:

> The metaphor of "flow" is one that many people have used to describe the sense of effortless action they feel in moments that stand out as the best in their lives. Athletes refer to it as "being in the zone," religious mystics as being in "ecstasy," artists and musicians as aesthetic rapture. Athletes, mystics, musicians, and artists do very different things when they reach flow, yet their descriptions of the experience are remarkably similar. (p. 29)

Csikszentmihalyi has worked at great lengths to encourage the notion that "flow," or a heightened sense of experience, can be enjoyed by anyone in everyday life through work, play, interaction with others, or even solitude. Yet, he also cautions that sustained "flow" only happens when there is a strong match between an individual's skills and the challenges faced. In other words, simply taking on new challenges will not produce flow. Similarly, an individual cannot experience the internal sense of effortlessness of flow if they lack the necessary skills to perform expertly.

Csikszentmihalyi (1990) argues that "flow" is not exactly synonymous with expertise. However, the resemblance of his description of "flow" is remarkably similar to descriptions of expertise.

> It ('flow') must be earned through trial-and-error experience by each individual, generation after generation. . . . It is not enough to know how to do it; one must do it, consistently, in the same way as athletes or musicians who must keep practicing what they know in theory. (p. 21)

Regardless of whether the concepts of "flow" and expertise are the same, Csikszentmihalyi's description of optimal experience is significant, particularly in how it underscores the following: (a) Excellence is a process that takes time, practice, and thorough skill development; and (b) optimal performance of expertise (called mastery) is characterized by an apparent effortlessness and grace.

The Characteristics Experts Share

Research psychologists Frensch and Sternberg (1989) say a main problem with the expertise literature is that it does not have a commonly accepted definition of expertise. Researchers Ericsson and Lehmann (1996) point out that however expertise may be defined, it is generally assumed that experts possess a unique combination of the innate talents and the motivation necessary for the rigorous training and practice required to achieve excellence. Such a position is confirmed in the definition of expertise offered by Frensch and Sternberg (1989): "the ability, acquired by practice and experience, to perform qualitatively well in a particular task domain" (p. 158). While this definition helps clarify our understanding of the construct, it is like any definition in that it reduces a complex phenomenon to a few highlights. A brief definition of the term "expertise" is like a snapshot picture: It provides some compelling information, but nowhere near as much as is contained in the real-life, organic complexity that the picture represents.

Owing to the complexity of the construct, perhaps the clearest picture of expertise comes from the numerous research psychologists since the 1970s who have devoted considerable time and energy describing the nuances of expertise. Among these researchers (e.g., Glaser & Chi, 1988), there seems to be an ever-growing consensus that experts can be identified by a limited set of well-studied and established characteristics that are generalizable across different domains. In the overview of the book *The Nature of Expertise* (Chi, Glaser, & Farr, 1988), Glaser and Chi outlined seven characteristics of expert performers:

1. *Experts excel mainly in their own domain.* There is little empirical evidence that experts in one domain can achieve expertise in another nonrelated domains. In fact, the available research indicates just the opposite. Voss and Post (1988), for example, revealed through their analysis that expert chemists solved political science problems no better than novices, discussing the salient issues in concrete, basic terms rather than in the detailed, abstract terms that they used in solving a chemical problem regarding moles, molecules, and the periodic table of elements.

Glaser and Chi (1988) reasoned that the simplest explanation for expertise is a high degree of specialized knowledge, typically obtained through years of exposure and study. Expert physicians, for example, are capable diagnosticians largely because of the volume of information that they have studied and retained over years of coursework, residency, and practice. It should be pointed out, however, that this characteristic of expertise is not limited to academia nor does it require advanced degrees. For example, expert taxi cab drivers can generate secondary or tertiary routes quickly while driving, while novice drivers tend to stick to one route (Chase, 1983).

2. *Experts perceive large meaningful patterns in their domain.* This characteristic refers to experts' ability to see larger, global patterns where less experienced individuals might see fewer meaningful patterns or perhaps just chaos. This is related to the "chunking" phenomenon described earlier in relation to chess masters. Experts in psychological assessment, for example, can often see patterns and profiles in personality inventories that are often overlooked by beginning therapists and graduate students. This same ability to see in data what novices may overlook has also been observed in architects (Akin, 1980), radiologists (Lesgold, Rubinson, Feltovich, Glaser, Klopfer, & Wang, 1988), and programmers (McKeithen, Reitman, Reuter, & Hirtle, 1981). More than anything, this characteristic indicates experts' ability to organize large amounts of information seamlessly, sometimes as though seeing information that is absent to the untrained eye.

3. *Experts are faster than novices at performing the skills of their domain.* Glaser and Chi (1988) suggest that experts' greater fluency in completing tasks depends on the task. For manual tasks such as typing, repetitive factory work, and craftsmanship, experts' speed is generally correlated with the amount of time spent practicing the task. For example, expert potters can create their pottery more quickly, and usually more artistically, than can novices. This is due to the number of years spent learning their craft—the different clays, wheel speeds, shaping instruments.

In analytical areas that require more reasoning than dexterity, the most likely explanation for experts' increased speed is their ability to see larger, meaningful patterns rather than disparate, isolated pieces of data. By seeing their domain in "chunks," experts save the time required by novices to piece information together.

4. *Experts have superior memory.* In the modern film classic *Amadeus,* Mozart's "adversary" Salieri presents the emperor of Austria with an honorary piece of music to welcome a young and irreverent Mozart to the Austrian palace. According to the film (Zaentz & Forman, 1984), the emperor was himself a novice pianist and asked Salieri's permission to play the new piece as Mozart entered the palace chambers. Salieri agreed, and the emperor set about fumbling his way through the music as the young prodigy came to greet the palace notables. After he very roughly completed playing the entrance march, the emperor presented Mozart with the music score. "Keep it if you'd like, sire. It's already in here," Mozart replied, pointing to his head. The incredulous and emphatic emperor replied to the young composer, "With one listening?" and challenged Mozart to show the court his virtuosity. Without missing a note, young Mozart replayed the piece note for note without once looking at the score and even radically embellished the work, humiliating Salieri in front of those present.

Mozart was an expert in his field and arguably the greatest composer in history. While it is possible that he was blessed with a photographic memory that greatly enhanced his powers of recall, cognitive researchers have found that experts do not necessarily possess larger short-term memories than other people. Rather, experts function in their domains with "automaticity," or as though the skills required to excel come forth automatically, without a great deal of effort or thought. This occurs through thousands of hours of practice. Because experts' skills are so automatic, they have greater mental resources freed up for storage, retrieval, or other executive mental functions.

5. *Experts see and represent a problem in their domain at a deeper (more principled) level than novices.* Research on this topic (e.g., Chi, Feltovich, & Glaser, 1981) has shown that while both experts and novices tend to organize problems in similar conceptual categories, novices' categories tend to be based on more superficial features while experts' tend to be based on meaningful, solution-based features. For example, Chi et al. (1981) found that expert physicists used principles of mechanics to organize a group of physics problems, while novices categorized the same problems using a less central ordering scheme.

6. *Experts spend a great deal of time analyzing a problem qualitatively.* One of the more robust findings in the expertise literature concerns the differences observed between experts' and novices' problem-solving strategies. From many fields like physics and psychology, researchers have found that experts tend to spend greater amounts of time than novices at the beginning of a problem-solving situation, trying to understand a problem from multiple viewpoints before attempting to implement a solution. Anecdotally, maybe they use the time to "really" understand the problem—understand in terms of depth, complexity, detail, and thoroughness.

In the field of diagnostic psychology, for example, researchers such as Hill and Ridley (2001) at Indiana University have shown that those mental health clinicians who arrive at their diagnostic impressions later in the therapy process are more accurate in their diagnoses than those who arrive at diagnoses earlier. Other researchers have spent time specifically studying the mental processes of this incubation period and have revealed some interesting findings. Paige and Simon (1966), for instance, discovered that experts, when faced with a problem, will start by quickly building mental representations of the essential elements of the problem. In so doing, experts not only define the problem's key aspects, but also identify the qualities of the problem from which potential solutions can be abstracted and ultimately implemented. Paige and Simon suggest that experts' abilities to quickly conceptualize a problem and its inherent solutions reduce the amount of time they spend on unreasonable or untenable solutions.

To illustrate the manner by which experts add time-saving constraints to their problem solutions, Voss and Post (1988) asked political scientists specializing in the Soviet Union to articulate what they would do (imagining themselves as Soviet Ministers of Agriculture) if crop productivity had been low for several consecutive years. As opposed to beginning political scientists, the experts generally used about 25 percent of their solution to elaborate on the initial problem, identifying genuine concerns that might limit solutions. This amount of time spent by experts eliminating unrealistic options stands in stark contrast to novices who spent about 1 percent of their solution time doing the same thing. Experts have found a way to separate the possible from the not possible, thereby freeing up their time and energy for solutions that may work.

7. *Experts have strong self-monitoring skills.* Experts seem to have better professional self-identities regarding their skill level. For instance, experts are generally more apt than novices to know the limits of their knowledge about a problem that they are facing, and they tend to be better judges about the difficulty of the problem they are attempting to solve. Expert therapists, for example, will likely see very quickly how long a certain type of client may require treatment, while a novice practicum student often has little idea about the specifics of the treatment needed.

According to Glaser and Chi (1988), experts' ability to accurately predict problem difficulty is ultimately related to experts' greater knowledge base about a given domain. This is used to increase efficiency and accuracy. Experts, by accurately assessing problem difficulty, have the advantage of knowing how much time they need to allocate to different aspects to complete the task.

Can Anyone Be an Expert?

While the above discussion paints a fairly clear picture of what an expert looks like, it fails to answer the question of how one goes about developing expertise. Inherent in the question of how expertise develops, is another: Who can be an expert? Early ideas of expertise, after the concept had begun to separate itself from a pure link with experience, suggested that it was a generalized phenomenon closely related to notions of intelligence and analytical aptitude (Glaser & Chi, 1988). That is, if someone were highly intelligent or expert in one domain, the intelligence and expertise would carry over to other domains. However, extensive research in the expertise literature has not supported this claim. Instead, as illustrated by the expert characteristics given by Glaser and Chi above, researchers now believe that the development of expertise is "domain specific" (Chi, Glaser, & Farr, 1988): Experts are experts because they have a great deal of knowledge about, and skills within a specific domain.

In many ways this notion regarding the development of expertise demystifies the concept of expertise and some of the more prejudicial ideas about the process of acquiring such an elite designation. It also begs the following question: Can anyone become an expert, or do those who obtain the status of expert in their field harbor special characteristics that place them head and shoulders above the average person?

In the early 1980s, William Chase set out to answer just such a question. Chase studied exceptional ability in the area of memory using traditional memory tests in which the average college student is capable of remembering about eight digits. He then trained two "normal people" to remember and repeat random numbers from these memory tests (Chi, Glaser, & Farr, 1988), using a technique similar to the "chunking" technique used by master chess players described earlier. (Chase taught the subjects to place numbers into groups of three or four using the format of running times—e.g., 4 minutes and 55.2 seconds. He then taught subjects to use higher order chunks to remember long sequences of each of these three- or four-number grouped chunks). After eight months of practice, Chase's best subject could repeat 80 numbers (Chase, 1983).

In the end, Chase's "experts" demonstrated near photographic memory when it came to numbers. Interestingly, however, such "expertise of memory" did not carry over when it came to letters. The importance of this work is demonstrated with the following quote: "Chase found that what appears to be very exceptional, perhaps a photographic memory, could be obtained presumably by any normal person whose practice was sustained over many days and who applied a systematic method of coding information into memory" (Posner, 1988, p. xxx).

In a similar manner, Simon and Gilmartin (1973) reminded expertise researchers that master chess players spent anywhere from 10,000 to 20,000 hours staring at chess positions in an effort to acquire some 50,000 different patterns that can be quickly recalled and utilized during competition. As Posner put it: "To put this in perspective, the student who spends 40 hours a week for 33 weeks spends 1,320 hours a year studying. Imagine spending more than 10 years in college studying one subject, chess, and you get some appreciation of the time commitment of master-level players" (Posner, 1988, pp. xxi–xxii).

While expertise by definition implies exceptional performance or superior ability, it does not mean that the development of expertise is limited to those with superior genetic stock or God-given prowess. To become an expert, one does not have to be gifted or talented or possess some sort of inherent intellectual inclination toward superior performance. The evidence suggests that the ordinary person can achieve expertise. However, the ordinary person must invest extraordinary amounts of time, practice, and commitment to develop expertise. To paraphrase Thomas Edison, expertise is 99 percent perspiration and 1 percent inspiration. How does someone begin this extraordinary commitment?

The Development of Expertise

In 1986, Hubert Dreyfus, a philosopher, and brother Stuart, a computer scientist, both professors at the University of California, Berkeley, proposed a model of expertise development in response to the focus and fervor over the "expert" computer systems developed and used in corporate training. The Dreyfuses argue that such "expert" systems are inherently different than the types of expertise exhibited by human beings and further suggest that a computer's expertise will never be able to mimic the intuition observed in human experts in fields as diverse as chicken "sexing" (being able to tell the difference between male and female chicks) and forestry.

The Dreyfuses point out that humans and computers operate fundamentally differently and hence develop expertise in two ultimately nonconverging fashions. Humans, the Dreyfuses point out, develop a new skill by learning and carrying out its constituent rules and regulations. In baseball, for example, a pitcher must first learn about balls and strikes, batters, and position players before attempting to win a ball game. However, Cy Young Award-winning pitchers rarely if ever stop to analyze baseball's rules while pitching in an important game. Rather, an expert pitcher or catcher will review an entire situation at once and intuitively know which type of pitch will work in certain fielding situations and with certain hitters. They can then focus at a deeper level on "simply" throwing the right pitch.

In contrast, a computer processes bits of information one piece at a time—albeit in a remarkably fast manner—based upon the rules and orders it was given, before outputting a solution. A computer, for all its uses and facility in processing orders, cannot learn, discard rules on its own, or think holistically or intuitively. The best that a computer might be able to achieve, at least according to the Dreyfuses, is a kind of "competence" characterized by speed and the creativity and ingenuity of its programmers.

The Dreyfuses (1986) posit that humans move through the following five stages on their way to expert performance in a domain: novice, advanced beginner, competent, proficient, and expert. In their model, the Dreyfuses propose that an individual moves from an "objective and context free" set of principles for governing their reasoning to a set of "subjective and contextual cues" that are used in determining decisions. Each stage is marked by a progression from more external to more internal mechanisms or decision rules for guiding behavior.

The Dreyfuses (1986) describe the novice stage as one in which the beginner may adhere to rules with little regard for the overall situation in which they occur:

> The beginning student wants to do a good job, but lacking any coherent sense of overall task he judges his performance mainly by how well he follows learned rules. . . . Like the training wheels on a child's first bicycle, these first rules allow the accumulation of experience, but soon they must be put aside to proceed. (p. 22)

In the field of therapy and counseling this might be likened to students who cling tightly to one counseling theory with little regard for the particular issues presented by their clients. Instead of operating from "client databases," the novices operate from their a priori databases of counseling theory and may adhere to the guidelines of a theory with little regard for the contextual elements of their clients. As students move to stage two—advanced beginner—they are better able to integrate the contextual elements of their clients with their "a priori theoretical database" (Fook, Ryan, & Hawkins, 1997, p. 401).

In the competence stage ". . . people learn, or are taught, to adopt a hierarchical procedure of decision-making" (Dreyfus & Dreyfus, 1986, p. 24). In therapy and counseling, this is the stage when practitioners begin to move away from rigid adherence to textbook theory. Rather, the competent practitioner will instead integrate knowledge of theory with experience as a practitioner to determine which set of factors is important to examine in the counseling/therapy work. "In general, the competent performer with a goal in mind sees a situation as a set of facts" (Dreyfus & Dreyfus, 1986, p. 24), and does not, like the novice, choose a course of action based on only objective, context-free rules (Dreyfus & Dreyfus, 1986).

The next stage, proficiency, is marked by the "intuition" experts in a domain seems to share. As the Dreyfuses state, "The two highest levels of skill . . . are characterized by a rapid, fluid, involved kind of behavior that bears no apparent similarity to the slow, detached reasoning of the problem-solving process" (p. 27). In essence, the Dreyfuses argue that the proficiency stage is characterized by "holistic similarity recognition," or the "ability to use patterns without decomposing them into component features" (p. 28). According to the Dreyfuses, the expert's ability to holistically and effortlessly understand and use patterns and situations is the reason why artificial intelligence programs will never adequately simulate human performance at the highest cognitive levels: Computers cannot intuit like humans can. Computer programs, no matter how quick and efficient, will never be able to linger in the "deep situational involvement" that enables humans to—with adequate training and discipline—eventually ascend beyond the "ground rules" into new and uncharted territories.

The final stage, expertise, is characterized by growth through all the other stages and the accumulated experience of reflective practice. In this stage, one can effortlessly operate from a mature understanding based on experience and critical reflection (Dreyfus & Dreyfus, 1986). To still use the example of the developing counselor, one who has reached the expert level has acquired what Skovholt and Rønnestad (1995) called accumulated wisdom. At this stage the counselor has long since let go of externalized textbook theories of counseling to guide his or her actions and is instead operating from an internal, personalized theory of counseling developed from years of practice, experience, reflection, and intuition.

Other models of expertise development, in addition to the Dreyfuses' five-stage model, have been offered by different researchers. Most, however, seem to draw fairly similar conclusions. One such model was developed by Schmidt, Norman, and Boshuizen (1992), who used clinical decision-making theory as a basis for articulating a four-stage novice to expert model. A key aspect of the model is the "hierarchical decision making" (p. 24) concept introduced in Dreyfus and Dreyfus' (1986) competence stage. Much like the Dreyfuses model, the Schimidt et al. model postulates that the difference between the novice and expert stages is knowledge acquisition: Earlier stages are characterized by the acquisition of knowledge primarily through academics sources, while the expert stages are characterized by knowledge that becomes more "clinically usable" and more "case specific" (Locke & Covell, 1997, p. 242). The person at the expert stage operates in the realm of "accumulated knowledge" and may appear to function in a "highly idiosyncratic" (Locke & Covell, 1997, p. 242) manner suggesting a unique and creative integration of knowledge and skills.

The Dreyfuses and Schmidt et al. models posit a similar conceptual progression of novice to expert. The novice operates from academic, theoretical knowledge. The expert works from accumulated wisdom and experience. In essence, based upon the brief summary of the Schmidt et al. model found in Locke and Covell (1997), the major difference between these two models seems to be language. The clinical decision-making model—which evolves around the development of knowledge structures—is highly cognitive and uses terms such as templates and scripts (Locke & Covell, 1997), while the Dreyfus and Dreyfus model uses the language of intuition. Language aside, the models are highly consistent in their view of expertise development.

Human Judgment and Decision Making

Another way to understand expertise and mastery is to examine human judgment and decision-making research. Kenneth Hammond (2000a), professor emeritus of psychology at the University of Colorado, attempted to understand human judgment and decision making by integrating six theories of human decision making: Decision Theory, Behavioral Decision Theory, Psychological Decision Theory, Social Judgment Theory, Information Integration Theory, and Attribution Theory. By integrating these six approaches Hammond attempted to reconcile the more "ephemeral" truths of wisdom and common sense with the study of cognition and the scientific method. Much of Hammond's work preceded that of Dreyfus and Dreyfus and their focus on intuition as a valid concept in the study of expertise.

The focus of Hammond's work was not so much the development of expertise as it was decision making. His work has implications for improving decision-making processes and includes language and ideas that closely approximate the work of expertise scholars. For instance, Hammond recognized that many decision-making approaches clearly illustrated methods for enhancing the judgments of the novice: "Whether or not these methods help decision makers think better, almost everyone claims that such methods make decision makers wiser about their particular problem . . ." (2000b, p. 107). Hammond's integrative review shows that decision-making theories help decision makers: (a) Decide what information is important and not important for decision making and (b) discern what information is still needed to reach an optimal conclusion. According to Hammond, these aspects represent the essence of the decision-making processes, in that they force the decision maker to create order from previous uncertainty.

In many ways, this work is a precursor to the work of Dreyfus and Dreyfus and other studies of expertise that examine such concepts as "intuition," "accumulated wisdom," and "domain-specific knowledge." In addition, Hammond's discussion of decision making in the realm of uncertainty foreshadows an important part of the development of expertise within the fields of therapy and counseling. For therapy and counseling practitioners, working with clients is an example par excellence of decision making in the face of complex ambiguity. Here one's expertise is based on adaptability in a world of novel situations and minimal structure.

"Routine" versus "Adaptive" Expertise

To better understand individuals who can solve very challenging problems, Holyoak (1991) made a distinction between "routine" and "adaptive" experts. Holyoak described routine expertise in terms of having the ability "to solve familiar types of problems quickly and accurately" (p. 310), but having only limited ability in applying knowledge to new problems. In contrast, adaptive experts use their expert knowledge for solving novel problems or situations.

Holyoak (1991) suggests that adaptive expertise ultimately develops from a "deeper conceptual understanding" (p. 310) of knowledge than routine expertise and is facilitated by certain conditions. First, Holyoak asserts that adaptive expertise seems to develop when individuals are confronted with the variable or unpredictable nature of ill-structured problems. In addition, deeper understanding is facilitated when there is no direct pressure to accomplish a goal while potential solutions are freely explored: "Understanding can result from sensitivity to internally generated feedback, such as surprise at a predictive failure, perplexity at noticing alternative explanations for phenomenon, and dis-coordination due to lack of explanatory links between pieces of knowledge that apparently should be related"(p. 310).

Other conditions facilitating deep understanding include encouragement to move to a deeper level and the motivation to explain the task to others. In essence, adaptive expertise is more easily developed when learning focuses on "understanding" as opposed to "solving." According to Holyoak (1991), learning for the purpose of understanding is more open for exploration of varied alternatives, allowing the learner to adapt a new path as needed.

Holyoak (1991) has posited that the study of expertise has entered a new phase characterized by an integrated, holistic perspective. This new phase of research has been described in terms of "symbolic connectionism" because of its emphasis on viewing problem solutions to be the integration of simultaneously activated, simpler cognitive schemas or networks. Scholars such as Locke and Covell (1997) have further asserted that this new generation of studies is particularly helpful in deriving inferences from complex sets of relational knowledge. Such a perspective has clear significance for the study of expertise in the "softer" fields such as counseling and psychotherapy that are easier to intuitively "understand" than they are to "solve" (using Holyoak's aforementioned distinction).

With this rubric of symbolic connectionism, expertise development, as Locke and Covell (1997) have illustrated, can be likened to the well-studied intellectual development of students through the college years: As undergraduates progress through their academic careers, they move from the memorization of relevant facts (a study strategy frequently observed in high school students and first-year undergraduates) to the synthesis and understanding of the whole picture (which is characteristic of college seniors and graduate students). In a similar manner, symbolic connectionism posits that experts distinguish themselves with their ability to integrate new knowledge with old, and synthesize complex sets of data into a relational whole.

Emotional Expertise

The distinction offered by Holyoak (1991) between adaptive and routine expertise describes the distinction between ill-structured and well-defined problem areas. With ill-structured problems that lack a clear or correct answer, the challenge is learning how to develop the ability to adapt and then perform. In contrast, well-defined problems are characterized by an agreed upon solution and search protocol. The latter of these two types of problems may be more appropriate for the development of routine expertise.

As mentioned previously, this adaptive view of expertise is particularly relevant when understanding the development of expert performance in ambiguous and ill-structured fields such as therapy and counseling. However, even the "relational" or emotional domains suggested by "symbolic connectionism" are obscured by the reliance with this model of expertise on human thought and cognition. Holyoak (1991) himself has admitted that is it is unclear where domains concerning human relationships or emotion are represented in his approach (to defining expertise) or any of the other approaches to expertise.

Some progress has been made in Goleman's (1995) work on emotional intelligence. Goleman notes that emotionally intelligent individuals know how to express themselves at the right level, at the right time, while ideally striving to enhance long-term goals versus achieving the sometimes reckless satisfaction of an immediate emotional reaction. Goleman's work withstanding, major areas in which expert therapists might be expected to excel—such as building relationships and having a high degree of emotional maturity—have been virtually overlooked by previous models of expertise development.

To address this shortcoming in the literature, we have previously proposed a model of expertise for master therapists (which will be discussed in more detail in Chapters 3 and 7) that specifically addresses three domains of knowledge—Cognitive (C), Emotional (E), and Relational (R)—vital to the success or failure of therapists and counselors. This model suggests that one must develop expertise in all three areas to reach the level of master therapist. The CER model appears to be among the first therapist expertise models to discuss domains such as emotional or relational expertise, and represents a necessary first step in discovering the potential pathways by which therapists and counselors achieve their unique form of expertise in such a highly ambiguous field. Next we will explore other models of expertise found in the therapy and counseling literature.

References

Akin, O. (1980). *Models of architectural knowledge.* London: Pion.

Anderson, J. R. (1990). *Cognitive psychology and its implications.* New York: W. H. Freeman and Co.

Chase, W. G. (1983). Spatial representations of taxi drivers. In D. R. Rogers & J. H. Slobada (Eds.), *Acquisition of symbolic skills* (pp. 391–405). New York: Plenum.

Chase, W. G., & Simon, H. A. (1973). The mind's eye in chess. In W. G. Chase (Ed.), *Visual information processing* (pp. 215–281). New York: Academic Press.

Chi, M. T. H., Feltovich, P. J., & Glaser, R. (1981). Categorization and representation of physics problems by experts and novices. *Cognitive Science, 5,* 121–125.

Chi, M. T. H., Glaser, R., & Farr, M. J. (Eds.). (1988). *The nature of expertise.* Hillsdale, NJ: Lawrence Erlbaum Associates.

Chi, M. T. H., Glaser, R., & Rees, E., (1982). Expertise in problem solving. In R. J. Sternberg (Ed.), *Advances in the psychology of human intelligence* (Vol. 1, pp. 1–75). Hillsdale, NJ: Lawrence Erlbaum Associates.

Christianson, G. E. (1996). *Isaac Newton and the scientific revolution.* London: Oxford University Press.

Csikszentmihalyi, M. (1990). *Flow: The psychology of optimal experience.* New York: Harper & Row.

De Groot, A. D. (1966). Perception and memory versus thought. In B. Kleinmuntz (Ed.), *Problem solving research, methods and theory* (pp. 19–50). New York: Wiley.

Dreyfus, H. L., & Dreyfus, S. E. (1986). *Mind over machine.* New York: Free Press.

Ericsson, K. A., & Lehmann, A. C. (1996). Expert and exceptional performance: Evidence of maximal adaptation to task constraints. *Annual Review of Psychology, 47,* 273–305.

Fook, J., Ryan, M., & Hawkins, L. (1997). Towards a theory of social work expertise. *British Journal of Social Work, 27,* 399–417.

Frensch, R. A., & Sternberg, R. J. (1989). Expertise and intelligent thinking: When is it worse to know better? In R. J. Sternberg (Ed.), *Advances in the psychology of human intelligence* (Vol. 5, pp. 157–188). Hillsdale, NJ: Lawrence Erlbaum Associates.

Glaser, R., & Chi, M. T. H. (1988). Overview. In M. T. H. Chi, R. Glaser, & M. J. Farr (Eds.), *The nature of expertise.* Hillsdale, NJ: Lawrence Erlbaum Associates.

Goleman, D. (1995). *Emotional intelligence.* New York: Bantam Books.

Hammond, K. R. (2000a). Coherence and correspondence theories in judgment and decision making. In T. Connelly & H. Arkes (Eds.), *Judgment and decision making: An interdisciplinary reader* (pp. 53–65). New York: Cambridge University Press.

Hammond, K. R. (2000b). *Judgments under stress.* New York: Oxford University Press.

Hill, C. L., & Ridley, C. R. (2001). Diagnostic decision-making: Do counselors delay final judgments? *Journal of Counseling & Development, 79*(1), 98–118.

Holyoak, K. J. (1991). Symbolic connectionism: Toward third-generation theories of expertise. In K. A. Ericsson & J. Smith (Eds.), *Toward a general theory of expertise: Prospects and limits* (pp. 301–335). New York: Cambridge University Press.

Larkin, J. (1981). Enriching formal knowledge: A model for learning to solve textbook physics problems. In J. R. Anderson (Ed.), *Cognitive skills and their acquisition.* Hillsdale, NJ: Lawrence Erlbaum Associates.

Larkin, J. H., McDermott J., Simon, D. P., & Simon, H. A. (1980). Expert and novice performance in solving physics problems. *Science, 208,* 1335–1342.

Lesgold, A., Rubinson, H., Feltovich, P., Glaser, R., Klopfer, D., & Wang, Y. (1988). Expertise in a complex skill: Diagnosing X-ray pictures. In M. T. H. Chi, R. Glaser, & M. J. Farr (Eds.), *The nature of expertise* (pp. 311–342). Hillsdale, NJ: Lawrence Erlbaum Associates.

Locke, T. F., & Covell, A. J. (1997). Characterizing expert psychologist behavior: Implications from selected expertise literature. *Educational Psychology Review, 9*(3), 239–249.

McKeithen, K. B., Reitman, J. S., Reuter, H. H., & Hirtle, S. C. (1981). Knowledge organization and skill differences in computer programmers. *Cognitive Psychology, 13,* 307–325.

Morrow, L. (1999, December 31). The most important people of the millennium. *Time, 173–176.*

Newton, I. (1931). *Opticks: or a treatise of the reflections, refractions, inflections, and colours of light.* New York: McGraw-Hill.

Paige, J. M., & Simon, H. A. (1966). Cognitive processes in solving algebra word problems. In P. Kleinmuntz (Ed.), *Problem solving* (pp. 119–151). New York: Wiley.

Posner, M. (1988). Introduction: What is it to be an expert. In M. T. H. Chi, R. Glaser, & M. J. Farr, (Eds.), *The nature of expertise.* Hillsdale, NJ: Lawrence Erlbaum Associates.

Richman, H. B., Gobet, F., Staszewski, J. J., & Simon, H. A. (1996). Perceptual and memory processes in the acquisition of expert performance: The EPAM model. In K. A. Ericsson (Ed.), *The road to excellence: The acquisition of expert performance in the arts and sciences, sports, and games* (pp. 167–187). Hillsdale, NJ: Lawrence Erlbaum Associates.

Schmidt, H. G., Norman, G. R., & Boshuizen, H. P. (1992). A cognitive perspective on medical expertise: Theory and implications. *Academic Medicine, 65*(10), 611–621.

Simon, H. A., & Gilmartin, K. (1973). A simulation of memory for chess positions. *Cognitive Psychology, 5,* 29–46.

Skovholt, T. M., & Rønnestad, M. H. (1995). *The evolving professional self: Stages and themes in therapist and counselor development.* New York: Wiley.

Voss, J. F., & Post, T. A. (1988). On the solving of ill-structured problems. In M. T. H. Chi, R. Glaser, & M. J. Farr (Eds.), *The nature of expertise* (pp. 261–285). Hillsdale, NJ: Lawrence Erlbaum Associates.

Zaentz, S. (Producer), & Forman, M. (Director). (1984). *Amadeus* [Film]. (Available from Warner Home Video. A Time Warner Entertainment Company. 4000 Warner Boulevard, Burbank, CA 91522).

2

Expertise in Therapy and Counseling

THOMAS M. SKOVHOLT

MATTHEW HANSON

LEN JENNINGS

TABITHA GRIER

In Chapter 1, we explored expertise in a broad sense, as a construct that can transcend the boundaries between disciplines, performance areas, and career fields. This broad-based approach mirrors the expertise literature, which has sought the common threads of experts across fields.

While this approach serves a valuable purpose in finding the foundation for human excellence and superior achievement, a question remains. Do the corollaries and descriptors of expertise outlined thus far apply to therapists and counselors. Some (e.g., Dawes, 1994) have suggested that achieving expertise in this "ill-structured" field is close to impossible. How, such authors question, can a field such as therapy—with its ambiguities and subjective interpretations—produce experts in the same way that "hard sciences" such as physics or mathematics can?

Skeptics point to the fact that there is no "gold standard" or agreed upon definition of "expert" or "master" therapist or generally recognized process by which one achieves expertise in this field. Further skepticism seems warranted when authors and researchers inadvertently or even consciously equate experience with expertise. While there appears to be some correlation between these two constructs, experience and expertise are certainly distinct, as practitioners and students of the profession can surely attest. We can all think of anecdotal examples where highly experienced professionals never reach "expert" status.

The relationship between experience and expertise in the mental health professions has received little research attention. One notable exception was a study published by Orlinsky et al. (1999), who used survey research to explore the relationship between experience and expertise in the context of therapists' perceptions of their own professional development. The huge sample ($n = 3,958$) was international, and participants ranged in age from 22 to 90. The sample included psychologists, psychiatrists, and people in other medical and mental health-related fields. The authors defined development as ". . . attainment of increasing expertise in a task that therapists perceive as highly challenging in its complexity" (p. 204), and they examined three major questions: (a) What is the relationship between perceived therapeutic mastery and level of professional expertise? (b) What is the relationship between currently experienced growth and level of professional experience? and (c) What is the relationship between a therapist's perceived mastery and currently experienced growth as a therapist?" (p. 204).

The researchers found that perceived mastery was positively related to therapists' years in practice. However, growth seemed to occur at the same level regardless of years in therapy, with novices and veterans reporting roughly the same amounts of growth. In addition, Orlinsky et al. (1999) found a moderate but consistent positive correlation between perceived mastery and currently experienced growth.

This study does have some limitations that make accurate interpretation of the results difficult. Notably, therapists' perceptions were not contrasted with any objective measures of performance and relied exclusively on self-report. With this limitation in mind, Orlinsky et al.'s (1999) study shows that self-reported feelings of mastery seem to indicate a sense of efficacy or self-confidence regarding one's therapeutic work.

While confidence or efficacy may be necessary parts of mastery, they are clearly not synonymous. In fact, Bernard and Goodyear (1998) state that the constructs of expertise and confidence are often independent. These authors note that experience is often a conduit for an inflated sense of confidence apart from mastery and use the example of "paraprofessional" counselors who feel highly competent and qualified to perform difficult tasks although they have had little formal training.

Still, one major contribution of the Orlinsky et al. (1999) study is that the authors move away from defining expertise exclusively in terms of years of experience. In their study the authors attempt to define mastery, through their perceived mastery scale, in the traditional sense of master craftsperson. Orlinsky et al. attempt to put forth a definition of therapeutic expertise, which takes into account an understanding of in vivo therapeutic dynamics with precision and skill. Their definition includes: ". . . understanding . . . what happens moment-by-moment during therapy sessions, [having] precision, subtlety, and finesse in therapeutic work, and [the] ability to guide the development of other psychotherapists"(p. 211).

The concepts in this definition such as "subtlety," "finesse," and "precision" remain somewhat vague. In addition, the methods used by these authors to study therapists' mastery may not fully capture the construct. As several authors have shown (e.g., Dreyfus & Dreyfus, 1986; Jennings & Skovholt, 1999), expertise in an ambiguous field like therapy and counseling is likely to be highly related to the ability to critically reflect on and learn from experience. In contrast, perceived expertise seems to be more reflective of confidence. Thus, although the authors were able to distinguish therapeutic expertise from experience, the connection between expertise and self-confidence needs further exploration.

Human Nature as Complex Ambiguity

The complex ambiguity of the helping professions certainly contributes to the ill-defined nature of acquiring expertise in these fields. Many of these fields struggle when trying to clearly distinguish experts from others. Fook, Ryan, and Hawkins (1997) explored this topic of expertise in social work. Fook and her colleagues conducted a qualitative study of thirty experienced social workers to identify characteristics of expertise in that field. In many regards, the finding presented by Fook et al. resembles the findings of other expertise researchers. For example, Fook and colleagues found that social work "experts" had confidence in their professional identity as social workers. These experienced social workers also displayed the ability to deal with complexity and quickly prioritize relevant factors when working with clients. In addition, Fook found that experts tended to have an awareness of the practical constraints involved in their cases and used minimal "formal" theory in their decision-making process.

Fook and her colleagues also concluded, however, that expertise within social work is particularly difficult to define and standardize because it occurs within changeable, unpredictable situations and depends on personal values and ideologies. Like other expertise researchers, the authors also disputed the idea of a universal expertise, and instead suggested that expertise is domain specific.

Fook and her colleagues used the Dreyfuses' (1986) model of expertise to guide their thinking, culling from that model the notion that "the learner progresses from detached abstract and consciously analytic behavior in a situation, to involved, skilled behavior which is based on unconscious and intuitive recognition of similarities with past experiences" (p. 401). Using the Dreyfuses' model, Fook and colleagues suggest that experts seemed to fit into one of three areas: (a) those who had a clear sense of the contextual "rules" of a particular situation versus more "context-free" rules; (b) those who were confident in their own professionalism and professional identity as social workers; and (c) those who believed in their ability to influence a difficult situation. This categorization of subjects lead Fook et al. to conclude that the development of expertise, at least in an "ill-structured" field such as social work, is likely based more on the development and use of wisdom and intuition (to borrow phrases from the Dreyfus brothers) than on the use of ". . . articulated theoretical frameworks" (p. 407).

Are wisdom and intuition central to expertise in therapy and counseling? The findings of Fook and her colleagues, while still only representing one study in one field, strongly suggest that the hallmark of social work expertise is having the ability to handle unpredictability and uncertainty and to remain flexible in the face of chaos in order to solve problems. There is no single way to handle all tasks. Tolerance for the illusive—ambiguity, anxiety, disorder, conflict, ambivalence, paradox—is essential for expertise in the helping professions. Without question, given the similarly complex and ambiguous nature of the therapy and counseling profession, expertise here should be characterized by similar—if not identical—characteristics. Fook and colleagues illustrated that expertise in fields such as social work and therapy and counseling is as much about process skills as positive outcomes.

"Embracing the Ambiguity": Optimal Therapist and Counselor Development

As those in the professions know so well, therapy and counseling are brimming with ill-structured problems and a sometimes overwhelming confluence of solutions. Clearly, this is one reason why it has been so difficult to operationalize the nature of therapy and counseling expertise.

Rønnestad and Skovholt (1991) note that one common error of novice counselors in efforts to deal with the ambiguity of the field is "premature closure," a phenomenon that can easily thwart professional development (Rønnestad & Skovholt, 1991, 2001; Skovholt & Rønnestad, 1992, 1995). Rønnestad and Skovholt describe premature closure as the tendency to latch on to one simplistic solution, theory, or frame of reference with which to view clients in order to avoid being cognitively or emotionally overwhelmed.

While not examining therapists in particular, Acredolo and Horobin (1987) performed a systematic study of premature closure and the development of relational reasoning among school children. In their study, Acredolo and Horobin defined premature closure as the "tendency to offer only a single solution to any problem that, because of insufficient or ambiguous information, logically permits more than one solution" (p. 13). With their sample of first, third, and sixth graders, the authors looked at how soon children could identify ill-structured problems in which no one right answer existed.

The researchers found dramatic differences in both relational reasoning and avoidance of premature closure (Acredolo & Horobin, 1987, p. 19) between the sixth graders and the other age groups. Differences were significantly reduced, however, when the authors gave "corrective feedback training" (explaining to the child the nature of an error) to the first and third graders. Interestingly, the authors suggest that the ability of the younger children to entertain solutions to problems with more than one answer may have gone undetected in part because of "cognitive overload." Acredolo and Horobin explain that cognitive overload happens when there are excessive demands on working memory and executive mental functioning. The authors suggest that such cognitive overload likely occurred in the younger children and led to subjects' premature closure.

Like young children who have the capacity to avoid premature closure, but do not, the novice therapist or counselor can also struggle. With this in mind, the results of the corrective feedback training used by Acredolo and Horobin (1987) may have important implications for therapist/counselor training where novices can be primed or sensitized to the existence of the ill-structured problems as well as the multiplicity of response patterns. Such training might serve to enhance novices' cognitive schema to the point where they can flexibly adapt the idea of employing multiple response patterns without fear of cognitive overload, thus helping to preempt the comfort of prematurely cutting off alternatives. The study by Acredolo and Horobin (1987) provides instructional strategies for students to problem solve in ambiguous situations. The importance of such instructional strategies for therapist and counselor training and the development of expertise seems worthy of exploration.

Rønnestad and Skovholt (1991) and Skovholt and Rønnestad (1995) address the issues of premature closure in their discussion of optimal practitioner development versus pseudodevelopment. The authors describe pseudodevelopment as the result of premature closure in which a developing practitioner avoids or aborts anxiety-inducing experiences, challenges, and complexities. The authors further define premature closure as ". . . interrupting the reflection process before the assimilation/accommodation work is completed" (Skovholt & Rønnestad, 1995, p. 135).

In their discussion of premature closure within the context of professional development, Rønnestad and Skovholt (1991) presented a Development/Stagnation Model of practitioner growth. Rønnestad and Skovholt argue that at the heart of this model—and correspondingly at the heart of successful practitioner development—is an awareness of the complexity often present in the therapeutic endeavor. Such "complexity awareness" precludes latching on to simplistic or reductionistic solutions, instead setting the stage where one can continuously strive toward mastery of the highly ambiguous, difficult to understand phenomena. As Skovholt and Rønnestad (1995) indicate, "Professional development presupposes an openness and awareness to these phenomena and processes, and presupposes a continual search to arrive at a more profound understanding of them" (p. 126). Thus, having an awareness of the complex ambiguity of the work lays the foundation for optimal therapist/counselor development.

Skovholt and Rønnestad's assertion that highly developed practitioners possess a "complexity awareness" not often seen in less seasoned therapists closely resembles the findings of other expertise researchers. On the other hand, therapeutic practice presents some unique challenges not typically experienced in other, "harder" fields such as chemistry or physics. Of particular importance, Skovholt and Rønnestad (1995) suggest that professional growth or stagnation can hinge on the type and intensity of the practitioner's motives to enter the profession in the first place. Practitioners whose primary motives revolve around themes of avoiding isolation or the need for power, for example, are those most at risk for professional stagnation. In contrast, practitioners whose primary motives for entering the profession reflect more altruistic or caring motives are setting the necessary foundation for personal and professional development.

Rønnestad and Skovholt (1991) and Skovholt and Rønnestad (1995) suggest that the relationship between functionality and intensity of motives is best understood as curvilinear: One route to stagnation is the presence of weak and dysfunctional motives. On the other hand, one may be excessively motivated and still en route to stagnation or pseudodevelopment. This occurs when the intensity of one's motives for entering the profession is high, but the motives for entering the profession are dysfunctional in nature. In this context, "functional" motives are typically conscious and include such desires as "wanting to help people," "wanting to understand people," and "wanting professional status" (Henry, Sims, & Spray, 1971). By contrast, dysfunctional motives are frequently unconscious in nature and can be seen in the need to continue the role of the negotiator in one's family of origin, compensating for loss themes in childhood, expressing voyeuristic tendencies, and avoiding isolation.

There are other factors that make the study of optimal practitioner development challenging. For example, many practitioners' motives for entering the profession may be largely unconscious. Additionally, optimal practitioner development often requires the ability to endure and sustain painful emotions and leave the comfort of the familiar to traverse into the territory of the unknown. Hence, while expert practitioners must possess the same qualities of experts in general, they must do so in the midst of pain, suffering, and emotional distress—features not as intensively seen in most other disciplines.

Along with complexity awareness and motive functionality, Skovholt and Rønnestad (1995) also describe the optimal practitioner as highly congruent, both personally and professionally. Skovholt and Rønnestad explain that highly developed practitioners have internalized an awareness of a developmental "metagoal." In this context, "internalization" is akin to the Rogerian concept of "genuineness" in that it refers to an alignment between personality, values, life philosophy, theories, and applied methods. An awareness of a developmental "metagoal" refers to the continuing quest for higher levels of congruence over the professional life span. The ". . . long-term career goal is to become more fully oneself in a highly competent way . . ." (Skovholt & Rønnestad, 1995, p. 131).

Overall, Skovholt and Rønnestad (1995) argue that optimal practitioner development is contingent upon several factors. First, it is important for developing practitioners to work within a structure that provides opportunities for innovation and support when facing complexities and challenges. In addition, the structures most conducive to growth offer the developing therapist or counselor balanced opportunities for, to use Piaget's terms, assimilating and accommodating new knowledge. Ultimately, this is all part of the "support/challenge balance," where counselors are not only provided with experiences that stretch and even exceed the confines of what they know, but are supported while navigating through what they do not know.

For advanced practitioners, this process becomes infinitely more complex. Skovholt and Rønnestad (1995) suggest that one way to endure this process is by creating "developmental contracts" to provide structure for experiences and factors that are facilitative of professional growth. Such contracts can provide fertile avenues for adapting and providing corrective feedback similar to what Acredolo and Horobin (1987) found so useful in helping young students avoid premature closure and cognitive overload. Developmental contracts can provide a framework useful for developing therapists to navigate the ill-structured problems of therapy and counseling. Supervisors can also provide feedback that is relevant and corrective, and that promotes development instead of stagnation within this realm of therapist/counselor ambiguity (Skovholt & Rønnestad, 1995).

The "Myth" of the Expert Therapist?

Although suggestions from Skovholt and Rønnestad (1995) may be useful for understanding optimal therapist/counselor development, they do not directly address an important question: Can expertise can be achieved in therapy/counseling in a way similar to other fields and disciplines? One of the most salient critics of the notions of therapy/counseling expertise is Dawes, a research psychologist at Carnegie Mellon University. Citing several relevant research articles, Dawes (1994) argues that the available literature indicates that experts simply do not exist in therapy and counseling. It is the contrary, he says. Someone who wants to consult a professional in mental health for emotional help would do just as well to find an empathetic "neutral" person who will listen and relate, or someone well-versed in the basic principles of behavior change. Ultimately, Dawes argues that ". . . much of the success of all therapy may be influenced by the fact that the client is taking action and no longer feels helpless in the face of disruptive emotional pain" (p. 75).

One of the empirical cornerstones of Dawes' assertion comes from an article published in a 1977 issue of *American Psychologist* where the results established psychotherapy as an effective means of interpersonal assistance. The authors, Smith and Glass (1977), used a then new technique, meta-analysis, and found that someone chosen at random from an experimental group that had received therapy was twice as likely to be better off emotionally than someone chosen at random from a control group. As a point of comparison, consider the fact that most *medical* studies (e.g., heart medication clinical trials, etc.) cannot reach this same level of significance (Dawes, 1994).

In addition to their major findings regarding the overall efficacy of psychotherapy, Smith and Glass offered three additional conclusions that challenged conventional therapeutic wisdom:

1. Therapists' credentials—no degree, Ph.D., or M.D.—were largely if not entirely unrelated to the effectiveness of the therapy.
2. The type of therapy used in treatment (e.g., cognitive behavioral therapy, humanistic therapy, etc.) was largely if not entirely unrelated to the effectiveness of therapy. (As a side note, certain types of behavioral techniques were found to be especially well-suited for treating some very specific behavioral problems and phobias).
3. The overall length of the therapy was unrelated to its overall success or failure.

Dawes observes that the psychological community readily embraced Smith and Glass's finding indicating the effectiveness of therapy, but remained comparatively silent regarding the significant details. Curious about the validity of the original meta-analysis and the replicability of the finding, Landman and Dawes (1982) analyzed the research literature just as Smith and Glass had (though using even more stringent criteria for their own study) and found nearly identical results: Without question, therapy worked. Yet, whether its effect requires a highly trained expert was yet to be confirmed.

Another classic study supporting Dawes's conclusion came from Strupp and Hadley (1977). For their analysis, Strupp and Hadley recruited undergraduate students who were experiencing nonclinical levels of either depression or anxiety. The researchers then randomly assigned fifteen students to a group of highly trained, credentialed psychologists or to a group of "empathic," nonclinically trained professors from the university. To their surprise, Strupp and Hadley found that the students in both groups scored statistically equally on multiple measures of mental health and well-being. The researchers did find that the students who saw the trained professionals scored higher on one measure of optimism about life, but the differences were slight, and underwhelming considering the battery of measures on which the two groups scored equally.

Of course, one could argue that a group of caring professors represent a cadre of highly skilled helpers. Therefore, they should be able to produce positive results when helping students. Perhaps a more refined research question is: How can first-year, beginning practicum students in the helping fields—with very little skill or professional knowledge—successfully help clients? Perhaps therapy/counseling is a field where experience level has very little to do with some successful client outcomes. For example, a first-year college student suffering a sudden relationship loss may feel great relief after receiving an hour of empathetic listening from a beginning practicum student.

Dawes's (1994) conclusions about the "myth of expertise" in therapy and counseling and the research supporting that conclusion are worth considering. Ultimately, Dawes claims that the effects of therapy are almost entirely determined by the client:

> I suggest that it may be the actions of the clients themselves in "taking up arms"—that is, in doing something about the problems addressed in therapy—that result in a change in life itself that has a "therapeutic" effect (p. 61).

But is this the sole determinant of the effectiveness in therapy? Can we attribute the whole of clients' success to their own actions, knowing that there are legitimate differences in the quality of therapists, or is the picture a bit more complicated? Is it possible, for instance, that certain experienced therapists are better able to elicit client change or evoke client motivation than other, more novice practitioners?

Searching for Expertise in Therapy and Counseling

Evidence presented in the current book suggests that there are certain therapeutic features that characterize expert therapy practitioners and that these differences do make an important difference in the quality of the therapeutic experience.

The idea that expert therapists/counselors are in some meaningful ways qualitatively different from novices seems sensible. The postulates observed in the general expertise literature suggest such an idea. Anecdotal evidence from those in the therapy/counseling profession know from their own experience that they are much more competent now as seasoned professionals than they were as novices. However, empirical research supporting this idea has been slow to accumulate though there has been more work in recent years.

In one of the first empirical studies to analyze expertise in counseling, Strong (1968), a prominent counseling psychologist at the University of Minnesota, hypothesized during the 1960s that change in counseling was largely attributable to the influence the counselor had on his or her client. Accordingly, if counselors were able to establish a base of social power (by being perceived by clients as expert, attractive, and trustworthy), they could use this influence to bring meaningful client change (Strong, 1968).

Strong's (1968) theory has received research support. Direct support comes from a line of evidence showing that counselors perceived by their clients as more expert, attractive, and trustworthy have an increased ability to be influential or impactful (Heppner & Claiborn, 1989). Indirect support comes from a different line of counseling research showing that clients' values tended to converge with those of their counselors over time, indicating another dimension of counselor influence (e.g., Beutler, Arizmendi, Crago, Shanfield, & Hagaman, 1983).

These findings highlight two important factors regarding expertise in therapy/counseling: (a) The "sense of expertise" a practitioner is able to convey to clients has an important influence on therapy outcome, and (b) practitioners have considerable power through influence in shaping the beliefs and values of their clientele. Both points are significant in helping researchers and practitioners understand the processes of therapeutic change. Yet, neither point specifically addresses the question of what expert practitioners "look" like—what they do, how they relate—compared to novice practitioners.

One such attempt to distinguish novice from expert counselors came from Martin, Slemon, Hiebert, Hallberg, and Cummings (1989), who explained that "it is through experience that experts acquire an adequate knowledge for conceptualizing situational information in ways that permit effective conceptualization, problem solving, and action" (p. 395).

In an attempt to test their idea that experienced and novice counselors differed qualitatively on important dimensions Martin and his colleagues had eleven experienced and twelve novice counselors "map" their thoughts and cognitions after several sessions with two actual clients per counselor. Martin et al. hypothesized that novice and experienced counselors would conceptualize counseling in general and their client's specific problems differently—with experienced counselors providing more nuanced, detailed, and accurate accounts than less experienced practitioners.

Martin and colleagues (1989) then recorded the responses of each of the counselors regarding his or her thoughts about counseling in general (e.g., "Generally speaking, what happens to help clients during counseling?") and regarding specific clients (e.g., "What are the most important things to consider with respect to the client's problems?") (p. 395).

Martin et al. (1989) found that experienced counselors tended to conceptualize cases in a more general manner (i.e., relating their experience of a particular client to broader therapy principles), whereas novices tended to conceptualize cases pertaining to specific counseling situations (i.e., analyzing the immediate counseling situation in which they are immersed). In other words, experienced counselors have an extensive storage of knowledge of counseling in general and can and do draw upon this knowledge efficiently and parsimoniously to determine the best course of action regarding specific client problems. Novices, by contrast, lack this abstract knowledge of counseling and need to engage in more extensive conceptualizations for each client.

To further explicate their results, Martin et al. (1989) published a follow-up study in which the authors did a content analysis of the same data. Content analysis is a qualitative research method used to extract broader "themes" or ideas from the data. Martin and his colleagues focused broadly on the consistency of responses and the subjects' use of "domain-specific" concepts (i.e., knowledge "about") versus procedural concepts (i.e., "how to" knowledge) in response to specific client questions.

The researchers found that experienced counselors displayed greater consistency in the concepts they used than novices and used a more "interactional" approach. In other words, experienced counselors displayed a greater awareness of the complex social and interpersonal context within which client problems are ensconced, and used more domain-specific concepts than novices. Interestingly, experienced counselors failed to use any procedural ("how to") concepts when analyzing clients, indicating that experienced counselors were not especially concerned about how to conduct their counseling sessions, but were rather conceptualizing clients at a broader, more abstract, more inclusive level. Conversely, novices used many procedural concepts when analyzing a session, indicating a greater preoccupation with the "how to" when conducting a counseling interview.

Martin et al. (1989) concluded that their findings were congruent with data regarding the development of expertise in other fields. That is, with the necessary training and ultimately experience, counselors developed deeper, more meaningful mental representations of their clients' presenting concerns that enabled them to conceptualize each particular client in a clearer and more efficient manner.

One study that supports the results obtained by Martin et al. (1989) was conducted by Kivlighan and Quigley (1991). In their study, Kivlighan and Quigley showed expert and novice group counselors a videotape of a group counseling session and then asked subjects to make judgments about the similarity or difference between each of the various pairs of group members.

Results of their study indicated that experienced therapists had more complex conceptualizations of group members than novice counselors. For example, the experts rated the group members in three dimensions (dominant/submissive, friendly/unfriendly, and supporting therapeutic work/hindering therapeutic work), whereas novices rated members along two dimensions (dominant/submissive and high/low participation). Ultimately, Kivlighan and Quigley (1991) made conclusions similar to those of Martin and colleagues:

> Since knowledge is organized into broader and more complete structures in memory, experts are able to make broader inferences, unify superficially disparate problems by underlying, often subtle features, and make qualitatively more sophisticated critical judgments. (p. 415)

Hillerbrand and Claiborn (1990) failed to support the conclusions of Martin et al. (1989). Hillerbrand and Claiborn compared the reasoning skills used by expert and novice counselors when making a diagnosis. Experts were rated by their peers as possessing above-average diagnostic abilities. Novices were graduate students enrolled in counseling psychology programs. Subjects were required to diagnose three case studies, each of which varied in terms of "problem structure" (i.e., the extent to which the information in the cases was clear, unambiguous, and readily solvable).

The researchers predicted that expert counselors would provide more accurate and numerous diagnoses and clearer rationale for their analyses. Surprisingly, the researchers found that a greater number of diagnoses were given by both experts and novice counselors for the well-structured cases and fewer diagnoses given for the ill-defined scenarios. Further, the authors found no difference between experts and novices in terms of the accuracy of the diagnoses across case types.

These results indicate that differences in the clarity of clients' presenting problems may affect all practitioners, seasoned or not. Therapy, as discussed before, is a complex, sometimes very ill-defined process that progresses in fits and spurts, without the linearity seen in other fields.

Why weren't significant differences found between experts and novices in the Hillerbrand and Claiborn study? And why are there discrepancies in the findings of these studies, which purport to measure the same phenomenon?

One possible explanation is that there are truly no significant differences between the two groups (or significances large enough to measure statistically). As mentioned previously, this is the conclusion drawn by some (e.g., Dawes) that challenges the idea that expertise can be achieved in such a "soft," ill-defined field. Hillerbrand and Claiborn (1990) offer another possible explanation that might account for the lack of consistency across studies. These authors suggest that the use of written, hypothetical case studies fails to capture the "live" experience encountered in the counseling room, and hence does not provide an accurate portrayal of how experts and novices actually act and interact with clients.

Another possible explanation for the Hillerbrand and Claiborn results concerns the nature of behavioral prediction itself. In a classic article, the eminent research psychologist Paul Meehl (1954) showed convincingly that predicting behavior (including behaviors such as those encountered in a therapeutic session) is a notoriously difficult and unreliable endeavor and may never be as accurate as some clients and therapists might hope. In other words, it seems immanently plausible, given the findings presented by Meehl, that therapists and other behavioral specialists may never achieve a high rate of success in predicting how long mental health disorders will last and when clients will implement the necessary changes in their lives to bring improvement. If this is true, perhaps pursuing diagnostic perfection—at least in terms of predicting behavioral change—is a fool's errand on the road to characterizing expert therapist/counselor behavior.

If expertise in therapy and counseling is not ultimately synonymous with highly accurate diagnoses and prediction, what does constitute expertise in this field? Are "expert" therapists synonymous with "effective" therapists? Equating expertise with effectiveness does have some intuitive appeal to it, but, as Dawes and others have shown, effectiveness is an extremely difficult construct to measure, given that sometimes in psychotherapy a client may feel worse before feeling better.

Perhaps expertise shows up in practitioners' ability to relate to extremely challenging clients and work with such clients in the presence of highly charged, emotionally unstable circumstances as suggested by Skovholt, Rønnestad, and Jennings (1997). The perspective suggesting that expertise in therapy and counseling may be inextricably linked to the therapists' exceptional ability to form relationships is finding support in the empirical literature. For example, a large study conducted by Luborsky, McLellan, Woody, O'Brien, and Auerbach (1985) revealed that significant therapy success was determined most by "a helpful relationship with the counselor." Other studies have found that the contribution of the therapist surpasses the contribution of the client in promoting and achieving mental health (Teyber & McClure, 2000). Teyber and McClure conclude that "... eliciting factors that enhance the therapist-client relationship may be the most appropriate focus for future research" (p. 68). They go on to say, "In many studies, what therapists say and do in the therapy hour that promotes a good working alliance has proven to be the single most important contributor to change and positive treatment outcome. ..." (p. 70).

In an exhaustive review of the research, Wampold (2001) affirmed the primacy of the therapist's ability to form relationships in distinguishing successful therapy:

> ... the particular treatment that the therapist delivers does not affect outcomes. Moreover, adherence to the treatment protocol does not account for the variability in outcomes. Nevertheless, therapists within treatment account for a large proportion of the variance. Clearly, the person of the therapist is a crucial factor in the success of therapy. (p. 202)

Some of the therapist/counselor effectiveness literature further supports this notion: Effective practitioners have well-developed social skills. They are caring, nurturing, sympathetic (e.g., Wicas & Mahan, 1966; Demos & Zuwaylif, 1966) and have a strong need to affiliate with others (e.g., Wiggins & Moody, 1983; Wiggins & Weslander, 1979).

Using information reviewed in the present chapter, we can tentatively offer a description of the expert therapist/counselor. A more detailed portrait of the master therapist is offered in the remaining chapters. Interpersonally, the effective counselor appears to be mature, self-assured, optimistic, generally satisfied (Jackson & Thompson, 1971), and able to form meaningful relationships with sometimes difficult, demanding clients. Simultaneously, therapists and counselors at the top of their profession seem to possess an intellectual curiosity and flexibility that allows them to feel comfortable confronting the complexities of human nature (e.g., Goldberg, 1992).

While these attributes paint a picture of warm, conscientious, and intellectually bright individual, they do not complete the portrait of expertise in this challenging profession. Bearing in mind some of the methodological limitations suggested above (e.g., small sample sizes used in studies, difficulties in clearly defining elusive terms such as "expert," and "effective"), initial findings regarding the achievement of expertise in counseling seem fairly consistent with findings on expertise in other domains.

Experienced therapists/counselors show both a greater number of conceptualizations and increased complexity when seeking to understand their clients (e.g., Cummings et al., 1990). Expert therapists/counselors also seem to have a broader knowledge of the therapeutic process in general and are less concerned with the specifics of the moment-by-moment (e.g., Martin, et al., 1989). Experts view themselves as knowledgeable, confident, and able to clearly understand client problems (Hillerbrand & Claiborn, 1990).

The literature suggests that experts are experienced in the therapy/counseling domain. They can see further because they have stood on the shoulders of giants and have taken the time to let their skills develop and mature. Expertise, like wisdom, takes time and experience. As Goldberg states in his book *The Seasoned Psychotherapist: Triumph*

Over Adversity, "Although being an experienced psychotherapist doesn't guarantee us wisdom, it does give us an excellent opportunity for it" (1992, p. 147).

The terms "expert," "effective," and "master" all attempt to describe the "best of the best" in the therapeutic professions. The literature to date has not yet offered a clear and comprehensive definition of practitioner expertise. The purpose of this book is to offer both questions and answers. We strive in these pages to provide the readers with a realistic description of excellence in therapy and counseling. This search for the essence of excellence is important because therapy and counseling help reduce emotional suffering experienced by people everywhere.

References

Acredolo, C., & Horobin, K. (1987). Development of relational reasoning and avoidance of premature closure. *Developmental Psychology, 23*(1), 13–21.

Bernard, J. M., & Goodyear, R. K. (1998). *Fundamentals of clinical supervision* (2nd ed.). Boston: Allyn and Bacon.

Beutler, L. E., Arizmendi, T. G., Crago, M., Shanfield, S. B., & Hagaman, R. (1983). The effects of value similarity and clients' persuadability on value convergence and psychotherapy improvement. *Journal of Social and Clinical Psychology, 1*(3), 231–245.

Cummings, A. L., Hallberg, E. T., Martin, J., Slemon, A., & Hierbert, B. (1990). Implications of counselor conceptualizations for counselor education. *Counselor Education and Supervision, 30*, 120–134.

Dawes, R. (1994). *House of cards: Psychology and psychotherapy built on myth*. New York: Free Press.

Demos, G. D., & Zuwaylif, F. H. (1966). Characteristics of effective counselors. *Counselor Education and Supervision, 5*, 163–165.

Dreyfus, H. L., & Dreyfus, S. E. (1986). *Mind over machine*. New York: Free Press.

Fook, J., Ryan, M., & Hawkins, L. (1997). Towards a theory of social work expertise. *British Journal of Social Work, 27*, 399–417.

Goldberg, C. (1992). *The seasoned psychotherapist: Triumph over adversity*. New York: W. W. Norton & Co.

Henry, W. E., Sims, J. H., & Spray, S. L. (1971). *The fifth profession*. San Francisco: Jossey-Bass.

Heppner, P. P., & Claiborn, C. D. (1989). Social influence research in counseling: A review and critique. *Journal of Counseling Psychology, 36*, 365–387.

Hillerbrand, E., & Claiborn, C. D. (1990). Examining reasoning skill differences between expert and novice counselors. *Journal of Counseling and Development, 68*, 684–691.

Jackson, M., & Thompson, C. L. (1971). Effective counselor: Characteristics and attitudes. *Journal of Counseling Psychology, 18*, 249–254.

Jennings, L., & Skovholt, T. M. (1999). The cognitive, emotional, and relational characteristics of master therapists. *Journal of Counseling Psychology, 46*(1), 3–11.

Kivlighan, D. M., & Quigley, S. T. (1991). Dimensions used by experienced and novice group therapists to conceptualize group processes. *Journal of Counseling Psychology, 38*, 415–423.

Landman, J. T., & Dawes, R. M. (1982). Psychotherapy outcome: Smith and Glass' conclusions stand up to scrutiny. *American Psychologist, 37*, 504–516.

Luborsky, L., McLellan, T. A., Woody, G. E., O'Brien, C. P., & Auerbach, A. (1985). Therapist success and its determinants. *Archive of General Psychiatry, 42*, 602–611.

Martin, J., Slemon, A. G., Hiebert, B., Hallberg, E. T., & Cummings, A. L. (1989). Conceptualizations of novice and experienced counselors. *Journal of Counseling Psychology, 36*, 395–400.

Meehl, P. E. (1954). *Clinical versus statistical prediction*. Minneapolis, MN: University of Minnesota Press.

Miller, W. R., & Hester, R. K. (1986). Inpatient alcoholism treatment: Who benefits? *American Psychologist, 41*, 794–805.

Orlinsky, D., Rønnestad, M. H., Ambuehl, H., Willutzki, U., Botersman, J., Cierpka, M., Davis J., & Davis, M. (1999). Psychotherapists' assessments of their development at different career levels. *Psychotherapy, 36*(3), 203–215.

Rønnestad, M. H., & Skovholt, T. M. (1991). The professional development and stagnation of psychotherapists and counselors. *Tidsskrift for Norsk Psykologforening, 28*(7), 555–567.

Rønnestad, M. H., & Skovholt, T. M. (2001). Learning arenas for professional development: Retrospective accounts of senior psychotherapists. *Professional Psychology, Research & Practice, 32*(2), 181–187.

Skovholt, T. M., & Rønnestad, M. H. (1992). Themes in therapist and counselor development. *Journal of Counseling & Development, 70*(4), 505–515.

Skovholt, T. M., & Rønnestad, M. H. (1995). *The evolving professional self: Stages and themes in therapist and counselor development.* New York: Wiley.

Skovholt, T. M., Rønnestad, M. H., & Jennings, L. (1997). In search of expertise in counseling, psychotherapy, and professional psychology. *Educational Psychology Review, 9*, 361–369.

Smith, M. L., & Glass, G. V. (1977). Meta-analysis of psychotherapy outcome studies. *American Psychologist, 32*, 752–760.

Strong, S. R. (1968). Counseling: An interpersonal influence process. *Journal of Counseling Psychology, 15*, 215–224.

Strupp, H., & Hadley, S. (1977). A tripartite model of mental health and therapeutic outcome with special reference to negative effects in psychotherapy. *American Psychologist, 32*, 187–196.

Teyber, E., & McClure, F. (2000). Therapist variables. In C. R. Snyder & R. E. Ingram (Eds.), *Handbook of psychological change.* New York: Wiley, 62–87.

Wampold, B. E. (2001). *The great psychotherapy debate: Models, methods, and findings.* Mahwah, NJ: Lawrence Erlbaum Associates.

Wicas, E. A., & Mahan, T. W. (1966). Characteristics of counselors rated effective by supervisors and peers. *Counselor Education and Supervision, 6*, 50–56.

Wiggins, J. D., & Moody, A. (1983). Identifying effective counselors through client supervisor ratings and personality-environmental variables. *The Vocational Guidance Quarterly*, 259–269.

Wiggins, J. D., & Weslander, D. L. (1979). Personality characteristics of counselors rated as effective or ineffective. *Journal of Vocational Behavior, 15*, 175–185.

The Cognitive, Emotional, and Relational Characteristics of Master Therapists

LEN JENNINGS

THOMAS M. SKOVHOLT

Characteristics of Master Therapists[1]

In the last few decades, the focus of many researchers has been on identifying the complex factors that constitute effective psychotherapy. Factors explored include client variables, therapist variables, client-therapist personality matching, the therapeutic alliance, and "common factors" across various therapeutic modalities (Miller, 1993). In particular, the therapeutic alliance is considered to play a central role in producing effective psychotherapy outcomes (Beutler, Machado, Neufeldt, 1994; Horvath & Symonds, 1991; Luborsky, McLellan, Woody, O'Brien, & Auerbach, 1985). Sexton and Whiston (1994) state in the first line of their abstract, "the quality of the counseling relationship has consistently been found to have the most significant impact on successful client outcome" (p. 6).

Assuming that the personal characteristics of the therapist influence the quality of the therapeutic alliance, it may be useful to understand more fully the qualities effective therapists bring to their work. Even more helpful would be to identify the characteristics of master therapists—those considered the "best of the best" among mental health practitioners.

In reviewing the literature on therapist effectiveness, the majority of studies employed neophyte therapists or even therapist trainees as participants. The few investigations that did study experienced therapists revealed scant information on the personal characteristics of effective therapists. Wicas and Mahan (1966) found effective therapists to be more self-controlled and sympathetic toward others compared to less effective therapists. Jackson and Thompson (1971) reported that effective therapists held more positive attitudes toward themselves, clients, most people, and therapy than did ineffective therapists. Studying two therapists intensively, Ricks (1974) found major differences in the success of the two therapists treating disturbed adolescent boys and attributed these differences to therapist personality differences and the handling of countertransference reactions by the two therapists. Wiggins and Weslander's (1979) research revealed that highly effective therapists reported greater job satisfaction than did less effective therapists. Luborsky et al. (1985) found a significant relationship between patient outcomes and therapeutic alliance and stated that "the major agent of effective psychotherapy is the personality of the therapist, particularly the ability to form a warm and supportive relationship" (p. 609). Although Luborsky et al. (1985) asserted that the personality of the therapist is critical in forming therapeutic alliances that make therapeutic successes possible, therapist effectiveness research has yielded only minimal information on what these therapeutic personality characteristics may be.

Even the few studies seeking to define characteristics of master therapists have revealed little. Harrington (1988) found that Diplomates of the American Board of Professional Psychology (defined as master therapists) scored similarly to each other on 30 of 37 subscales of the Adjective Check List. With Diplomates sharing 30 descriptors, the results of this study served to cloud, not clarify the definition of master therapists. Goldberg (1992) interviewed twelve psychiatrists recommended by colleagues as exceptional therapists. Goldberg found that as a group, these therapists seemed to be sensitive, caring, and dedicated to their clients' welfare and their own personal and professional growth. They seemed pleased by their career choice and reported being helped by a competent mentor and rejuvenated professionally by mentoring others. Finally, Albert (1997) interviewed twelve psychiatrists nominated by their colleagues as expert clinicians and found that the therapists' flexibility, sensitivity, ability to create a place of sanctuary for the client, and ability to create a therapeutic alliance were all important in providing effective psychotherapy.

Apart from therapist efficacy, another potential factor in being a master therapist relates to the knowledge and skill base of the therapist and the cognitive processes that help organize and access that knowledge base. Although the literature on therapist expertise is limited, interest has increased recently in this line of research. Hillerbrand (1989) defines the expert therapist as a person who:

> . . . is able to conceptualize clients, integrate factual information into performance, and recognize interpersonal processes. Expertise consists of the cognitive skills of comprehension and problem solving. That is, the ability to identify and understand incoming information and then cognitively process this information for the purpose of reaching a conclusion or solution. (p. 292)

Similar to expertise research in other domains, research on differences between expert and novice therapists suggests that expert therapists have more complex schemata and tend to notice more subtle features of problems than novice therapists (Martin, Slemon, Hiebert, Hallberg, & Cummings, 1989). This promising line of research is not without problems, however. For instance, many of the studies purporting to study therapist expertise utilize years of experience as the main criteria for judging expertise (Cummings, Hallberg, Martin, Slemon, & Hiebert, 1990; Kivlighan & Quigley, 1991;

Martin et al. 1989). However, years of experience have not been found to clearly differentiate levels of expertise (Skovholt, Rønnestad, & Jennings, 1997).

In an attempt to better define the term master therapist, the present study focuses on the question: What are the personal characteristics of master therapists? More specifically, this study asks: What are the characteristics of therapists considered outstanding by their professional colleagues? Despite the lack of a clear definition, the term master therapist is used frequently in the mental health lexicon to describe therapists considered to be "the best of the best" among fellow practitioners. Whereas much of psychotherapy research has focused on neophyte therapists (Goldberg, 1992), we believe that a considerable amount can be learned about potentially efficacious therapist characteristics by studying highly experienced, well-regarded therapists across various professional mental health disciplines.

Qualitative methodology was used in this study of master therapists. Many methodologists consider qualitative designs to be the most effective means for exploratory phases of investigation (Hoshmand, 1989; Patton, 1990). Because of the exploratory nature of the current study and the desire to gain a better understanding of a complex human construct (i.e., master therapists), qualitative interviews were chosen as the data gathering method. Please see Appendix A for a detailed description of the ten master therapists and methodology used in this study.

Results

The findings are organized under three domains representing key attribute areas of master therapists: cognitive, emotional, and relational. Within each domain, there are three categories. Below, selected quotes from the ten master therapists are offered as "raw data" to best illustrate both category and domain.

Cognitive Domain

Category 1: Master Therapists Are Voracious Learners. Continuous professional development seems to be a hallmark of the master therapist. When speaking about learning and knowing, many respondents used terms such as "hunger" or "thirst." Their voracious appetite for knowledge appears to be an intense source of development. One respondent said:

> I can't stay content in what I know. And I get embarrassed at how much I seek out other learning experiences. My family is forever kidding me about it. Because I do take classes, I still do. . . . Oh, my joke is that when I die, they ought to put on my epitaph, "Now her question is answered." Like the curiosity of what the death experience would be. So curiosity has been a big thing all my life.

Another respondent shared how a love for learning is a source of renewal:

> [I] go to workshops, give workshops, teach in consultation groups. All those kinds of things that take energy, take interest, take wanting to know more. . . . I love getting

together with people, reading and talking about what we're reading. Some people don't like that at all, and I just love it . . . It provides constant energy for one thing and I think what happens in our field is that we can get tired and exhausted, but I think that's one of the things that keeps me feeling high-energy and [it creates] a lot of interest and love for what we do, and it's exciting.

One respondent captured the never-ending quality and excitement of pursuing knowledge with this statement:

The more we know the more we know we don't know. Right? We have that equation in front of us all the time. Knowledge leads to the unknown. But, it's interesting and it's fascinating and it's all right, that search . . . [but] the searching never stops. There's never going to be a known.

Respondents had a similar fascination with the unknown early in their careers as well. Fueled by a personal drive and innate curiosity, the once-neophyte psychotherapist eagerly sought out new learning experiences. For example, one respondent said:

When I was a very young or hatching therapist, . . . I was interested in all of it [psychotherapy] and I tried everything. I learned a little bit of every imaginable theory and then watched the places where it failed . . . being open to try things and open to seeing the failures of the different approaches.

Similarly, another respondent stated:

I tried on styles [therapy approaches] just like kids try on clothes. Some of them worked, some of them a little bit, and some of them worked sometimes.

Finally, one respondent advised:

. . . go through as many rites of passage as you possibly can. . . . try to broaden yourself as much as you possibly can . . . you've got to open yourself up to as much as possible.

Category 2: Accumulated Experiences Have Become a Major Resource for Master Therapists.   Over time, the respondents, with an average of 29.5 years of professional experience, have rich life and work experiences that they draw upon in their work. These experiences seem to have increased the respondents' depth and competence as human beings and mental health practitioners. The benefits of experience were cited frequently during the interviews. For example, one respondent shared how a returning client noticed the development of character and expertise the respondent had gained over the years:

I was really lucky just two years ago, a fellow that I had seen seventeen years ago called me and said that he wanted to come back into therapy . . . probably about three months into it, he said, "Boy, you're really different." And, I said, "You know what, I'd like to hear it." And it was wonderful. He said, "You've just got so much more of yourself, and there's so much more of you in the room, and I'm getting so much more out of this. You know, my sense of you back then was that you were going by the book." And I was, because that's all I knew how to go by.

The same respondent went on to say how years of experience were so useful:

I'm a lot older. I've got a lot more experience, and as much as I used to want to believe, when I was younger, that age and experience didn't count, . . . it counts a lot, in terms of your ability to empathize and understand a wider range of things.

Similarly, another respondent said:

I just think that there's no exchange for the experience. You can be smart at 21 but it's still not quite the same as somebody who's 61.

Another respondent shared how relying on experience can mean getting through difficult sessions:

A long stretch of someone being very, very, angry or being really critical of you, or disappointed in what you are doing, is very hard to face for the very first time. The time comes when you can say, "I know what this is."

Experience has helped this respondent in a general sense:

Well, I think my knowledge base is much broader and deeper. I probably have learned as much about what people are about in therapy experiences—more probably—since I got my Ph.D. than in preparation for the degree. . . . [I am] able to address more problems, more complexities.

Finally, one respondent explained how the value of many years of experience is sometimes taken for granted:

Most of the great therapists, the ones who have big names, who write and so forth, what they're doing is talking about techniques and stuff that most of them take for granted. Because they've been doing it so long and talking about it for so long, they just assume that everybody else has that [too].

Although respondents gained greatly from accumulated experience, most agreed that experience alone did not guarantee optimal professional development. Several respondents shared that it was a commitment and openness to learning from one's experiences that counted. One respondent stated:

I don't think years of experience by itself does it. . . . I might have the same year of experience twenty times. So [one] needs to put that together with good consultation and a good collegial system so that you actually are learning from what you're doing, [learning] more about yourself and about how you are impacting people.

Another respondent had a similar response:

> You know, experience by itself, I don't think it suffices. I think experience can be a medium or vehicle that one uses for self-reflection and a deeper understanding, or not. Experience in itself doesn't necessarily enhance one's ability. . . . Maybe the difference between those that become better at the trade or art . . . is being able to really recognize and reflect upon it [experience], and observe themselves. . . .

Another respondent emphasized self-esteem as a key factor that makes one more willing to learn from his or her experiences:

> I think it takes a certain amount of self-esteem and openness to be able to use it [experience] to grow. . . . The ones who have learned the most . . . have been strong enough to look at themselves without seeing themselves as nothing, if they make a mistake . . . mistakes are our greatest pieces for learning.

Category 3: Master Therapists Value Cognitive Complexity and the Ambiguity of the Human Condition.   Respondents do not merely tolerate ambiguity and complexity, they seek it out. One respondent said it would be fun to be a meteorologist and deal with complex systems such as the weather. Another reads about chaos theory as a leisurely pursuit. When therapists are on the "cutting edge" of understanding human life, they are likely to encounter complexity and the unknown. The respondents seemed to welcome the complexity and ambiguity. For example, one respondent said:

> None of us ever arrive when we're in this business of working with people. . . . There's always an AIDS, the thing around the corner. There's always that level of complexity. . . . And the minute you start thinking things are simple, you better quit the business [psychotherapy]. That [reminds me of] my favorite quote, by the way, "If the brain was simple enough for us to understand it, we'd be too simple to understand it."

Similarly, another respondent said:

> It's almost a cliché, but it really is true, the more you learn, the more you discover what you don't know. . . . You have to continually approach every situation with an openness of not knowing what's going to happen. . . . It seems to create an increasing openness to possibilities instead of a closing down. There is something about me personally that has never really been fond of dogma. I have never swallowed any point of view "hook, line, and sinker."

Another respondent describes how an openness to ambiguity and complexity is an asset for a therapist:

> I think part of our difficulty sometimes is trying to make something too simple that really is complex, and clients will say that very often to me, you know, it's all these things and more. So, be open to not knowing and to an ambiguous situation, so that you can

hear what it is that's emerging, rather than laying something on the situation. You know, I used to take comfort when I thought I knew, because "now I can relax because I know." And, then realizing that it's the opposite, when you don't know, then you can listen more curiously and have more of an openness about what all might be coming here. So, I think the ambiguity is a part of that, it helps you stay curious about sorting it out and understanding it, finding out more.

The same respondent shared how complexity and ambiguity are so often present:

. . . You think you're being really empathic and somebody sees it as an empathic failure and gets angry. . . . You think that you're doing such a good job and somebody thinks it's lousy, or you thought you did a rotten job and then you get thirty-five referrals from the person, because you helped them so much. I think that's really humbling, because it makes you aware that you don't know. There are so many factors involved.

Similarly, respondents use complex and multiple criteria in judging therapy outcomes. Respondents recognize the difficulty of assessing a process as complex as psychotherapy. Like other therapists, respondents look for positive changes in clients' behaviors, cognitions, and feelings as evidence of efficacious therapeutic outcome. However, respondents shared a number of sophisticated and somewhat idiosyncratic methods for judging effective outcome. For example, one respondent said:

On some levels, I don't think psychotherapy has an end point. I think that successful therapies have continued internally for clients. And I think I wouldn't have known it in the earlier years, but after having practiced so many years, I've had the opportunity to have people who knew me fifteen years ago come back because of life circumstances or whatever, and quite clearly they have had an ongoing process with me even though we didn't meet for fifteen years. So it [psychotherapy] is in some ways a process that activates something internally for people, and I think therapy that truly ends on the last meeting day maybe wasn't psychotherapy.

Emotional Domain

Category 4: Master Therapists Appear to Have Emotional Receptivity Defined as Being Self-Aware, Reflective, Nondefensive, and Open to Feedback. Respondents spoke of engaging in personal therapy, peer consultation, and supervision to obtain various sources of feedback in order to heighten their awareness of themselves and others. Respondents seem to constantly be striving to learn more about their work and themselves. For example, one respondent spoke of a need for continuous self-reflection and feedback:

[I need to be] fully aware of myself and my own motivational system, what's moving me inside. . . . So, I get a chance to look at myself on the outside over and over and over again, through personal therapy, through lots of supervision, through ongoing consultation. That helps incredibly.

Their openness to feedback includes feedback from clients. One respondent shared a critical incident in which valuable feedback from a client was offered and received:

> My clients have taught me a lot. Early in my career, I saw a couple for a year, and what she complained about was his drinking. What he was basically saying was "I wouldn't be drinking if you didn't bug me so much." And, I knew absolutely nothing about alcoholism at that point. They kind of faded out [of therapy] and I don't blame them when I look back on it, because we didn't do much. A year later, she called me to make an appointment, and came in, sat down, and said "I just want to tell you face-to-face how destructive you were to us." And, that was one of the most powerful things that could have happened. I mean, I am forever grateful. It was incredibly hard to hear, but I had a sense that I had really done a lousy job and there was something about her being strong enough to come back. I was embarrassed. . . . It made a powerful impression. . . . I knew it was true, and that I had a lot to learn. And I think that the other part was that I was incredibly impressed with the fact that she had the guts to do it. And I thought, you know, if she had the guts to do it, then I've got the guts to learn from it. . . . It colored my absolute commitment to learn about what I didn't know.

Another respondent shared:

> I was just thinking about one who was here this morning, who said, "Stop interrupting me, you keep interrupting me." And I was. It was partly because I was really wanting to make a connection with him, because I felt the stronger one was his spouse but you know, there it was . . . and for me to say, "What's going on with me that I'm doing this?"

The following are more examples that illustrate the respondents' use of self-reflection. One respondent said:

> . . . I know how I am feeling or how I am reacting in a given situation. Being skilled at observing myself helps me to observe other people. . . . My own personal analysis is a centerpiece of that particular kind of self-knowledge.

Another respondent held a similar view of the importance of being aware:

> I think that self-awareness is really the key to helping you understand if you're getting in the way or not getting in the way, of facilitating or not facilitating, being with and not being with.

Related to humility, all respondents were quite willing to state their limitations and did so in a nondefensive manner. It appears that knowing and being able to talk openly about limitations may be one indication of a highly competent therapist. For example, one respondent explained:

> I'm much better at identifying if I'm not helping somebody and they need to get someplace else. So, that I can help them by the process of recognizing that I can't help them. One of the things that I tell people when they are looking for another therapist is to

really ask them, "What can't you do?" and boy, if they don't have something they can't do, get out!

The next respondents openly addressed their limitations as well. One respondent revealed:

> . . . there might be people who are too much like me for me to see them clearly and there are people with life experiences that are so dramatically different than mine, a culture gap that I cannot bridge. I think there are some kinds of personality clashes that are just inevitable. I think there are people that come from very lively, noisy families that respond to my relative quiet as a negative judgment. I can't change my manner enough to go out and feel comfortable like they want me to.

Another respondent stated:

> I'd probably be all right with people who need someone who is very Rogerian, but I wouldn't be all right with someone who just needs confrontation, because I have a hard time with that one.

Category 5: Master Therapists Seem to Be Mentally Healthy and Mature Individuals Who Attend to Their Own Emotional Well-Being.   As one indicator of emotional health, respondents strive to act congruently in their personal and professional lives. Many respondents described themselves as congruent, authentic, and honest. For example, one respondent said:

> My integrity or my believability rests on what I do in my work and what I do in my personal life. . . . I don't go to work and come home and live a different life. . . . I fully require in my personal life and in my professional life a kind of absolute—and in this sense, it's rigid—but, absolute honesty. . . . It's not that you're making a dedication to the client, it's that you're making a dedication to a congruent life. . . . It's a life in which the inside and the outside match. It's when what people think you are, it's who you are.

Another respondent described a similar value:

> . . . If I happen to reframe something the client is telling me or whatever else that I may happen to do, I'm doing it within the sense of rapport that we have, and doing it with integrity. I'd never do it to shape or to trick or to deceive. It is honoring the integrity of a relationship. . . . Whatever relationship I have, whether it's with a friend that I'm having dinner with, or I am negotiating a price on a used car with a car dealer or I am planning a vacation with my wife, or I'm talking with a client about his or her life, I'm going to be honest.

One respondent stated:

> . . . I'm authentic, what you see is what you get kind of thing. . . . I think it's pretty hard for me to fake things.

As another indicator of emotional health, respondents seem to have a healthy perspective on their sense of importance. Most respondents displayed a genuine sense of humility and were not self-centered or grandiose in presentation. They appeared to be comfortable with themselves and held a realistic perspective on their importance in the world. In short, respondents seemed to have struck a healthy balance between confidence and humility. For example, one respondent said:

> It is an odd piece of humility. And it isn't the "Euria Heap humble" humility, it is sort of like saying "I am not that important." I mean what goes on here is important. But it is the actor [client] over there. And we are both experts. And if I make a mistake they can also do some things to make it better. So I am not that responsible.

Respondents' perspectives on their own importance may be related to sensing their place in a vast universe and an appreciation for the human condition. For example, one respondent said:

> I think it [being a good therapist] takes some personal qualities, including humility. And by humility, I mean having a perspective on yourself as having a place in the universe . . . in a very big universe. I don't mean to detract from myself, I just see my place. . . . Whoever should come through my door shows me another aspect of what it is to be a human being, like I am a human being . . . we're much more alike than different.

Another example of the respondents' healthy perspectives relates to the title "master therapist." Although respondents were honored to be nominated by their colleagues as master therapists, most respondents would not feel comfortable identifying themselves by that title. Besides humility, there were a number of reasons offered for being cautious about calling oneself a master therapist. For example, one respondent said:

> I had a reaction to the whole idea of master therapist. A curious concept that almost had dangers involved in it. For the client or patient, it leads to an almost automatic idealization which can get in your way. And I think if one begins to think of oneself as a master therapist, it can lead to grandiosity. It can pave the way to all sorts of misuse of power.

Capturing the humility and broader sense of perspective characteristic of this group, one respondent said:

> . . . [When] you have the opportunity to study with all different kinds of people, I think the mystique of master therapist gets lowered. You realize that each of us has something to offer and some of us work well with some folks, and some beginning folks starting out work well with some folks we wouldn't work well with . . . the concept of a master therapist, I think, [is] ambiguous in the sense of who's a master at one thing isn't at something else, and who is at one point in time, isn't at another point in time.

In addition, respondents attend to their well-being through personal therapy and other self-care practices. Respondents take preventive action to protect what they consider their most important therapeutic tool—themselves. They understand that maintaining their emotional well-being is an ongoing process and have found numerous ways to do so such as with personal therapy, exercise, and practicing spirituality. One respondent, wanting to be sure of "practicing what one preaches" concerning self-care, said:

> I exercise every day. I try to do what I encourage other folks to do. I have a strong support system. I have a lot of long-term good friends that I meet with regularly, that I do things with. I have quiet time every day, where I have a chance just to be with myself. I eat well. I would feel really fraudulent to not do [these things]. . . . To not do it would not be good self-care, I think.

Another respondent said:

> I don't do it [self-care] for the client. I do it because I can't live with myself, knowing things are off and not addressing them. . . . Earlier in my life it was about therapy. Today it's about more of a spiritual piece, it's more about what I do in terms of my physical well being. As I get older, I have to pay more attention to that than what I used to, which all affects how I feel emotionally.

Another respondent spoke of the importance of taking breaks from work:

> If you start getting burned out, that's when you're in trouble. And to me, that's just not taking very good care of yourself. And I don't know how, but I figured out years ago that I needed to get away and go on vacations and take a break about every three months. And if I don't do that, my first symptom, I start double booking. I go out there, . . . it's been as bad as three people [waiting]. And then I really know I have got to get out of here!

Finally, one respondent thought that a good therapist:

> . . . must be well fed and well loved. Basically, have a life out there that is working.

Category 6: Master Therapists Are Aware of How Their Emotional Health Affects the Quality of Their Work.   Respondents are keenly aware of how their emotional health affects their work. One respondent offered a convincing argument for the saliency of the therapist's emotional health when observing:

> See, one of my firm beliefs is that the only way, the only hope we have of becoming good therapists is if we're willing to look at our own stuff. Because we can learn all the skills in the world and if we're in this long enough, we learn plenty of skills, but, if we haven't gotten our own stuff cleared out of the way, we're going to be acting that out on our clients over and over and over again. . . . [There needs to be a] commitment to getting [our] own psychological shit out of the way, with whatever that's going to take. And the understanding that we have to be willing to do that all of our lives, because practically every hour that we see somebody, there's something hitting on our old stuff.

Another respondent highlights the dangers of not attending to one's emotional well-being as a therapist:

> It is up to me to do everything I can to maintain my own emotional health so that I can actually be available to my patients without needing them. I think one of the ways therapy goes awry is that the therapist starts to use the patient for their own emotional sustenance . . . regulation of the therapist's self-esteem, all those sorts of things.

Recognizing and utilizing transference and countertransference reactions seem to be an important part of respondents' work. One respondent explained:

> If I am off-centered, I have this kind of checklist that says, "Is it me or my client, or is it us?" . . . my main way of experiencing life is kinesthetic, so that if I start to feel queasy, that is when my brain finally gets the signal, "Look at this."

Another respondent emphasized the importance of recognizing transference/countertransference as a normal process of therapy. Believing that not recognizing this process could lead to boundary violations, the respondent said:

> . . . a lot of sexual issues always come up in therapy, the patient's sexual feelings and fantasies. But if the therapist is not aware of similar feelings and fantasies, . . . then something surprising or unpredicted can occur. But if the therapist is well tuned to this as an interaction, and something that is inevitable and, of course, it's here and, of course, we pay attention to it and, of course, we talk about it, then it is neutralized.

Another respondent shared how countertransference is utilized:

> With countertranference what needs to be understood is that if I am sitting here afraid of you, I have to look at two things: what's going on for me and who are you reminding me of in my past. That's 50 percent of what I look at. But the other 50 percent is what is it about you, how can I use my countertransference reaction to learn something about you. If in fact, I am reacting like I did to my father, let's just pay attention to that and see if there are some of those qualities or whatever. If I am reacting that way, it isn't just a matter of "Boy I really have to look at my stuff." That's one piece of it. The other piece of it is looking at whether there is something about you that I can also use in your therapy.

Relational Domain

Category 7: Master Therapists Possess Strong Relationship Skills.   In their families of origin, many respondents developed skills of listening, observing, and caring for the welfare of others. This may have given the respondents a ten- to fifteen-year head start on developing relational skills. For example, one respondent said:

> My father would always come to me for solace when he was upset with my mother. My mother would come to me when she was upset with him, and I was always trying to help both of them. So maybe that created a need to be needed . . . to be there for people [was] well-ingrained very early.

One respondent described the process of family role assignment:

> ... [many] therapists ... grew up in a family structure where they were defined as the caretakers ... in the system sense, that was their family job. And so, they were trained into that role, so they had to be sensitive to everybody's needs, ... sensitive to conflict and ... take on the impossible task of problem solving.

Another respondent said:

> ... [I] didn't have an alcoholic dad, stuff like that, but there was tension between my parents and I was always trying to figure out what was going on, so I end up working with marriages.

One respondent shared:

> I think most of us therapists got started when we were 2 ... I know I got labeled as a nosy kid. I was forever curious about people and what made them tick. And what would make them feel better. And being a midwestern female, I was into making them feel better. So I do think there are people who get started as therapists very young ... they were trained by their families.

The same respondent gave an example of an early experience behaving compassionately:

> ... there are stories about me before he [her father] died, I am 4 or 5, going in one day when he was in bed sick, and without saying anything pulling down the shade because the sun was shining in his eyes. So I had it [emotional sensitivity], and I don't know where that came from precisely.

In addition, the respondents' own emotional wounds seemed to have increased their sensitivity and compassion to others. Respondents shared personal accounts of suffering and how their experiences increased their sensitivity to others. For example, one respondent said:

> I have been through a hard five years; during which time I sold my house, moved into another place, had my last surviving sibling die of a brain tumor and my mother and an aunt die. So I was picking myself up and kind of holding on to myself for a while. And the interesting thing is, when I was in the most pain, I was a very good therapist. And it was like the bank robbers who sandpaper their skin so that they can really be sensitive to the movements of the machine they are trying to break open. . . . I think I was more sensitive to what my clients were doing.

One respondent said having wounds was a necessary condition for being a good therapist:

> ... I don't know that anybody can really do therapy well until they know vulnerability, unless they are aware of their woundedness ... it's exceptionally helpful in terms of [developing] compassion, and a deeper sense of respect for somebody else's experience, which is different than your own.

Another respondent said:

> Probably every therapist goes through periods of crisis or illness or something like that. In general, I think that [if] the therapist's life is one of deprivation and isolation and pain, I don't think it would work. However, I think that probably nobody becomes a therapist [who] hasn't had a lot of emotional pain in their life. I think this profession wouldn't be of interest if someone didn't know about emotional pain on a very personal level.

One respondent was interested in what people do with their emotional wounds to increase their effectiveness as therapists and stated:

> You can be very wounded and still be open to learning. I know lots of people who have had horrendous backgrounds, who are wonderful therapists and have used their wound-edness and their growth from it to be more empathic, to understand, to really help the other person heal. Or, you can be so wounded that you're totally defended. Again, it . . . it depends on what you do with it . . . I've seen people that are less . . . I mean, when you look at their backgrounds, it's less harsh and yet they're more defensive than some of the ones who've gone through just amazing things and have come out the other end of it.

During the interview process, respondents exuded warmth, respect, caring, and a genuine interest in people. Respondents seem to have highly developed social skills that enable them to relate well with others. One respondent described relationship skills this way:

> Well, I think I have a pretty natural capacity for empathy, which is the starting place for most relationships. The ability to put myself in the other person's shoes and to imagine that even if I haven't lived a life anything like theirs, I have the capacity to imagine what that would be. I am terribly responsible and reliable. I think I create an environment where people can visit pain and count on me to be there, both in terms of time and space, and be predictable. . . . I think it [empathy and predictability] creates a safe environment. People bring in problems that are frightening and abhorrent to themselves and to most people in their lives. I try to create a situation where these problems are approachable, something that can kind of counteract the person's embarrassment or shame or whatever and be able to go on to address the problems. I think the empathy has the effect of helping someone be empathic to themselves.

One respondent stated that forming a good working relationship means:

> . . . being free to love, free to care about people . . . and not worry about being hurt.

The same respondent described a person considered to be a master therapist this way:

> . . . I think everybody that worked with him on the most part really felt that they were the most important person in the world to him then, and they were.

It seems that outstanding therapists have a gift for helping the client to feel special. One respondent described characteristics that communicate interest in the client:

> What I hear back from people I work with is that I really care about them, that I'm really involved with them. I care what happens. I think about what goes on and then share that. I pay attention to what's happening with them from moment to moment in therapy, and I'm respectful. I give room for them to have whatever feelings they have, to challenge me, to get mad at me, to question me.

Category 8: Master Therapists Hold a Number of Beliefs about Human Nature That Help to Build Strong Working Alliances. Although the respondents represented a variety of disciplines and theoretical orientations, all agreed on the necessity of establishing a strong working alliance. One respondent spoke of the relationship's importance:

> Therapy is a real partnership, as I view it. . . . I think we generate an alliance that allows us to do what, without it, we could not otherwise do. . . . That's where the healing is, in the use of the relationship.

Some spoke of the relationship as therapy itself. For example, one respondent explained:

> The core of psychotherapy to me is the development of that relationship and the connection, and so it's the development of a relationship . . . the purpose of which is to heal or help the other person. . . . Psychotherapy is the relationship, as opposed to a technique that I do or whatever else. It's really about forming and working in the in-between.

Another respondent held a similar view:

> . . . if I don't feel like I can join them, then I probably would not be effective.

One respondent highlighted the importance of shared responsibility between the therapist and client:

> One of the things that I have heard is that it's really up to the client, whether they change, that we're just here to facilitate that, or to help them. It's not ours if they change or don't change. . . . But, I really believe that this is a two-person operation, so that it is about us together if change happens or doesn't happen. So, I don't think about it as if something is successful, that I did it. You know, I think it's something that we did together, and I think that if it's not working, it's something we're not doing together.

Moreover, respondents firmly believe in their clients' ability to change, which may instill hope and strengthen the working alliance. Respondents have a deep respect for their clients' right to self-determination and believe that client change is possible. In fact, one respondent explained how change is inevitable:

> The very fact that they're sitting in this office means that they've got a push to make things better, and that's what you have to support all of the time. . . . It's a part of the function of the human cell, if you want to get down to that [level]. . . . Growth is part of life.

So there will always be growth, just like change is a constant, there will always be change. The issue isn't whether there will be change, the issue is whether you can steer it a little bit, you know, help it go in one direction as opposed to another. . . . Help them choose what direction they want to go, and then help them make it go in that way and you don't define for them what direction it should go. I think you always have to give people a choice. And, our basic mission is to help them see their choices, and if they want to make bad choices. . . . My job is to help them see that that's what the consequence will be if they do that.

Another respondent sees competence in every client:

See, they are adults who are walking around out there. They come in here for an hour. So they are competent, and what they want is some way to have less pain and be more competent.

Last, one respondent gave an example of how a good therapist allows the client to search for answers:

And, another thing he [author Sheldon Kopp] said that impacted me . . . was "A client comes into the room and throws himself at your feet, sort of hanging on to your ankles, hoping that you will save them. A good therapist will step back and let them fall on their face, and be there for them when they learn how to pick themselves up." . . . but they've got it in them to learn how to do for themselves, and that you're there to stand beside them . . .

Category 9: Master Therapists Appear to Be Experts at Utilizing Their Exceptional Relationship Skills in Therapy.   Not only do respondents provide safety and support, they can also challenge clients when necessary. After establishing a relationship through warmth and safety, respondents seem to be able to address very difficult and painful client issues. Respondents seem to have a strength of character and a personal power that enables them to face tough issues and challenge clients when needed. For example, one respondent said:

I think that part of the reason that I probably get good feedback has to do with both being supportive and also being challenging. . . . I guess that I'm both gentle and strong, and I can be really soft and compassionate. But if need be, I can also be strong. I'm someone that [a client] can push against and I won't fold over.

Another respondent shared:

. . . in terms of what the attraction is, I think people feel safe. I think people feel very attended to. I do think that I have a lot of clarity, which gives people a lot of security. I think people feel very affirmed, if they're doing something that's different, new, or hard. If anything, I tend to overdo it by giving them support and encouragement. I do think people feel challenged, both cognitively and affectively. I think I'm warm, I think I'm loving. I think the biggest thing is I'm not afraid to go where I need them to go. I'm not afraid to ask . . . and I think that helps them not be afraid.

A third respondent commented:

> One of my half-joking kind of things is a description of what a therapist's task is. A therapist is a tsetse fly on the ass of humanity. What you are in many ways is a professional irritant, you see, because you're the person who has to ask the bad questions, the embarrassing questions, the nosy questions . . . You're the person who has to ask the person to look at things in ways they don't want to look at them, or to look at things that they don't want to look at.

Another common characteristic was that respondents expressed no fear of their clients' strong emotions. Respondents expressed their willingness to be with clients during very intense moments. One respondent explained that the therapist can be present with the client's pain only to the degree that the therapist has dealt with his or her own pain:

> If a therapist is afraid of their own pain, they cannot stay with their clients in their pain, they'll cut them off. And, what the client learns from that, because they pick up on your discomfort, is that there's something wrong with them for having that kind of pain. It's so important not to be afraid of someone's pain.

Another respondent explained:

> I can lead you into your darkness and not be afraid to do that.

One respondent helps certain clients eventually move on from their pain by not getting too impressed with their pain. The respondent explained it this way:

> . . . once in a while I get cynical and say what we are having here is the Academy Award for pain. People kind of treasure their pain and think that my pain is more exquisite that your pain. And I work not to get impressed with that. To acknowledge pain and to pay attention to it, but then to say "And what's next?" . . . That is a mistake I have made a lot. Get so impressed with someone's horrendous stories . . . that I don't do anything. I had a client who brought in pictures of the Asian holocaust when Japan went into Nanking. Pictures of heads lined up and, you know, I said, "Would you rather be a person who didn't feel this pain?" She went right back into realizing that made her a much deeper person. So I will pay attention to it but. . . . I try not to get seduced by it. . . .

One respondent described an ability to handle client anger:

> . . . clients can get very angry, they don't often, but they can and they know it's okay. And, usually, they say, "You know, I'm not really angry with you," and I say, "Yeah, I know. It's okay."

In addition, respondents seem to have become skilled at the art of timing, pacing, and "dosage" when working with clients. With years of experimenting and learning from mistakes and successes, respondents have a finely tuned sense of judgment related to the timing and intensity of their interventions. One respondent gave an example of dosage:

> You see, if she [a client] had gotten mad at me, then I would have pulled back and done something else. Part of it is a gestalt concept of dosage. That you have to put out the right level of experiment. Because if it isn't enough, it is not going to get the adrenaline going and if it is too much, they get overwhelmed.

Similarly, a respondent said that with experience:

> . . . you trust that you won't overrespond, or underrespond, or that the range will be narrow. Everybody overresponds and underresponds, but the range is narrow [with expertise].

Another respondent shared an attention to the timing of interventions this way:

> I probably, at different points, would not put that [self-disclosure] out until we had enough alliance to hold it . . . that's a part of the timing and pacing process. . . .

Discussion

Only a few researchers—such as Harrington (1988), Goldberg (1992), Skovholt and Rønnestad (1995), and Albert (1997)—have sought to tap the wealth of knowledge and wisdom that seasoned, well-regarded practitioners possess. Similarly, the present authors sought to identify and illuminate the characteristics of master therapists—those considered the "best of the best" among their professional colleagues.

Based on the current findings, it appears that becoming a master therapist is more than just an accumulation of time and experience. The master therapists in this sample seem to continuously capitalize on and proactively develop a number of characteristics in an effort to improve professionally. These master therapists appear to be voracious learners who are open to experience and nondefensive when receiving feedback from clients, colleagues and others. The master therapists seem to use both experience and intelligence to increase their confidence and comfort when dealing with complexity and ambiguity. In addition, they appear to be quite reflective and self-aware and use these attributes to continue to learn and grow personally and professionally. These master therapists seem to possess emotional maturity and strength of character that come from years of active learning and living. Finally, the master therapists appear to be able to relate superbly with others, which, one can assume, often leads to a strong working alliance and positive therapeutic outcomes.

There is strong convergence between the research results reported here and those of other research. For example, many of the themes embedded in the nine categories of the present result are similar to the stages and themes presented by Skovholt and Rønnestad (1995). Regarding the qualities that develop competence and expertise, there is strong agreement between the results reported here and other reports in the literature (Colton & Sparks-Langer, 1993; Neufeldt, Karno, & Nelson, 1996; Rønnestad & Skovholt, 1991, 1997; Schon, 1983, 1987; Skovholt & Rønnestad, 1995, Tremmel, 1993; Ward & House, 1998; Worthen & McNeill, 1996). A central tenet in this literature involves an embracing of complexity and reflecting on this complexity in order to grow professionally. The underlying concern here is how to use experience to increase competence and move toward expertise. The alternative is "misuse of experience," where the practitioner is not impacted by it but just routinely repeats the same process over and over again.

Ward and House (1998) discussed the embracing of complexity in the education and supervision process when they described how professional growth for the practitioner in training comes through "experiencing increased levels of emotional and cognitive dissonance" (p. 23). They add that:

> counselors are encouraged to reflect in the moment of action when situations do not present themselves as given, and clinical direction must be constructed from events that are puzzling, troubling, and uncertain (Schon, 1983). It is this recognition of discomfort in response to professional experiences that highlights the reflective learning process and . . . encourages supervisees to willingly explore dissonant counseling experiences. (p. 25)

This emphasis on facing complexity and working through it through reflection is central to the Uncertainty-Certainty Principle of Professional Development (Rønnestad & Skovholt, 1997). Here the supervisor's orientation is to always present a searching stance through the uncertainty while also presenting the certainty of specific techniques and ideas to the novice.

Regarding implications of the present study, we offer the following scenarios, posed as questions, for consideration. Could it be that some therapists have the cognitive ability to understand the dynamics of difficult cases, but lack the relationship skills needed to establish a therapeutic alliance with their clients? Could it be that some therapists relate extremely well with their clients, but their own emotional needs interfere with their clients' work? Could it be that some emotionally healthy therapists do not have the cognitive wherewithal to understand the complexity of their clients' problems?

Based on the current research findings, we propose the CER model of the master therapist. It is hypothesized here that those who go on to become master therapists have developed (C) cognitive, (E) emotional, and (R) relational domains to a very high level and have all three domains at their service when working with clients. The CER model of the master therapist consists of a blend of this three-legged expertise stool, which includes cognitive attributes (cognitive complexity and voracious appetite for learning), emotional attributes (emotional receptivity and maturity), and relational attributes (interpersonally gifted).

Three suggestions for future research are offered. First, although the therapist expertise research has offered a substantive contribution to the understanding of the cognitive processes of a therapist (Cummings et al., 1990; Hillerbrand & Clairborn, 1990; Kivilghan & Quigley, 1991; Martin et al., 1989), the present findings suggest that therapist expertise researchers expand the definition of expertise to include the emotional and relational domain of the therapist. Again, we suggest that expertise in psychotherapy is much more than a cognitive dimension. The cognitive domain is only one leg of the three-legged expertise stool. We believe that all three legs (i.e., cognitive, emotional, and relational) are needed for a solid base in order to perform as an expert in psychotherapy (Skovholt, Rønnestad, & Jennings, 1997).

Second, although the present research highlights a number of potentially desirable therapist characteristics, future researchers will want to explore whether master therapists actually achieve better results than other therapists on measures such as establishing a therapeutic alliance, reducing clients' symptoms, and satisfying clients.

Finally, it appears that many of the master therapist characteristics highlighted in this study are related to concepts such as Rogers' (1961) "fully functioning" person, Maslow's (1970) "self-actualized" person, Skovholt and Rønnestad's (1995) senior therapist in the integrity stage of therapist development, and Erikson's (1963) ego integrity stage of human development. In the future, researchers may want to explore commonalties between master therapists and highly functioning individuals found in a variety of professional fields, those who have achieved a high level of maturity and wisdom acquired through their experiences. Our study may have tapped personal characteristics resulting from optimal human development, regardless of career field.

The results of this study should be interpreted in light of several limitations. As with any qualitative design, the findings are not generalizable beyond the context of this group because the sampling method focused on an information-rich versus representative subject pool (Patton, 1990). In addition, the sampling method may have excluded some outstanding therapists who are lesser known among their colleagues. Next, although attempts were made to minimize experimenter bias by employing a collaborative data analysis between the researchers and the respondents, there was still subjectivity throughout the research process.

Another limitation was the lack of diversity in the research sample. Although the sample was fairly representative of the northern state in which the study was conducted, future researchers would do well to incorporate the richness of a diverse subject pool.

If future research replicates our findings, then these characteristics of master therapists may serve as guideposts for therapists and therapist training programs seeking to promote optimal therapist development. For therapists, the results suggest attending to several areas of personal and professional development. Therapists are encouraged to seek out opportunities for continuous learning, feedback, and reflection. Therapists would do well to keep an open mind when dealing with complexity and ambiguity in their work. Therapists are encouraged to attend to their own emotional well-being, seek their own therapy when necessary, and continue to hone their relational skills. Training programs may want to consider elevating the saliency of the personal characteristics of prospective students to a level on par with the emphasis given to the candidate's cognitive abilities (e.g., GRE scores, GPA). Moreover, training programs can strive to provide a learning environment to further develop these desirable characteristics in their trainees. Overall, the results of this study highlight the importance of developing the emotional and relational domain, as well as the cognitive domain of the therapist.

References

Albert, G. (1997). What are the characteristics of effective psychotherapists? The experts speak. *Journal of Practical Psychology and Behavioral Health, 3*, 36–44.

Beutler, L. E., Machado, P. P., & Neufeldt, S. A. (1994). Therapists variables. In S. L. Garfield & A. E. Bergin (Eds.), *Handbook of psychotherapy and behavior change* (4th ed., pp. 229–268). New York: Wiley.

Colton, A. B., & Sparks-Langer, G. M. (1993). A conceptual framework to guide the development of teacher reflection and decision-making. *Journal of Teacher Education, 44*, 45–54.

Cummings, A. L., Hallberg, E. T., Martin, J., Slemon, A., & Hiebert, B. (1990). Implications of counselor conceptualizations for counselor education. *Counselor Education and Supervision, 30*, 120–134.

Erikson, E. (1963). *Childhood and society* (2nd ed.). New York: W. W. Norton & Co.

Goldberg, C. (1992). *The seasoned psychotherapist*. New York: W. W. Norton & Co.

Harrington, K. M. (1988). *Personal characteristics of diplomates defined as master therapists*. Unpublished doctoral dissertation, University of Minnesota.

Hillerbrand, E. (1989). Cognitive differences between expert and novices: Implications for group supervision. *Journal of Counseling and Development, 67*, 293–296.

Hillerbrand, E. T., & Claiborn, C. D. (1990). Examining reasoning skill differences between expert and novice counselors. *Journal of Counseling and Development, 68*, 684–691.

Horvath, A. O., & Symonds, B. D. (1991). Relation between working alliance and outcome in psychotherapy: A meta-analysis. *Journal of Counseling Psychology, 38*, 139–149.

Hoshmand, L. L. S. T. (1989). Alternate research paradigms: A review and teaching proposal. *Counseling Psychologist, 17*, 3–79.

Jackson, M., & Thompson, C. L. (1971). Effective counselor: Characteristics and attitudes. *Journal of Counseling Psychology, 18*, 249–254.

Kivlighan, D. M., & Quigley, S. T. (1991). Dimensions used by experienced and novice group therapists to conceptualize group process. *Journal of Counseling Psychology, 38*, 415–423.

Luborsky, L., McLellan, T. A., Woody, G. E., O'Brien, C. P., & Auerbach, A. (1985). Therapist success and its determinants. *Archive of General Psychiatry, 42*, 602–611.

Martin, J., Slemon, A. G., Hiebert, B., Hallberg, E. T., & Cummings, A. L. (1989). Conceptualizations of novice and experienced counselors. *Journal of Counseling Psychology, 36*, 395–400.

Maslow, A. (1970). *Motivation and personality*. New York: Harper & Row.

Miller, L. (1993). Who are the best psychotherapists? *Psychotherapy in Private Practice, 12*, 1–18.

Neufeldt, S. A., Karno, M. P., & Nelson, M. L. (1996). A qualitative study of experts' conceptualization of supervisee reflectivity. *Journal of Counseling Psychology, 43*, 3–9.

Patton, M. Q. (1990). *Qualitative evaluation and research methods* (2nd ed.). Newbury Park, CA: Sage Publications.

Ricks, D. F. (1974). Supershrink: Methods of a therapist judged successful on the basis of adult outcomes of adolescent patients. In D. F. Ricks, M. Roff, & A. Thomas (Eds.), *Life history research in psychopathology*. Minneapolis: University of Minnesota Press.

Rogers, C. (1961). *On becoming a person*. Boston: Houghton Mifflin.

Rønnestad, M. H., & Skovholt, T. M. (1991). En modell for profesionell utvikling og stagnasjon hos tetapeuter og radgivere. *Tidsskirft for Norsh psykologforening*. [A model of the professional development and stagnation of therapists and counselors]. *Journal of the Norwegian Psychological Association, 28*, 555–567.

Rønnestad, M. H., & Skovholt, T. M. (1997). Berfliche entwicklung und supervision von psychotherapeuten [Professional development and supervision of psychotherapists]. *Psychotherapeut, 42*, 299–306.

Schon, D. A. (1983). *The reflective practitioner: Toward a new design for teaching and learning in the professions*. San Francisco: Jossey-Bass.

Schon, D. A. (1987). *Educating the reflective practitioner: Toward a new design for teaching and learning in the professions*. San Francisco: Jossey-Bass.

Sexton, T. L., & Whiston, S. C. (1994). The status of the counseling relationship: An empirical review, theoretical implications, and research directions. *The Counseling Psychologist, 22*, 6–78.

Skovholt, T. M., & Rønnestad, M. H. (1995). *The evolving professional self.* Chichester, England: Wiley.

Skovholt, T. M., Rønnestad, M. H., & Jennings, L. (1997). In search of expertise in counseling, psychotherapy, and professional psychology. *Educational Psychology Review, 9*, 361–369.

Tremmel, R. (1993). Zen and the art of reflection practice in teacher education. *Harvard Educational Review, 63*, 434–458.

Ward, C. C., & House, R. M. (1998). Counseling supervision: A reflective model. *Counselor Education and Supervision, 38*, 23–33.

Wicas, E. A., & Mahan, T. W. (1966). Characteristics of counselors rated effective by supervisors and peers. *Counselor Education and Supervision, 6*, 50–56.

Wiggins, J. D., & Weslander, D. L. (1979). Personality characteristics of counselors rated as effective or ineffective. *Journal of Vocational Behavior, 15*, 175–185.

Worthen, V., & McNeill, B. W. (1996). A phenomenological investigation of "good" supervision events. *Journal of Counseling Psychology, 43*, 25–34.

4

Master Therapists' Construction of the Therapy Relationship

MICHAEL SULLIVAN

THOMAS M. SKOVHOLT

LEN JENNINGS

The long war among theoretical orientations in counseling and psychotherapy has come to a truce. Numerous studies have found that all approaches can produce positive change, but consistent superiority of one approach has not been found. As Asay and Lambert (1999) state in their review of the outcome research:

> The conclusions reached here do not offer strong or widespread support for the field's pursuit of model-driven, technical interventions and approaches. On the contrary, much of what is effective in psychotherapy is attributable to pantheoretical or common factors, those shared by many schools of therapy. (p. 23)

The most important pantheoretical variable appears to be the client—"the client's capacity for self-healing is the most potent common factor in psychotherapy" (Tallman & Bohart, 1999, p. 91). One other major variable of promise is that of the therapist. There is now strong evidence for the therapist's effect on client outcome. For Luborsky, McLellan, Woody, O'Brien, and Auerbach (1985), significant counseling success was determined most by "a helpful relationship with the counselor." In research studies, the contribution by the therapist surpasses all but the contribution by the client (Teyber & McClure, 2000).

In an exhaustive review of the research, Wampold (2001) affirms the neglected but critical therapist effect in his chapter titled "Therapist Effects: An Ignored but Critical Factor." In the chapter, Wampold says:

> . . . the particular treatment that the therapist delivers does not affect outcomes. Moreover, adherence to the treatment protocol does not account for the variability in outcomes. Nevertheless, therapists within treatment account for a large proportion of the

variance. Clearly, the person of the therapist is a crucial factor in the success of therapy. (p. 202)

A highly effective therapist does seem to make a difference. We know this implicitly as people and consumers when we actively search for a really good practitioner: a doctor, dentist, attorney, or therapist. We know that some are better than others. Yet, this notion of exploring the therapist variable has been less of a focus in contemporary research. Wampold (2001) states ". . . it is productive to identify those characteristics that differentiate more competent from less competent therapists—yet surprisingly, little research has been directed toward this goal" (p. 186).

Reviewing the research that points out the critical importance of the therapist and the therapeutic relationship, Teyber and McClure (2000) say, "Eliciting factors that enhance the therapist-client relationship may be the most important focus for future research" (p. 68). They go on to say, "In many studies, what therapists say and do in the therapy hour that promotes a good working alliance has proven to be the most important contributor to change and positive treatment outcome" (p. 70).

The present research investigates the working alliance as constructed by a sample of the best of the best, a group of master therapists.

Background

The recognition of the importance of the therapeutic relationship has a long and varied history. The therapeutic relationship has been given an important theoretical role in psychoanalysis (Freud, 1912, Greenson, 1967), humanistic therapy (Rogers, 1957), and social influence theory (Strong, 1968). In recent history, the therapy relationship has primarily been studied through formulations of the therapy alliance (Bordin, 1979). Formulations of the therapy alliance have been developed into a variety of scales, including the Working Alliance Inventory (Horvath & Greenberg, 1994), the Penn Helping Alliance Scale (Luborsky, Crits-Christoph, Alexander, Margolis, & Cohen, 1983), the Vanderbilt Therapeutic Alliance Scale (Hartley & Strupp, 1983), and the California Psychotherapy Alliance Scales (Marmar, Horowitz, Weiss & Mariaza, 1986). Horvath and Luborsky (1993) report that there are at least eleven different alliance scales in use. The scales, to varying extents, incorporate aspects of earlier formulations of the therapy relationship.

What therapist contributions to the therapy relationship are associated with an optimal therapy relationship? The interplay between therapist, client, and therapist-offered therapy conditions is complex. As summarized in this section, optimal therapy relationships are associated with the therapist's judiciously offering therapy conditions based on an accurate assessment of the client's relationships needs.

The research literature on the therapy alliance is extensive. Bachelor and Horvath (1999) report that more than 100 empirical studies have been carried out. However, relatively few studies examine the effect of therapist variables on the therapy alliance (Al-Darmaki & Kivlighan, 1993), and there were no studies found that explored the qualities of the therapy alliance from the therapist's point of view.

Several therapist variables that bear on the therapy relationship have been studied. These include: (a) therapist theoretical orientation (Krupnick et al., 1996; Luborsky et al., 1985), (b) therapist experience (Mallinckrodt & Nelson, 1991), (c) therapist personal characteristics (Blatt, Sanislow, Zuroff & Pilkonis, 1996; Dunkle & Friedlander, 1996; Kivlighan, Patton & Foote, 1998), (d) therapist activities (Horowitz, Marmar, Wiess, DeWitt & Rosenbaum, 1984; Kivlighan, 1990), (e) therapist actions to address poor therapy relationships (Foreman & Marmar, 1985; Kivlighan & Schmitz,, 1992; Safran & Muran, 1996), and (f) training to increase therapist skill in the therapy relationship (Henry, Strupp, Butler, Schacht, & Binder, 1993).

It is remarkable that across the varied therapist variables, it is the therapist's ability to form a strong therapy relationship that is most associated with good therapy outcomes. For example, therapist theoretical orientation does not predict successful therapy; rather, it is the best therapists from any theoretical orientation that have the most successful therapy outcomes. As Luborsky et al. (1985) state: "The highly consistent finding of nonsignificant outcome differences among conceptually different therapies suggests that the specific type of therapy may be less potent in affecting change than the therapist factors" (p. 609). Similarly, Krupnick et al. (1996) found that "even within different approaches, the therapeutic relationship may be established in similar ways" (p. 536).

What are the qualities or characteristics of therapists that form strong therapy relationships? The research literature provides only a few indicators. Mallinckrodt and Nelson (1991) found therapist ability to form good therapy relationships increased as therapist experience increased, but their study design included relatively inexperienced interns and students. Dunkle and Friedlander (1996) found that therapist personal characteristics and social skill attainment, not therapist experience, predicted good therapy relationships. A study by Kivlighan et al. (1998) was designed to examine the divergent findings of the previous two studies and found that a client variable, client's comfort with intimacy, moderated the association between therapist experience and strong client-therapist relationships, where less comfortable clients fared better with more experienced therapists.

A major theme from the research is that therapists who adapt their relationship stance to their client's relationship needs are more adept in forming stronger therapy relationships. It is not surprising that an interactive factor—therapists' effective actions vary depending on client variables—is key to understanding therapist contributions to the therapy relationship. The therapy alliance is conceptualized as a process variable to which both therapist and client make contributions (Bordin, 1979). Because of the importance of the client's contribution to the relationship, the burden for the therapist is to create a therapy relationship environment that is flexible and sensitive to client differences.

In the studies reviewed, a uniform approach by therapists to meet client relationship needs was generally not effective. For instance, the training program described by Henry et al. (1993) was unsuccessful in improving alliances primarily because therapists adhered too rigidly to the prescriptions of their training and avoided a more intuitive, flexible approach to their clients. The importance of moderating effects of client variables on the impact of therapist experience reported in Kivlighan et al. (1998), and on effective therapist actions reported in Horowitz et al. (1984), support the notion that therapists who can differentially respond to clients' levels on various dimensions are more effective. A conclusion that can be drawn from the above examples is that a model of therapist-offered therapy relationship should have the following characteristic: It should be flexible and adaptable to complex and variable client relationship needs.

However, the research-based studies reviewed do not describe optimal therapist-offered relationship conditions. With the exception of Bachelor's (1995) qualitative study of client's perceptions of therapist-offered alliance types, all of the research-based studies reviewed use as their operative definition of the alliance a measure of the therapy alliance. In many of the studies, the therapist alliance score is not used in the statistical analyses because of the poor correlation of these measures with both client alliance scores and with therapy outcome (Bachelor, 1991; Horvath, 1994). Generally, the research-based studies reviewed correlate a therapist variable (e.g., characteristic or technical activity) and client-rated alliance. As a consequence of this research strategy, there is no comprehensive presentation of what the relationship means to the practicing therapist and how therapists may intentionally make use of the relationship.

In contrast, clinically based approaches to describing optimal therapy relationships may provide new research avenues. One promising approach is given in a special section of the journal *Psychotherapy* where distinguished therapists and theorists from a variety of therapy orientations (Beutler & Consoli, 1993; Dolan, Arnkoff, & Glass; Lazarus, 1993; Mahoney & Norcross, 1993; Mahrer, 1993; Norcross, 1993) describe tailoring the therapist's relationship stance to meet the unique needs of the client.

Lazurus (1993) typifies this approach when he advocates that it is as important for therapists to have a flexible repertoire of relationship styles as it is for them to have a range of technical interventions. Pointing out the need for therapists to differentially relate to clients, he states, "The fact that it is essential for therapists to tailor their interpersonal styles and stimulus values to different clients has not been given much (if any) attention in most psychiatric and psychotherapy training programs" (Lazurus, 1993, p. 405).

The articles in *Psychotherapy* cited above provide descriptions of therapy stances from several theoretical orientations: multimodal (Lazarus), cognitive behavioral (Dolan, Arnkoff, & Glass), experiential (Mahrer), and eclectic (Beutler & Consoli). Several conclusions, drawn by considering the articles as a whole, are relevant to the present study: (a) Descriptions of relationship stances vary widely between proponents of different theoretical positions, (b) salient relationship stances are related to client variables as assessed within each theory, and (c) assessments of salient client variables vary widely between different theories.

The third conclusion, that there is little concordance between theorists as to which client variables are critical for purposes of matching relationship stances, is not surprising. Mahoney and Norcross (1993), in a commentary on the theorist's discussions of relationship stances, reflect that in the general research literature, "more than 200 client variables have been proposed as potential match-making markers." They state further, "The number of permutations for every possible interaction of matching algorithm among patient, therapist, and treatment is endless without some empirical- or theory-driven guidance" (p. 424). It appears clear that the state of current research is such that it is premature to limit the potential client variables to which a therapist may need to adapt. However, the need for a flexible strategy to respond to the variety of client variables remains.

The therapist's capacity for flexibility may well depend on the therapist's level of expertise and experience. Mahoney and Norcross (1993) state, "It is the talented (and perhaps the relatively rare) clinician who is able to respond effectively to the unique needs of different clients and settings" (p. 424). The literature on therapist expertise, according to Mahoney and Norcross (1993), suggests that expert therapists have greater improvisational skills, are more self-regulating, and have a more flexible repertoire of skills than do novice therapists. However, they also point out that there is probably a limit to any therapist's capacity for flexibility, and this understanding "should help us guard against grandiose expectations and capricious posturing on the therapist's part" (p. 424). Complementing the use of a flexible repertoire of relationship stances is the use of "judicious referral." The therapist who is aware of his or her personal range of relationship stances and the limit of that range should not impose a "relationship stance at the client's expense" (Mahoney & Norcross, 1993, p. 425).

Miller, Duncan, and Hubble (1997) discuss research findings that provide a context for understanding the importance of client variables in the therapy relationship. According to the authors, "extratherapeutic factors" of the client and his or her environment contribute 40 percent of the explained variance in therapy improvement measures. This percentage is the highest of any factor. The second highest percentage, 30 percent, is attributed to the therapy relationship. They suggest the importance of client characteristics for the therapy relationship lies not in therapist-offered relationship conditions but rather in the client's *perception* of those conditions. They state, ". . . the most helpful alliances are likely to develop when the therapist establishes a therapeutic alliance that matches the client's [relationship needs]" (Miller et al., 1997, p. 28). Therefore, effective therapists will strive to understand and value a client's individuality and will accommodate the therapy to the client's needs.

Therapist impact on the alliance has been studied as it occurs during the initial phase of therapy and during the middle phase of therapy. The alliance has been found to best predict therapy outcome during the first three sessions of therapy (Horvath & Symonds, 1991). The practical significance of this finding for therapists is that while a strong alliance may not guarantee a positive therapy outcome, a "good enough" alliance may be essential. Ratings of the alliance during the middle phase of therapy generally fluctuate, representing a theoretical rupture-repair cycle in the therapy relationship (Horvath, 1994). The significance of this rupture-repair cycle has been described by Bordin (1994), who refers to the middle phase of therapy as one of necessary "strain." According to Bordin (1994), strains are important to the therapy relationship for several reasons. If a therapy relationship is not strained, it may represent a too positive transference by the client and the failure of the therapist to engage the client in the difficult work of therapy. Furthermore, if the relationship does not undergo periods of strain, it is likely that the client has not been engaged sufficiently in the relationship to experience therapeutic change. Bordin (1994) differentiates between strains due to difficulties in forming a therapy alliance and strains occurring after the initial alliance has been established and states that the strain aspect of the alliance has been little researched.

Similarly, the areas of therapist characteristics and therapist actions contributing to the alliance have been subject to little research. Horvath (1994) in a review of research on the alliance, reports that "the impact of therapist's pretreatment characteristics on the alliance is only beginning to appear in the literature" (pp. 275–276). Regarding the contribution of therapist actions to the alliance, Horvath (1994), cites eight studies. Four of these are on the effect of counselor interpretations on the alliance with a general consensus among the studies indicating nonsignificant results. Studies of therapist characteristics and actions as they impact the alliance will be included in the literature review of this study. However, it may be stated here, following Horvath (1994), that there has been a dearth of studies relating counselor characteristics and actions to the alliance. And, as Horvath (1994) states, "the study of the relationship must ultimately focus on the specification of actions that promote and maintain the alliance to enable the therapist to use this knowledge for the benefit of the client" (p. 278).

The approach of this study was to examine the therapy relationship—a "co-constructed" (Sexton & Whiston, 1994) interactional phenomenon—through the lens of only one of its participants. This area needs conceptual clarification. Indeed, Sexton and Whiston (1994) conclude their review of research based on Gelso and Carter's (1985) definition of the therapy relationship with a call for contextualized, meaning-based (qualitative) research as the most effective means to realize the paradigm shift called for by Gelso and Carter (1985). In such a social-constructionist perspective "the mechanism of the construction of the relationship would become the focal point for both theory and practice (Sexton & Whiston, 1994, p. 63). Furthermore, they state "the primary focus of attention shifts from the identification of components of the relationship to the jointly determined meanings developed by the relationship participants" (Sexton & Whiston, 1994, p. 62).

Nevertheless, the value of eliciting therapists' constructions of the therapy relationship, especially expert therapists, is supported by the following argument: Therapists bring a perspective to the therapy relationship that is different than the clients' perspective, as evidenced by discrepancies in therapist and client ratings of the alliance (Horvath, 1994). It may be assumed that their perspective is guided by such factors as personal qualities, theoretical orientations, and expectations for therapy based on experience. It may be further assumed that these perspectives and expectations for the therapy relationship are applied in an individualized manner.

The purpose of the current study was to elicit from information-rich informants a description of important aspects of the therapy relationship. The study was exploratory and made use of a qualitative methodology. A model of the therapy relationship from the therapist's point of view was not present in current formulations of the therapy relationship. A model of an effective therapy relationship offered by the therapist was derived from the statements of the ten master therapists who comprise the information-rich informants of this study. The model, as developed from practicing master therapists, is intended to increase our knowledge of the therapist-offered therapy relationship and provide new variables for possible future study. Please see Appendix A for a complete account of the study's methodology.

Findings

Derived from the qualitative interviews, categories and domains will be presented and described. Themes have been incorporated into the text. Both the Safe Relationship Domain and the Challenging Relationship Domain contain three categories.

The Safe Relationship Domain

Category A: Master Therapists Evidence a Heightened Responsiveness to the Client. The themes of this category include being sensitive to clients at the beginning of therapy, using therapy techniques to suit client needs, and being nondefensive in hearing client complaints.

The master therapists described the importance that they put on the beginning of the therapy relationship. Particular importance was placed on the initial contact, even if this contact was a phone call. The therapists described the importance of careful listening and responding to the cues that the client is presenting. For example, one respondent described an empowering approach to clients in the initial meeting:

> It is truly listening and being interested and feeding back to them from the beginning what you are hearing. Because I have heard more clients come in saying that they felt hurt or disrespected if people are too curt with them—like they're not interested. . . . So what I say to them when they come in here is that . . . "Do you feel understood and respected?" So to me that's the most important. . . . It's like, right from the beginning, engage them in the process as an equal and a consumer . . . when you give them that, it's like they've got some power.

One master therapist told of foregoing intake formalities to respond to a client's immediate needs:

> When I do an intake, my first thing is "Why are you here? What is it that brought you into therapy?" Sometimes I won't even do an intake until the second session because they are so full of what it is they are upset about.

Another manifestation of heightened sensitivity of master therapists is their wise and judicious use of therapy techniques to meet individual client needs. One master therapist used the analogy of doing research with the client:

> The contract is one way to start, but then we proceed as we experience each other. What I usually say is "This is something we are going to do together. It is a kind of research, and we are both going to work on it together." They [the clients] have the final authority.

Another master therapist discussed her facility with a variety of therapy techniques, which are applied according to client need:

> I may use more than one approach. So I may use psychodynamic and nondirective [approaches] and then with someone [else] a different way. But if the need appears very clearly—let us say for behavioral therapy—then I am very proficient with that also.

An aspect of the master therapists' heightened sensitivity is their ability to hear and respond to clients' complaints. Master therapists' ability to respond to client concerns, even at times to elicit client expressions of such concerns, seems to be a reflection of their experience and maturity as therapists. As one master therapist stated:

> I wrote a paper about this about ten years ago. It said, and I still believe, an apology is one of the best therapeutic tools there is. And I think that so many of our clients who get screwed around by the system, they are so astonished by an apology that it begins to put the relationship back where it belongs.

One master therapist discussed her willingness to admit mistakes as a departure from how she was trained to respond to client complaints. Her training had taught her that client complaints were primarily "about" the client:

> The first thing is to really listen to what the person is saying to you in terms of how they are feeling about the rupture. Sometimes the rupture has to do with something that you actually did. I think very often in the past, the training has been, and emphasis has been, that [relationship problems are] about the client and about transference issues and to turn it back to the client.

Category B: Master Therapists Actively Collaborate with the Client.   Themes in this category involve gearing the therapy agreement to the client's understanding of the problem, mutually resolving impasses in the relationship, and working with clients to form a meaningful therapy termination.

One master therapist described the process of forming the therapy agreement in terms of writing a job description for the therapist:

> I do want to stay with what the client presents. I won't hesitate to point out patterns and invite somebody to go that broader level, but I don't want to enlarge the job description. If somebody comes and says, "I want to hire you to help me with my boss," I don't want to start saying, "Yes, and we'll work on all this other stuff too."

Another master therapist described establishing the therapy agreement as a cooperative process:

> It's probably not as formal as a therapy contract, as in some settings where they actually require contracts. I don't do this that formally. I usually ask what they are looking for and what their expectations are and give them some feedback of what I believe I can deliver. I try to convey that it is basically a cooperative process—so it isn't me establishing the terms and trying to deliver.

One respondent described varying the agreement according to client familiarity with therapy:

> So with more sophisticated clients it might be that some of those things [in formal agreements] are not necessary and I have to figure that out. I don't do anything without them.

while another respondent summed up his valuation of forming the therapy agreement:

> It immediately establishes a relationship.

When facing a lack of progress in therapy, master therapists openly discuss the difficulty and seek joint solutions. Master therapists described clients not following through on therapy tasks as an expected aspect of the process. The master therapists typically address the resistance directly, align themselves with the client in approaching the resistance, and view the resistance as an opportunity to learn about the client's difficulty in making needed changes. One master therapist said:

> I view resistance as a normal part of the process. I'm likely to find some way to explain it like, "You're here with a purpose in mind of addressing certain kinds of problems, and I see you defeating yourself or digging in your heels and not doing the things that would be most helpful to us in pursuing this problem." So I name what I see in the way of resistance and then inquire what the person thinks about that or feels about that or what they know about the way they are not doing what they need to do. But I would be reluctant to issue any kind of ultimatum about "You have to do this or else—we're not going to do this kind of work"—because I think the process of understanding a resistance is really a big chunk of the therapy. If you get through that, you're near the end of the tunnel.

"Meaningful" termination of therapy is seen as an extension and fulfillment of the therapy contract. Meaningful termination is defined as (a) a termination that is a mutual decision and (b) a termination process that is sensitive to the nature and stage of the therapy relationship. One master therapist discussed tying discussions of terminating with the client to the nature of the relationship:

> Out of the nature of the work comes the nature of the closing. If we've met for three times, we might stop and we might terminate in the same session that the idea of termination comes up. If we've been meeting for three years, we'll probably be talking about it [over time]. We'll probably be tapering off for a while and then talking about ending. It will be one of the background topics.

Another master therapist described arriving at the termination phase of therapy as an intuitive, yet mutual, process:

> Most of the time, what I find is that when it occurs to me that we're ready to end, it's also occurring to them . . . when they do bring it up, I'll ask them, "When did you first think about this?" They'll go back to almost exactly the same time that I was thinking about it. In that sense, I do think we arrive there pretty close together. What usually happens is that we talk about how many more times we need to meet. They'll give me some idea [of their thoughts] about that.

Category C: Master Therapists Seek a Strong, Deep Therapy Relationship.   The master therapists said that a strong therapy relationship is critical for therapy success. This view is described in three interrelated themes of the centrality of the relationship

to the therapeutic enterprise, the great value of a relationship that can withstand ruptures, and how profound healing occurs within a strong therapy relationship.

Master therapists' descriptions of the importance of the relationship ranged from the relationship *being* the therapy to the relationship as *necessary* for therapy. As one master therapist described it:

> I guess my response is—the relationship is the whole thing. This person's investment in our relationship gets to be one of the biggest motivations for pursuing difficult work, for being reliable, for facing pain.

Similarly, another respondent stated:

> I think that [the relationship] is the central aspect. In my view that's the most central part of psychotherapy. Everything else gets siphoned off from where I am in the relationship. . . . All the way along, I don't know if it [the relationship] is part of my technique, I think that is my technique.

Another master therapist talked of the therapeutic relationship as the primary tool in therapy:

> I guess I believe, and I have always maintained this, that the primary tool I use is the relationship. I have a lot of knowledge, I have a lot of skills, but they're wasted if the relationship isn't there. For me, it's the critical dynamic, and everything I'm doing is actually through that relationship.

Master therapists expressed the view that strains and ruptures in the therapy relationship are an expected occurrence. The desired outcome from working through relationship ruptures is a stronger, deeper relationship. The in-therapy experience of repairing a relationship provides a blueprint for the client's repairing other nontherapy relationships. For example, one master therapist described how she explains the importance of working through ruptures with clients:

> What I would say to clients is that a therapy relationship is like all other relationships. Even though sometimes we wouldn't want it to be, it is, and how we repair the rupture in our relationship can also help with ruptures occurring in other relationships. This could be a place where that could happen and serve as a model for that in other experiences.

Ruptures that arise from clients' reenacting prior negative relationship patterns are typically discussed by the master therapists as transference reactions. One master therapist discussed working through ruptures in the context of a client's having not resolved ruptures in previous therapy relationships:

> I just need to be willing to go there with somebody and explore the feelings of a falling-apart relationship and understand what that means in the context of their life history. If I don't chicken out, perhaps they won't chicken out, and we can sort through this together. . . . When somebody comes and tells me about how the last six therapists failed

them and they heard I was the best, I know that I too will fail, and the task will be whether I can work that out.

For the master therapists, client healing occurs because a strong therapy relationship provides a safe environment. Health and healing are seen as natural occurrences that antagonistic environments have thwarted. A strong, healthy, "deep" relationship provides an environment in which the natural process of healing takes place. For example, one master therapist describes how clients may come—through the therapy relationship—to change their experience of themselves:

> Often the people that come in to see you have never felt cared about, have never felt respected, doubt their own judgment, so that by your listening and your attentiveness, you begin the process of respecting them. . . . As they begin to trust you and begin to open up and look at their past history, they begin to see the pieces in their history that have not been helpful or have damaged them, and they can begin to see in a different way. You provide a different way of seeing without blaming . . . and you help them to learn to repair themselves in a relationship of respect.

Another master therapist described psychological healing as analogous to physical healing:

> I think of an old medical school image of how I would facilitate the healing of a wound by stitching it up and covering it up. But another kind of answer would be to let it granulate in and heal from the depth up, and that is more my version of how therapy works. You got an open, gaping wound for a long time. [It] heals from the inside out in the context of this relationship where it is safe and supportive and noninjurious.

Another master therapist described therapeutic healing as occurring because the client has the opportunity to find new symbolic value in his or her experience through the relationship:

> How does psychotherapy heal? . . . I think that one of the things it does is that it's a way in which people can symbolize their experience, put into symbolic form something that has not been put into symbolic form, just by talking about it . . . I think that [the symbolization] bridges the gulf of isolation and alienation that a person may feel from life—the traumas and the dehumanizing experiences or the injustices that they've experienced. It sort of reestablishes that kind of bridge back to humanity, reestablishes that sense of being in the human community. I think that all of this seems to build with reestablishing that kind of link. It has to do with having the opportunity to trust, to feel self-esteem, and to be part of a relationship.

The Challenging Relationship Domain

Category D: Master Therapists Use "Self" in the Therapy Relationship.
Themes here relate to how master therapists describe an awareness of their "selves" as an agent of change in the relationship. Accordingly, they stressed the importance of self-care

and congruency in their professional and personal lives. A distinguishing characteristic of master therapists is their use of themselves as agents of change in the relationship. One master therapist described the importance of therapist awareness of his or her own power in the relationship:

> We can't just do therapy intellectually. That therapy is a relationship, that therapy is about feelings and about history, and recognizing the power of our own psychological and emotional stuff in the process of therapy, we need to recognize the power of that.

Similarly, another respondent discussed the therapist's power needing to be tempered by the quality of the therapist as a person (in the context of a new therapist learning how to be a competent therapist):

> Learn the techniques because they are like arrows in a quiver, so you can pull them out and use them, and they give you power, you need the competence, but develop quality as a person.

Another master therapist emphasized accepting and using one's emotions, such as fear, therapeutically:

> The issue isn't whether you're afraid or not, it's whether you recognize the fear and accept it and use it therapeutically, because the trick is to use yourself therapeutically. Use as many aspects of yourself as you can as a therapeutic agent.

And another respondent described "filtering" the client's experience through himself:

> The therapist's job is to give, not to give the client an explanation, but to engage them in an experience . . . and their experience is, hopefully, of themselves in significant ways, not that it's not of you, but that it still gets filtered through you.

In addition, master therapists use core metaphors to convey their role in therapy. When describing their essential activities as therapists, the master therapists frequently employed a metaphor. A range of metaphors was used, with "guide" being mentioned most frequently. One master therapist stated:

> One of the metaphors I often use with my clients is the metaphor of "The Wilderness Guide," and the way I put that is they can hire me as a guide, because I know a lot about survival in the wilderness—my own, and I've traveled through a lot of wildernesses. I've got a compass; I can start a fire in the rain. I know how to make it through, but this is a new wilderness to me. I haven't been in this particular wilderness before, and so I can't quite predict what we're going to encounter.

Other metaphors include "good mother," "good parent," "helper," and "artist." Last, from a master therapist who used a detective metaphor:

> There are two kinds of therapists as there are two kinds of detectives. There is Sherlock Holmes, and there is Columbo. And Sherlock Holmes is very keen-minded, cuts to the

chase, and does it. And Columbo, who fumbles. I'm a Columbo. I frame the first interview as: We are going to "muck" around; we're going to have to get to know each other and what we can or cannot do here.

Category E: Master Therapists Intensely Engage the Client throughout the Therapy Relationship.

As presented in themes, master therapists engage clients in change by working with client motivation, pacing the therapy, expecting clients to progress, and maintaining the conditions for change.

Master therapists expertly make use of the relationship to increase client motivation. They describe working with client motivation in a variety of ways. For example, if the client comes to therapy because it is required, the therapist will attempt to form an alliance with the client to establish an intrinsic, rather than extrinsic, reason for the therapy. If the alliance cannot be established, the therapy does not go on. One master therapist described building a therapy relationship to effect client motivation:

> I know that I have to build a relationship in which I have leverage, then to use that leverage to help certain things happen. Sometimes the leverage is about becoming very important in somebody's life. Sometimes the leverage is my approval. Sometimes the leverage is my caring. It can take a lot of different manifestations, but I'm very aware that I'm building a relationship to create that leverage.

Two master therapists discussed increasing a client's motivation by focusing on the client's anxiety:

> I can say that I view it as my job to heighten the motivation and that I try to do that by getting them to invest in their growth—recognize that what they've done in the past hasn't worked and try to seal those doors off, to heighten sometimes the anxiety that helps them move towards the change they have to make. So I do heighten motivation.

And:

> Freud said, "You have to help them maintain a certain level of anxiety to keep them stay motivated to be in therapy," which is a very insightful, very interesting observation he made a long, long time ago. What he is saying, in a sense, is that you have got to keep the person looking at what they are struggling with. That is what I think he was talking about and how that affects every nuance of their existence. If you are doing that and helping them work on those things, then they will be motivated to continue to do the work.

Master therapists skillfully pace therapy interventions. They describe pacing interventions to enable clients to make changes at a rate that they can manage. For example, one master therapist told of skillfully responding to clients' wishes for too rapid change with patience and understanding. Another master therapist suggested introducing a wider perspective on the client's therapy issues, but only when the client is ready to hear:

> The issue isn't one of trying to "shoehorn" them into your way of seeing, the issue is trying to help them see how maybe what they are struggling with reflects other things

they may want to consider. It is to reframe the whole issue as you see it, but you have to do that at a pace in which they can hear it. You can't just lay it on them.

Another respondent told of waiting to discuss issues that other therapists might address at the beginning of therapy:

> I try not to deal with a lot of things that a lot of the other people say you have to go through ahead of time until they come up as issues, because I think when they come up as issues they are more important to deal with.

Master therapists described a precision and grace in becoming more active in therapy exactly when it is needed to move the therapy forward. Being more active may include therapists' being more verbally challenging, taking a more didactic approach, or setting limits. The circumstances that may give rise to the therapist's becoming more active include questionable client behavior or the therapist's perceiving that the client would benefit from a carefully applied "push." One master therapist illuminated a more "lecturing" stance with a client with whom she has a values conflict:

> I am very passionate about protecting the young and helpless, and if I see clients not doing that, then I have to say, "You know, you need a lecture from a mother's peak, and I am delivering it. You don't do this with kids." So I will take my stand. I won't throw a client out on that account, but I do make it clear that is not my value system.

Another master therapist told of setting firm ground rules for behavior in couples therapy. The ground rules for behavior also establish a therapeutic contract:

> What I generally do with couples who are verbally abusing each other is to say, "Stop this. You've got to stop that." The situation that comes to mind is one in which the wife would get into these temper outbursts, and she would degrade her husband, and he would get weepy and feel so injured and often sulk. Then she wouldn't respect him for being such a wimp. I said to her, "You've got to stop that." It was early in therapy. They had had a lot of therapy with someone else on that very topic. And I said, "Well, listen, I'm not even going to do therapy on this. It's preliminary in therapy." "Well," she said, "I have a right to my feelings, and I get angry." So we had to dialog about that, and I specifically said, "I'm not going to do therapy with you unless you agree with me. I'm not asking you for perfection; I'm asking you to establish a standard. It's off limits. It's out of bounds. It's a foul ball. You have no right to do it. If you can agree to that, we can start there."

Another master therapist communicated applying a therapeutic "kick" to a client:

> We were talking about some self-hypnosis or some meditation time. He said, "You know, any time we have done that here, it's really helped and made me feel a lot better. But when I try and do it at home, I don't know, I just don't follow through on it." I said to him at that point, "Now this is where I feel like I need to give you a kick in the butt. This is about you taking care of yourself, and what you're telling me is you don't take care of yourself. So I want to give you a kick in the butt." So that's an example of my

response . . . I leaned on my relationship with him, in essence, and said, "I expect you to follow through on this."

Category F: Master Therapists Maintain an Objective Stance in the Relationship.

Themes here focus on how master therapists remain objective within the powerful pulling forces of therapy. Master therapists have a perspective based on extensive experience. They maintain a more objective stance in the therapy relationship, which gives them a wider perspective on the client's experience. Master therapists view their task as attending to the context of the client's experience. Earlier, master therapists described the importance of being present in the relationship with clients. Here they are describing the necessity to be somewhat outside the relationship to increase client awareness of relationship patterns in their lives. One master therapist described this as "the therapist's task":

> Sometimes my task seems to me to be attentive to a larger range of their experience than they are identified with and to bring that in. It's present in them, but it isn't getting much priority in their self-system. I catch that and reinforce it in some way, but I am catching something that is present in their experience. I'm not putting something in their experience that is not there.

Another master therapist recounted asking clients to fill in "missing pieces." In this example, the therapist is not so much pointing out a larger perspective that is known but is more sensing that there is more than what the client has so far disclosed:

> I may say . . . "I need to know more about ta-da ta-da ta-da, which I want you to tell me more about next time so that I have a fuller picture because there are missing pieces here." I do that a lot, and I think this is true across the board with clients.

Another respondent similarly described sensing there is something more for the client to talk about:

> I think it's pretty common that there are directions or ways the client needs to go that are not obvious to them.

Regarding one particular client, the same respondent said:

> I'm clearly going down a path with her now which is not where her [initial] goal was. I also believe that she can't get to that goal without doing these pieces given the history of what she has tried to do and so forth. I'm literally educating her along the way with what I see so that it feels like a progression that makes sense to her.

Master therapists also bring clients' outside relationships into the therapy relationship, which is another means to increase clients' awareness of relationship patterns. One master therapist's example:

> If they are talking about something that is happening, I'll ask them, "Do you find that happening here?" Then we can move closer to the interpersonal relationship between us.

Master therapists view therapy as a series of phases. As a rule, master therapists described the phases as a beginning, a middle, and a termination. Within these three phases of the relationship, the master therapists conceived the nature and tasks differently. Thematically, master therapists locate clients within a temporal framework with expectations for tasks and progress according to the phase. However, they are also mindful of individual complexity and variations in moving through phases.

Several master therapists described distinct parts of the beginning phase of therapy, for example:

> At the beginning, if there is a good, positive connection, there is often some idolizing that goes on by the client, as they would do with their parents. For the first period of time, the positive idolizing is okay because it really helps you get into what's going on, and they trust you a lot.

Another master therapist described the beginning phase as more of an introduction:

> I think there's sort of an introductory phase, a getting to know all the manifestations of a problem or of how a person is constructed. Whether it's family of origin, or defense structure, what their strengths are, or what's all current. So I think there is sort of a generalized introductory phase.

The middle phase of therapy is often described by the master therapists as the working phase. The nature, or content, of the phase varies to some extent according to the master therapist's theoretical orientation. Overall, master therapists told of less rigidity of form and more authenticity. As one master therapist described the middle phase:

> If that phase [beginning] plays out successfully, then I think we move into the next phase, which is more trusting, less game playing . . . to see now whether it's okay not to be so guarded, in which the client can be thoughtless or angry or be embarrassed and let me in on it. I can be more exploratory. I can be a little more spontaneous. I can make a mistake because I'm not being so careful. At that level, there is something more authentic happening. At that level, what happens between us counts for a lot more.

Another master therapist said of the middle phase:

> There are different levels of intimacy that come, phases of intimacy, and some of those places involve increasing conflict where we are more able to identify the difference. Where I am not the same thing, the one they prayed for, and they are not the perfect client that I saw a glimmer of. We begin to engage our differentness, and we begin to experience conflict and some contesting and that kind of apprehension with each other.

Another master therapist illuminated the middle phase of therapy for work with both individual, and couples:

> I think the longest phase is the mid-phase, and I think of that as the working-through phase. Helping people to start identifying more of their feelings and also feelings that

they may feel ashamed of, looking at their part in the relationship issues, looking at areas where they may be blocked or stuck, areas of conflict. I think about that as being mid-phase. If you are doing couples work, it might be the phase where you teach them skills—things like identifying feelings, being able to share them with each other, being able to ask for what they need—those kinds of things where I think it is the working part of the relationship.

The master therapists discussed a variety of ways of ending therapy. They appear to be sensitive to clients' needs in terminating from therapy. The master therapists expressed specifically what is expected of the client and of the therapy in the termination phase. One master therapist talked of planning for termination "well in advance":

I believe in planning for termination well in advance. It doesn't always turn out that way as sometimes the patients have their own agendas going. . . . To set a date somewhere out there in advance, weeks or months depending on the intensity of the therapy. And between now and the termination time, that will be a major subject of our conversations, and it's important that they be paying attention to their feelings and fantasies and dreams in relation to the termination.

Another master therapist said termination comes by the nature of the work that was done in the therapy:

You're looking at how the person will continue to work once they leave—whether they will keep the relationship open so that they can come back, kind of a check-in point, which some people like to do, or whether this would be the end of our relationship.

Finally, one master therapist said that the end phase of therapy comes from experiencing a change in how each party in the relationship experiences the other:

At that point, there is a deeper commitment to work together where our differentness becomes a richness in what's happening here. My differentness from what they thought [I was] becomes an asset to them, and their differentness becomes a pleasure to me.

Discussion

Throughout the interview process, the master therapists verbally demonstrated their astute awareness of the therapy relationship. The six categories identified in the present study may be conceived as relationship stances employed by master therapists. Table 4.1 (p. 70) presents the correspondence of categories with the proposed relationship stances. Norcross (1993) describes relationship stances as forms of the therapy relationship, chosen by therapists, to meet individual client needs. Norcross compares choosing a relationship stance to choosing a clinical technique to match a client's presenting problem. He says, "It is widely acknowledged that psychotherapists . . . attempt to adjust their interpersonal style and stimulus value to meet the needs of the unique client and the singular circumstance" (p. 402).

TABLE 4.1   Correspondence between Categories and Relationship Stances

Categories	Relationship Stances
Safe Relationship Domain: Categories A, B, C	
A: Master therapists evidence a heightened responsiveness to the client.	Responsive Stance
B: Master therapists actively collaborate with the client.	Collaborative Stance
C: Master therapists seek a strong, deep therapy relationship.	Joining Stance
Challenging Relationship Domain: Categories D, E, F	
D: Master therapists use "self" in the therapy relationship.	Self Stance
E: Master therapists intensely engage the client throughout the therapy relationship.	Engaging Stance
F: Master therapists maintain an objective stance on the relationship.	Objective Stance

In the proposed model presented below, the relationship stances are grouped within the two domains. Each of the domains—the safe relationship domain and the challenging relationship domain—describes a complementary aspect of the therapy relationship.

Safe Relationship Domain

The master therapists' relationship stances within the safe relationship domain (comprising categories A, B, and C) have these elements in common: The client and his or her needs are the central focus, the therapist constructs the relationship to be a secure base from which the client may express feelings and explore new behaviors, and the client is able to feel the empathy and concern of another human being who is worthy of the client's trust. For many clients, the relationship stances contained in the safe relationship domain may contain the essential ingredients for the client to make necessary changes. In the responsive stance, the master therapist is warm and receptive, listens, and offers unconditional positive regard. The client-centered approach is seen as the theoretical framework that is most descriptive of the responsive stance. A master therapist using the collaborative stance emphasizes the client's partnership in the therapy alliance. Here, the therapist supports and encourages the client's involvement in setting the therapy agenda. The master therapist using the joining stance creates the relationship as a cocoon-like haven in which the client may heal. The therapist offers the conditions of trust necessary for the client to enter into such a relationship.

Challenging Relationship Domain

In contrast, the master therapists described another set of relationship stances within the challenging relationship domain (comprising categories D, E, and F). "Challenge" is considered the quality of requiring the full use of one's abilities, energy, or resources (*American Heritage Dictionary*, 1992). The challenging relationship domain describes more active relationship stances by the master therapists, relationship stances that overtly bring forth from clients' behaviors that approach clients' therapy goals. In the objective stance, the master therapist provides interpretations and information and evaluates progress. Goldfried and Safran (1986) describe the therapist's role of offering clients a more objective perspective on themselves and their world as a general clinical strategy common to all therapy orientations. The engaging stance emphasizes the master therapist's responsible role to move the therapy forward and the therapist's increased activity in guiding and directing the therapy. A description of the "team approach" in cognitive therapy illustrates this stance:

> The cognitive therapist implies that there is a team approach to the solution of a patient's problem: that is, a therapeutic alliance where the patient supplies raw data . . . while the therapist provides structure and expertise on how to solve the problems . . . The therapist fosters the attitude "Two heads are better than one" in approaching personal difficulties. When the patient is so entangled in symptoms that he is unable to join in problem solving, the therapist may have to assume a leading role. (Beck, Emery, & Greenberg, 1985, p. 175)

Finally, the master therapist employing the self stance emphasizes the therapist's role in the relationship of trust. The therapist intentionally makes use of his or her personality and personal resources to authentically relate to the client, but does not "lose" him- or herself in the relationship.

Theoretical Correlates to Proposed Model of Master Therapists' Relationship Stances

The consistent finding that the therapeutic relationship accounts for more therapy outcome variance than does technical interventions (e.g., Krupnick, Sotsky, Simmens, Moyer, Elkin, Watkins, & Pilkonis, 1996) makes it surprising that a prescriptive approach to the therapy relationship has not been the subject of more research activity. As Norcross (1993) states, "Although many experienced clinicians may intuitively try to tailor their relational stance to individual clients, there are few published attempts to systematize the process" (p. 402). Fortunately, a recent effort to examine the efficacy of relationship stances on therapeutic outcome has been undertaken by various researchers. Findings from the Task Force on Empirically Supported Therapy Relationships have made a significant contribution to our understanding of the impact relationship stances have on positive therapy outcomes (Norcross, 2002). Norcross (2001) summarizes the findings of the task force by stating that the "therapy relationship is crucial to outcome . . . can be improved by certain therapist contributions, and . . . can be effectively tailored to the individual patient" (p. 354). As an example, Beutler, Rocco, Moleiro, and Talebi (2001) note that for clients displaying high levels of resistance, the optimal therapist stance appears to be nondirective, while a more directive therapist stance is beneficial for clients' with low levels of resistance. Another example of therapist stances is offered by Prochaska and Norcross (2001), who prescribe relationship stances based on client readiness for change. In the early stages of change, the authors suggest a "nurturing parent" role. To help the client delve deeper and gain insight into his or her problems, the authors suggest the therapist take on a "Socratic" teacher role. Each of the five stages of readiness for change require that the therapist adapt to best facilitate client movement.

Another related model is Adaptive Counseling and Therapy (ACT) (Howard, Nance, & Myers, 1986), a system of prescribing relationship styles to task-readiness levels of clients. ACT has been utilized with humanistic, cognitive-behavioral, and psychodynamic psychotherapies (Nance & Associates, 1995). The ACT model (Howard et al., 1986) is similar in several respects to the findings of relationship stances noted in this study. ACT posits two dimensions of therapist activity—supportive and directive—that correspond to the safe and challenging relationship domains. In ACT, the two dimensions evolve into four therapist styles. The present findings derive six relationship stances from two domains. The ACT model has developed an assessment of client characteristics that is prescriptive of a preferred therapist style. The present findings, having no client database, do not match relationship stances with client characteristics. However, it appears from the interviews that a therapist stance may be chosen and applied according to the master therapist's assessment of client need. The proposed model of relationship stances derived from the master therapists' interviews was developed without knowledge of ACT. The many similarities support the construct validity of each of these models.

In addition, the present findings of master therapists' relationship stances are similar to Clarkson's (1994) theory of therapy relationship modes. Five types, or modes, of therapy relationships are described: (a) the working alliance, (b) the transferential/countertransferential relationship, (c) the reparative/developmentally needed relationship, (d) the I/You relationship, and (e) the transpersonal relationship. A primary aim of Clarkson's descriptions of relationship modes appears to be to connect the various modes of relationship with different therapy orientations. Clarkson's theory is offered here because it is similar to the present findings of relationship stances: The therapy relationship may take different forms, as intentionally constructed by the master therapist, in response to different client therapy needs.

Limitations

The intent of this study was to describe how master therapists construct the therapy relationship. The study was exploratory and preliminary, and as such, it carried several limitations. The study sample was primarily white, middle-aged, and in private practice. They were representative neither of therapists more generally nor of master or expert therapists who undoubtedly work in a variety of settings and are of diverse backgrounds.

The method of the study allowed for a "feedback loop" through the use of a second interview with the therapists to reflect on the initial formulation of themes and categories. Additionally, an auditor was extensively involved in the formulation and reformulation of the results. These are forms of triangulation that are encouraged to improve validity in qualitative studies. However, the internal validity of the study would have been augmented through other forms of triangulation (Hill, Thompson, &

Williams, 1997). For instance, collecting data from clients regarding the relationship stances that they experience with their therapists would have increased the validity of these formulations.

Implications and Recommendations

The importance of relationship stances found in this study may have implications for training. As evidenced in the literature review, there is a wealth of information available about the therapy relationship, generally, and a developing knowledge of therapist contributions to the relationship, specifically. A curriculum focusing on this literature, highlighting the efficacy of the therapy relationship in predicting good therapy outcomes, could be offered to students.

In clinical training, students could learn about flexible strategies for relationship stances in response to client variables. An important component of such learning would be the student's self-awareness regarding one's "relationship capacity." One's relationship capacity is not a static sum; nevertheless, students could begin to explore the following questions: Can I work with a hostile client, a dependent client, or an involuntary client? What would be my relationship stance toward clients with certain characteristics? Such questions may open up avenues of self-exploration of one's strengths and limitations.

Future research may incorporate a strategy of studying relationship stances, working alliance measures, and therapy outcome. General measures of therapist relationship skills—for instance, "therapist capacity for relationship" (Luborsky et al., 1985)—and measures of therapist social adjustment (Dunkle & Friedlander, 1996) have been found to correlate with alliance measures. However, these measures lack specificity and do not tell us why some therapists are more effective than others in forming therapy relationships. Therapist relationship stances may be operationalized and studied for their association with variables such as client relationship expectations.

In addition, we recommend that future studies continue to make use of information-rich informants. A strategy of exploratory, qualitative research is a recognized means to discover new variables, with information-rich informants an excellent source for identifying the most salient variables (Patton, 1990). A quote from a quantitative study comparing master therapists' interpersonal interventions illustrates the value of research with information-rich informants: "How do we as psychologists define the 'state of the art'? Is it by the treatment manuals included in clinical trials or is it by what master therapists, who have been nominated by those who wrote the manuals, actually do in clinical practice?" (Goldfried, Raue, & Castonquay, 1998, p. 809). Research with information-rich informants, such as in Goldfried et al.'s study, supports the notion that information-rich informants provide different data than other sources. Also, at higher levels of professional attainment, there is, ideally, a distilling of the best practice techniques.

This study was conducted with a view similar to Teyber and McClure (2000), who said, "In many studies, what therapists say and do in the therapy hour that promotes a good therapy alliance has proven to be the most important contributor to change and positive treatment outcome" (p. 70). Using a sample of master therapists, we have explored their construction of the working alliance. The master therapists' belief that effective therapy involves safety and challenge (which we conceptualized as the safe relationship domain and the challenging relationship domain) reminds one of the classic statement that an ideal climate for human development involves an optimal balance of support and challenge. Secondly, within each of the domains, we have suggested that master therapists use relationship stances. Within the safe relationship domain, the therapist is attuned to the client's needs (the responsive stance), is attentive to the client's participation in therapy (the collaborative stance), and is receptive to the client's deepest concerns (the joining stance). Within the challenging relationship domain, the engaging stance has the therapist employ a more directive role, the objective stance has the therapist reframe the client's experience in a larger context, and the self stance has the therapist employ his or her personality to effect client change. Perhaps master therapists are those who can use their talents as a gifted artist would—in a creative way where therapeutic tools such as timing, intensity, and relationship stances are applied optimally.

References

Al-Darmaki, F., & Kivlighan, D. M. Jr. (1993). Congruence in client-counselor expectations for relationship and the working alliance. *Journal of Counseling Psychology, 40,* 379–384.

American Heritage Dictionary of the English Language (3rd ed.). (1992). Boston: Houghton Mifflin.

Anastasi, A., & Urbina, S. (1997). *Psychological testing* (7th ed.). Englewood Cliffs, NJ: Prentice-Hall.

Asay, T. P., & Lambert, M. J. (1999). The empirical case for the common factors in therapy: Quantitative findings. In M. A. Hubble, B. L. Duncan, & S. D. Miller (Eds.), *The heart and soul of change: What works in therapy.* Washington, DC: American Psychological Association.

Bachelor, A. (1991). Comparison and relation to outcome of diverse measures of the helping alliance as seen by client and therapist. *Psychotherapy: Theory, Research, and Practice, 28,* 534–549.

Bachelor, A. (1995). Clients perception of the therapeutic alliance: A qualitative analysis. *Journal of Counseling Psychology, 42,* 323–337.

Bachelor, A., & Horvath, A. O. (1999). The therapeutic relationship. In M. A. Hubble, B. L. Duncan & S. D. Miller (Eds.), *The heart and soul of change: What works in therapy.* Washington, DC: American Psychological Association.

Beck, A. T., Emery, G., & Greenberg, R. L. (1985). *Anxiety disorders and phobias: A cognitive perspective.* New York: Basic Books.

Beutler, L. E., & Consoli, A. (1993). Matching the therapist's interpersonal stance to client's characteristics: Contributions from systematic eclectic psychotherapy. *Psychotherapy, 30,* 417–422.

Beutler, L. E., Rocco, F., Moleiro, C. M., & Talebi, H. (2001). Resistance. *Psychotherapy: Theory/Research/Practice/Training, 38,* 431–436.

Blatt, S. J., Sanislow, C. A., Zuroff, D., Pilkonis, P. (1996). Characteristics of effective therapists: Further analyses of data from the National Institute of Mental Health Treatment of Depression Collaborative Research Program. *Journal of Consulting and Clinical Psychology, 64,* 1276–1284.

Bordin, E. S. (1979). The generalizability of the psychoanalytic concept of the working alliance. *Psychotherapy: Theory, Research, and Practice, 16,* 252–260.

Bordin, E. S. (1994). Theory and research on the therapeutic working alliance: New directions. In A. O. Horvath & L. S. Greenberg (Eds.). *The working alliance: Theory, research, and practice.* New York: Wiley.

Clarkson, P. (1994). The psychotherapeutic relationship. In P. Clarkson & M. Pokorny (Eds.). *The handbook of psychotherapy* (pp. 28–48). London: Routledge.

Dolan, R., Arnkoff, D., & Glass, C. (1993). Client attachment style and the psychotherapist's interpersonal stance. *Psychotherapy, 30,* 408–412.

Dunkle, J. H., & Friedlander, M. L. (1996). Contribution of therapist experience and personal characteristics to the working alliance. *Journal of Counseling Psychology, 43,* 456–460.

Foreman, S. A., & Marmar, C. R. (1985). Therapist actions that address initially poor therapeutic alliances in psychotherapy. *American Journal of Psychiatry, 142,* 922–926.

Freud, S. (1912). The dynamics of transference. In *The standard edition of the complete works of Sigmund Freud* (pp. 97–108). London: Hogarth.

Gelso, C. J., & Carter, J. A. (1985). The relationship in counseling and psychotherapy: Components, consequences, and theoretical antecedents. *The Counseling Psychologist, 13,* 155–243.

Goldfried, M. R., Raue, P. J., & Castonquay, L. G. (1998). The therapeutic focus in significant sessions of master therapists: A comparison of cognitive-behavioral and psychodynamic-interpersonal interventions. *Journal of Consulting and Clinical Psychology, 66,* 803–810.

Goldfried, M. R., & Safran, J. D. (1986). Future directions in psychotherapy integration. In J. D. Norcross (Ed.), *Handbook of eclectic psychotherapy.* New York: Brunner/Mazel.

Greenson, R. R. (1967). *The technique and practice of psychoanalysis (Vol.1).* New York: International Universities Press.

Hartley, D. E., & Strupp, H. H. (1983). The therapeutic alliance: Its relationship to outcome in brief psychotherapy. In J. Masling (Ed.), *Empirical studies of psychoanalytic theories (Vol. 1),* Hillsdale, NJ: Lawrence Erlbaum Associates.

Henry, W. P., Strupp, H. H., Butler, S. F., Schacht, T. E., & Binder, J. L. (1993). Effects of training in time-limited dynamic psychotherapy: Changes in therapist behavior. *Journal of Consulting and Clinical Psychology, 61,* 434–440.

Hill, C. E., Thompson, B., & Williams, E. (1997). A guide to conducting consensual qualitative research. *The Counseling Psychologist, 25,* 517–572.

Horowitz, M. J., Marmar, C., Weiss, D. S., DeWitt, K. N., & Rosenbaum, R. (1984). Brief psychotherapy of bereavement reactions: The relationship of process to outcome. *Archives of General Psychiatry, 41,* 438–448.

Horvath, A. O. (1994). Research on the alliance. In A. O. Horvath & L. S. Greenberg (Eds.), *The working alliance: Theory, research, and practice* (pp. 259–286). New York: Wiley.

Horvath, A. O., & Greenberg, L. S. (1994). Introduction (pp. 1–9). In A. O. Horvath & L. S. Greenberg (Eds.), *The working alliance: Theory, research, and practice.* New York: Wiley.

Horvath, A. O., & Luborsky, L. (1993). The role of the therapeutic alliance in psychotherapy. *Journal of Consulting and Clinical Psychology, 61,* 561–573.

Horvath, A. O., & Symonds, B. D. (1991). Relation between working alliance and outcome in psychotherapy: A meta-analysis. *Journal of Counseling Psychology, 38,* 139–149.

Howard, G. S., Nance, D. W., & Myers, P. (1986). Adaptive counseling and therapy: An integrative, eclectic model. *The Counseling Psychologist, 14,* 363–442.

Jones, E. E. (1985). *Manual for the Psychotherapy Q-Sort.* Unpublished manuscript, University of California, Berkeley.

Kivlighan, D. M. (1990). Relationship between counselor use of intentions and clients perception of working alliance. *Journal of Counseling Psychology, 37,* 87–97.

Kivlighan, D. M., Patton, M. J., & Foote, D. (1998). Moderating effects of client attachment on the counselor experience-working alliance relationship. *Journal of Counseling Psychology, 45,* 274–278.

Kivlighan, D. M., & Schmitz, P. (1992). Counselor technical activity in cases with improving working alliances and continuing-poor working alliances. *Journal of Counseling Psychology, 39,* 32–38.

Krupnick, J. L., Sotsky, S. M., Simmens, S., Moyer, J., Elkin, I., Watkins, J., & Pilkonis, P. A. (1996). The role of the therapeutic alliance in psychotherapy and pharmacotherapy outcome: Findings in the National Institute of Mental Health Treatment of Depression Collaborative Research Program. *Journal of Consulting and Clinical Psychology, 64,* 532–539.

Lazarus, A. (1993). Tailoring the therapeutic relationship, or being an authentic chameleon. *Psychotherapy, 30,* 404–407.

Luborsky, L., Crits-Christoph, P., Alexander, L., Margolis, M., & Cohen, M. (1983). Two helping alliance methods for predicting outcomes of psychotherapy: A counting signs versus global ratings method. *Journal of Nervous and Mental Diseases, 171,* 480–491.

Luborsky, L., McLellan, T., Woody, G. E., O'Brien, C. P., & Auerbach, A. (1985). Therapist success and its determinants. *Archives of General Psychiatry, 42*, 602–611.

Mahoney, M., & Norcross, J. (1993). Relationship styles and therapeutic choices: A commentary on the preceding four articles. *Psychotherapy, 30*, 423–v426.

Mahrer, A. (1993). The experiential relationship: Is it all-purpose or is it tailored to the individual client? *Psychotherapy, 30*, 413–422.

Mallinckrodt, B., & Nelson, M. L. (1991). Counselor training level and the formation of the psychotherapeutic working alliance. *Journal of Counseling Psychology, 38*, 133–138.

Marmar, C.R., Horowitz, M. J., Weiss, D. S., & Mariaza, E. (1986). The development of the therapeutic alliance rating system. In L. S. Greenberg & W. M. Pinsof (Eds.), *The psychotherapy: A research handbook.* New York: Guilford.

Miller, S. D., Duncan. B. L., & Hubble, M. A. (1997). *Escape from babel: Toward a unifying language for psychotherapy practice.* New York: W. W. Norton Co.

Nance, D. W., & Associates (Eds.). (1995). *How therapists act: Cases combining major approaches to psychotherapy and the adaptive counseling and therapy model.* Washington, DC: Accelerated Development.

Norcross, J. (1993). Tailoring relationship stances to client needs: An introduction. *Psychotherapy: Theory, Research, and Practice, 30*, 402–403.

Norcross, J. C. (2001). Purposes, processes, and products of the task force on empirically supported therapy relationships. *Psychotherapy: Theory/Research/Practice/Training, 38*, 345–356.

Norcross, J. C. (Ed.). (2002). *Psychotherapy relationships that work: Therapist contributions and responsiveness to patient needs.* New York: Oxford University Press.

Patton, M. Q. (1990). *Qualitative research and evaluation methods* (2nd ed.). Newbury Park, CA: Sage Publications.

Prochaska, J. O., & Norcross, J. C. (2001). Stages of change. *Psychotherapy: Theory/Research/Practice/Training, 38*, 443–448.

Rogers, C. R. (1957). The necessary and sufficient conditions of therapeutic personality change. *Journal of Consulting Psychology, 21*, 95–103.

Safran, J. D., & Muran, J. C. (1996). The resolution of ruptures in the therapeutic alliance. *Journal of Consulting and Clinical Psychology, 64*, 447–458.

Sexton, T. L., & Whiston, S. C. (1994). The status of the counseling relationship: An empirical review, theoretical implications, and research directions. *The Counseling Psychologist, 22*, 7–78.

Strong, S. R. (1968). Counseling: An interpersonal influence process. *Journal of Counseling Psychology, 15*, 215–224.

Tallman, K., & Bohart, A. C. (1999). The client as a common factor: Clients as self-healers. In M. A. Hubble, B. L. Duncan & S. D. Miller (Eds.), *The heart and soul of change.* Washington, DC: American Psychological Association.

Teyber, E., & McClure, F. (2000). Therapist variables. In C. R. Snyder & R. E. Ingram (Eds.), *Handbook of psychological change.* New York: Wiley.

Tobin, S. (1990). *Multidimensional scaling analysis of the Psychotherapy Process Q-Sort.* Unpublished manuscript. University of Missouri, Columbia.

Wampold, B. E. (2001). *The great psychotherapy debate: Models, methods, and findings.* Mahwah, NJ: Lawrence Erlbaum Associates.

5 Emotional Wellness and Professional Resiliency of Master Therapists[1]

MARY A. MULLENBACH

THOMAS M. SKOVHOLT

This chapter focuses on the methods used by one group of mental health practitioners to maintain professional vitality. Jennings and Skovholt (1999) initiated a research project with ten peer-nominated mental health practitioners. The purpose of that initial study was to identify the components of mastery among this group of expert practitioners. Based on their findings, Jennings and Skovholt (1999) developed a model of expertise that included three components: cognitive, emotional, and relational. The authors also suggested that, in an attempt to develop a more comprehensive understanding of the qualities of highly effective therapists, future research should explore the emotional domain of practitioner development. Included in this domain are coping strategies and self-care practices geared toward preserving emotional wellness and insuring professional vitality. Their suggestion is particularly important given the multitude of stressors that currently confront mental health practitioners.

The debilitating effects of the counseling role on the practitioner have long been recognized as an occupational hazard (Freudenberger & Robbins, 1979). Areas of stress stem from external and internal sources such as professional and personal experience, client issues and behaviors, and the work environment. For example, practitioners engage in an ongoing series of professional attachments and separations (Skovholt, 2001). This process is often intensified by lack of client success, nonreciprocated giving within the counseling relationship, overwork, difficult client behaviors, discouragement due to the slow and uneven pace of the counseling process, constant exposure to the suffering of others, the practitioners' existing personal issues that emerge in response to involvement in the counseling process, isolation, and administrative demands from

[1]From Thomas M. Skovholt, *The Resilient Practitioner: Burnout Prevention and Self-Care Strategies for Counselors, Therapists, Teachers, and Health Professionals.* Published by Allyn and Bacon, Boston, MA. Copyright (c) 2001 by Pearson Education. Adapted by permission of the publisher.

agency and managed health care organizations (Dupree & Day, 1995; Farber, 1990; Kassam-Adams, 1995).

In addressing the hazards of the profession, Sussman (1995) stated: "Although it is rare that the problem is openly acknowledged, ample evidence indicates that the practice of psychotherapy poses significant dangers to clinicians" (p. 1). Based on his review, Sussman suggests that the work of psychotherapy exacts a "heavy toll" on the practitioner. Other researchers (Freudenberger, 1975; Neumann & Gamble, 1995) have also explored the effects of work-related stress on the practitioner. Often, these sources of stress are discussed in regard to their association with professional burnout or secondary traumatization.

According to many authors (Freudenberger & Robbins, 1979; Grosch & Olsen, 1994; Neumann & Gamble, 1995; Norcross, 1990), the effects of practitioner-related stress can be pervasive and include symptoms such as depression, negative self-appraisal, guilt, emotional detachment, anxiety, loss of meaning, omnipotence, callousness, a loss of authenticity, compulsivity, and various psychosomatic complaints. At the most advanced level, burnout represents an emotional exhaustion that reflects a profound psychological, physical, and spiritual depletion.

Farber (1983a) suggests that the cumulative effects of counseling can have a substantial negative impact on practitioners' self-identity, behavior, and attitudes outside of the work setting. These existing stressors may be intensified by current changes within the mental health profession such as issues connected to service delivery and the growing number of clients who present complex treatment issues such as comorbid diagnosis (Dupree & Day, 1995; Farber, 1990).

Review of the Literature

This section provides a brief summary of studies that explore factors that contribute to professional burnout and vicarious traumatization among mental health practitioners. It specifically discusses stressors related to professional and personal experience, difficult client behaviors and issues, work setting, and vicarious traumatization. Important variables that appear to promote professional resiliency are also highlighted.

Being a Novice as a Stress Factor

Numerous researchers cite work experience as a factor that impacts stress among practitioners. Farber and Heifetz (1981) noted higher levels of personal depletion among practitioners who had been in the field for one to three years versus those professionals who were more experienced. Rodolfa, Kraft, and Reilley (1988) obtained similar findings in their comparison between trainees and more experienced practitioners. In this study trainees reported significantly more stress connected to difficult client behaviors, counseling experiences, and their own beliefs and expectations. Ackerly, Burnell, Holder, and Kurdek (1988) found professional experience to be related to emotional exhaustion and depersonalization, with novice practitioners reporting higher levels of distress in these areas. Research by Pearlman and MacIan (1995) indicated that trauma practitioners with less experience showed more disruptions in cognitive schemas than did seasoned professionals.

One conclusion that can be drawn from these findings is that the early years of a practitioner's career represent a critical phase of professional development. It is one in which novice practitioners frequently report feeling overwhelmed and therefore at risk for becoming overinvolved in the counseling process (Farber, 1990). Sussman (1995) suggests that training programs historically have been remiss in preparing students for the occupational hazards of their future work. More effective education in this area would help to normalize events confronted in the first years of professional practice. Coster and Schwebel (1997) highlighted the importance of peer support within the work setting. Peer support is an especially salient variable for novice practitioners.

Personal Trauma History as a Stress Factor

Studies in this area investigate the influence of personal experience on practitioners' perception of stress. Research on this topic is focused in two areas: childhood trauma history and current life events. Researchers (Racusin, Abramowitz, & Winter, 1981) have suggested a relationship between childhood history and career choice, such that an individual may enter into a helping profession to deal correctively with an early history of distress. In their study, Pearlman and MacIan (1995) examined childhood trauma history as a factor in stress among practitioners. Results indicated that subjects with trauma history and less work experience reported higher levels of distress on both the general and specific measures. Subjects with trauma history and more experience reported significantly less general distress. One possible explanation offered by the researchers is that as experience and competence increase, symptoms abate.

It is noteworthy and perhaps very surprising that, given their high level of early trauma, subjects surveyed by Elliott and Guy (1993) reported less distress in adulthood as compared to subjects from other professions. It is possible that the effects of professional training as well as the subjects' greater likelihood to engage in their own personal therapy enhanced their coping abilities. Radke and Mahoney (2000) obtained similar findings in a survey that compared the personal lives of therapists and research psychologists. Their results suggest that the work of a practitioner is both stressful and deeply enriching.

Supportive Relationships as a Stress Reliever

Studies by Mahoney (1997) and Coster and Schwebel (1997) identified self-care practices among practitioners. A primary theme that emerged from their research is the importance that practitioners place on maintaining supportive relationships both within and outside of the work setting. These relationships included peer support, personal relationships, supervision, personal therapy, and ongoing contact with families of origin. Catherall (1995) suggests that peer support within the work setting is essential for the practitioner. Given the highly subjective and personal nature of practitioner-client interaction, it is helpful to access a colleague-level professional viewpoint. This resource may enable the practitioner to maintain a healthy perspective and appropriate boundaries within counseling relationships. Practitioners often use positive relationships outside of the work setting to maintain a balanced outlook in work as well as life.

Client Behaviors as a Stress Factor

Studies that investigated the impact of client behaviors on practitioners' perception of stress yield an interesting finding. Farber (1983a, 1983b) identified two dimensions of stressful client behavior: (a) psychopathological and (b) resistances. He found that the stress associated with each of these factors fluctuated significantly according to certain practitioner background variables. For example, client behaviors related to the psychopathological factor were more stressful for institutional-based practitioners than for private practitioners. A study by Deutsch (1984) yielded similar findings with reports of stress due to emotional arousal in the session more common among agency-based practitioners than for private practitioners. A conclusion that can be drawn from these results is that the dynamics of a counseling relationship are complex and may be influenced by several factors. Farber (1983b) suggests that one key factor in this relationship is the practitioner's attitude toward the client. In their study that examined practitioners' responses to difficult clients, Medeiros and Prochaska (1988) identified optimistic perseverance as being a successful coping strategy. The phrase "optimistic perseverance" describes those practitioners who are able to persist with difficult clients.

Positive Work Environment as a Stress Reliever

A consistent finding is noted among studies that explore the impact of work environment on practitioners' perception of stress. Practitioners who worked in agencies or managed health care sites reported higher levels of stress than private practitioners. In reviewing their findings, Savicki and Cooley (1987) suggest that work environments that promote well-functioning are those where practitioners receive encouragement from colleagues and support through supervisory relationships. Raquepaw and Miller (1989) suggest that institutional interventions that counter practitioner stress include decreasing paperwork and administrative duties, structuring the day to include breaks, improving work relations between staff members, and creating social support systems. These suggestions are aligned with those made by other researchers (Rosenbloom, Pratt, & Pearlman, 1995) who emphasize the role that work environment plays in supporting effective practitioners.

The role work environment plays as a factor in practitioner functioning is becoming increasingly important as changes within the mental health profession include issues connected to managed health care. Snibbe, Radcliffe, Weisberger, Richards, and Kelly (1989) note that practitioners are frequently caught between trying to meet clients' treatment needs at the same time they are expected to meet the expectations placed on them from health maintenance organizations (HMOs). Dupree and Day (1995) noted higher levels of job satisfaction reported by private practitioners compared to practitioners who worked in public sector and managed care settings.

Vicarious Traumatization as a Stress Factor

Secondary or vicarious traumatization represents an emerging area of concern for practitioners. Secondary traumatization is a term that refers to disturbing but predictable symptoms that represent a practitioner's response to repeatedly hearing about the suffering of others. Study in this area emerged out of research focused on burnout and post-traumatic stress disorder (PTSD). The DSM-IV (1994) defines the first criterion for PTSD as:

> The essential feature of post-traumatic stress disorder is the development of characteristic symptoms following exposure to an extreme traumatic stressor involving direct personal experience of an event that involves actual or threatened death or serious injury, or other threat to one's physical integrity; or witnessing an event that involves death, injury, or a threat to the physical integrity of another person; or learning about unexpected or violent death, serious harm, or threat of death or injury experienced by a family member or close associate. (p. 424)

Figley (1995) proposes that an individual, such as a mental health practitioner, can be harmed without actually being present when the event occurs. According to Saakvitne and Pearlman (1996), "Vicarious traumatization is the transformation of the therapist's or helper's inner experience as a result of empathic engagement with survivor clients and their trauma material. Simply put, when we open our hearts to hear someone's story of devastation or betrayal, our cherished beliefs are challenged and we are changed" (p. 25). This transformation is influenced by specific environmental factors and the process of their interaction with characteristics of the practitioner. McCann and Pearlman (1990) suggest that symptoms of burnout (e.g., numbing and avoidance patterns) may be the final result of repeated exposure to traumatic material that has not been assimilated or worked through. Vicarious traumatization represents a process in which a practitioners' view of self and the world is altered through repeated exposure to trauma material. It is an occupational hazard and yet some practitioners have been hesitant to discuss the perils inherent in their practice (Sussman, 1995). It is essential that practitioners understand the potential costs entailed in work with clients who present painful issues. This may best be accomplished through professional training programs that prepare the future practitioner specifically for this element of practice and stress the importance of balance in regard to caseload, work activities, and relationships. Once in the work force, it is critical that peer and supervisory support is available to normalize experiences, to facilitate an understanding of emotional reactions to trauma clients, and to provide an open environment that invites discussion (Pearlman & MacIan, 1995). Rosenbloom, Pratt, and Pearlman (1995) advocate for comprehensive organizational support that includes ongoing training and supervision, case conferences, biweekly seminars, and consultation.

Summary

The vast majority of studies that explore work-related factors among mental health practitioners have identified variables and experiences that are stressful and, as a result, increase the risk of burnout or vicarious traumatization in this group of professionals. A primary concern about this body of research is that it has concentrated almost exclusively on the negative in regard to the nature of the work and its potential effects on the practitioner (Ackerly, Burnell, Holder, & Kurdek, 1988; Farber, 1990). A second concern about this existing body of work is that it has relied heavily on survey research (Norcross, Prochaska, & DiClemente, 1986; Pearlman & MacIan; 1995; Rodolfa, Kraft, & Reilly, 1988). While this body of research has yielded much data, the information it provides is often of a superficial quality and questions exist in regard to the validity of its results. Although stressors have clearly been identified, much less is known about professional resiliency and actual coping strategies that enable practitioners to maintain a positive level of emotional wellness.

A multitude of variables impact mental health practitioners throughout the course of their professional development. While a substantial body of the research identifies specific stressors, fewer studies (Coster & Schwebel, 1997) have been completed that explore those factors and self-care practices that sustain professional vitality. The current study sought to investigate these key factors in a group of highly seasoned practitioners who are considered master therapists. The study explored how these individuals coped with critical incidents and key stressors throughout the span of their professional careers. For a more detailed accounting of the methodology used in this study, please see Appendix A.

Results

From the data analysis, we have identified twenty-three themes within five categories. The five categories are: (a) professional stressors, (b) emergence of the expert practitioner, (c) creating a positive work structure, (d) protective factors, (e) nurturing self through solitude and relationships (see Table 5.1).

Category A: Professional Stressors

Category A contains four themes that identify stressors that are confronted by the participants in their work.

Theme 1: Participants Are Stressed by Issues That Challenge Their Competency.
Participants reported an array of issues and events that represented a challenge to their sense of wellness. Sometimes, as in the case of a suicidal client, these experiences represented unpredicted critical incidents for the practitioners. Other, less intense events and issues were chronic in nature and occurred on an ongoing basis. Regardless of the specific experience, a commonality that ran through their reports was the participants' experience of feeling "tapped out" in regard to their level of competency or comfort level. One participant discussed the emotional impact of a client who committed suicide during a hospitalization:

> I know that she ended up in the hospital, I arranged it . . . So I, I took care of her safety, I felt. And I don't know what the heck they did; she was suicidal, and they weren't watch-

TABLE 5.1 Summary of Themes

Category A: Professional stressors
1. Participants are stressed by issues that challenge their competency.
2. A frozen therapy process is highly stressful for participants.
3. Peer relationships are breached.
4. Intrapersonal crises negatively impact the professional role.

Category B: The emergence of the expert practitioner
1. Early experiences introduced participants to the helping role.
2. Training experiences were inadequate in preparing the participants for the emotional demands of practice.
3. As novices, participants searched for a professional niche.
4. Participants learned role of limits and boundaries.
5. Over time, participants experienced less performance anxiety.
6. With experience, participants moved from theory to use of self.
7. Participants view attachment and separation as a natural process.
8. Participants understand human suffering at a profound level.

Category C: Creating a positive work structure
1. Mentor and peer support was critical at the novice phase.
2. Participants have ongoing and enriching peer relationships.
3. Multiple roles are a protective factor.
4. Participants create health-promoting work environments.

Category D: Protective factors
1. Participants directly engage highly stressful professional dilemmas.
2. Participants confront and resolve personal issues.
3. Highly engaged learning is a powerful source of renewal.

Category E: Nurturing self through solitude and relationships
1. Participants foster professional stability by nurturing a personal life.
2. Participants invest in a broad array of restorative activities.
3. Participants construct fortifying personal relationships.
4. Participants value an internal focus.

ing her, and she hung herself. And that was, and it was really hard; I just felt heartbroken, and I was so pissed at the psychiatrist.

One participant discussed her experience of dealing with the ongoing stressors that are related to working with chronically ill clients who don't progress:

Ah, I think of depression that doesn't lift. All kinds of interventions, I mean, some people have had therapy for years before they get to me. Some of them have had shock treatment, some of them have had medication, and nothing seems to be helpful. You know, people who have been searching for a long while and maybe you can help them make some inroads, but there are some people for whom it just feels like we don't have what's needed yet.

Other participants discussed their sense of feeling lost or depleted when working with specific client behaviors:

> And I'm realizing that, for example, I don't work well with addictives, people who are addictive. I find I get sucked into their dynamics, and I can't, I can't keep track that these people are also con people because they need to be.
>
> I've had a few men who have been very abusive . . . they're coming to me and the allegation of physical or sexual abuse may be in the air, but they haven't dealt with it at all, or maybe it hasn't been in the air at all. But I find myself angry at the end of those sessions. Those are, those are the people that I find myself, I feel used up rather than giving 100 percent; I feel like I've been stolen from; I feel like I've been taken from. It's totally unrewarding, like they don't give anything back.

Sometimes this sense of being tapped out resulted from the level of distress expressed by the client:

> I think it has more to do with when there's been a lot. So, for example, there are some weeks where it feels like you always thought you heard the worse that you could possibly hear and then someone comes in with something worse about what, what people are able to do to people that causes pain and distress . . . And sometimes it's just in waves.

Theme 2: A Frozen Therapy Process Is Highly Stressful for Participants.   Participants reported that they experienced a sense of "boredom" related to clients who were unmotivated or resistant to treatment. This experience of feeling bored within the therapeutic relationship was reported as a significant stressor. Participants stated:

> . . . for me the issues would be probably somebody is just really without any willingness whatsoever to reflect. It is always something outside of themselves, continuously so . . . mostly I think I lose interest.

> I think what's challenging, frankly, are the boring clients, you know, where it's time after time and very little is happening . . .

In reflecting on his work with clients who were resistant, one participant spoke about the need to deal with his own defensive response:

> Well, I find I don't mind their resistance; it's when I start getting resistant in the face of their resistance. I mean, I expect that they have the right, I expect them to get resistant. But then when they do their resistance in a way that engenders my resistance, then I don't like that.

Theme 3: Peer Relationships Are Breached.   Participants consistently reported that they derived a beneficial sense of support from their peer relationships, both within the work environment and in the broader professional community. Not surprisingly, breaches in these relationships are especially stressful. One participant stated:

Some of the most stressful times have been when I've accidentally ended up working with colleagues that I didn't feel compatible with, to come to work every morning and greet a face that you're not happy to see. Someone you don't trust or respect—who doesn't seem to trust or respect me—that's very hard but it's not my situation now.

Another participant discussed his struggle to stay engaged with peers in the broader professional community when discussing issues relevant to professional practice and integrity:

[Stressful to me are] my own relationships and associations with colleagues who, where we hit points of important divergence. And my willingness to stay present to those, to stay in a relationship with those colleagues and to stay present to the divergence without favoring a tendency to want to split off or isolate or withdraw.

In a similar way, a participant spoke about her negative response to conflicts between separate divisions in the psychological community:

They're both really good groups, and I think it's good for our practices and the community and everything else, but there are elements of competition and resentment and politics, I guess is what you'd call it, but I really dislike it, and when I'm caught in the middle of one of those frays, I'm very unhappy.

Theme 4: Intrapersonal Crises Negatively Impact the Professional Role.   Participants reported that personal life crises and related problems presented challenging situations in their professional role. Although the participants had developed proactive methods for coping with these issues, they reported a strong sense of discomfort when initially faced with this type of challenge. One participant described the unease that he felt when personal issues created a sense of incongruence in his perception of self:

. . . when I was experiencing a lot of tearing in relation to my own family, which I did some years ago, a long time ago. That was pretty difficult and, and I think the difficulty was having to redo my conception of myself while I was continuing to practice. And you really can't take yourself off line and decide to redo your conception of yourself and come back because it's always so closely integrated to whatever you're doing every place else.

Another participant described the hardship she encounters when she is in the process of resolving her own crises:

And so then I feel very spilt, I feel split in terms of what I need to attend to with clients and yet knowing this other thing is playing in my own life that, that is not going to resolve today in a phone call and is not going to resolve in a week, and it's going to be with me for whatever period of time. And so those, frankly, are torture chambers for me . . . when I'm sitting with clients and they're talking about anything that remotely is similar or identifies with or touches on, the anxiety just shoots up . . . how do I manage that level of anxiety and at the same time try to be here for my clients?

Category B: The Emergence of the Expert Practitioner

Category B contains eight themes that focus on aspects of the participants' professional experience, beginning with early events that reinforced the helper role, moving to the novice phase, and ending with the present. These themes highlight factors related to emotional wellness and resiliency in the participants' development as practitioners.

Theme 1: Early Experiences Introduced Participants to the Helping Role.   Participants reported childhood and family relationships and situations that were complex and frequently stressful. Their childhood years provided a degree of challenge that encouraged the development of innate helping traits, skills, and a personal resiliency that the participants carried into their adult lives. Participants offered a variety of impressions and insights regarding these early events and the effects on them as adults. One participant shared how challenges met in childhood provided the knowledge and confidence that she would later access as a practitioner:

> . . . of all the clients I've seen over the years, I would guess that I've only seen a few who come from a crazier family. The horrendous part about that is that it's taken a ton of work to understand my family, to understand the dynamics that were back then, and how to deal with it ongoingly. But at the same time that was a stretching experience. I mean, that's why I could go to school and say I don't expect to learn anything here and yet I know I'll be able to do this work because I'd already come out of that kind of an environment, I already knew that I would relate to a whole lot of the world—and easily to some extent. And I think a lot of it was shaped by that experience.

This same participant went on to note that:

> When there have been problems in my life, all the way through, the way that I have handled them is to become more confident. That's been the secret. And that has allowed me to come out on top over and over and over again.

One participant felt "immensely" impacted by her childhood in Israel where she lived with her parents who had fled the war:

> [It was] . . . a real-life laboratory for coping with stress and surviving and thriving, actually, because those who perish, perish. But those who survive, like my family and their friends eventually, actually thrive. And those were probably hardier people who somehow knew to see opportunities or how to look at things not always in blinders.

This participant went on to highlight the importance of her difficult early experiences:

> I think knowing you've lived through it . . . awful, awful experiences and . . . to that extent, helps you know that you'll get through it again.

Other participants cited a connection between their early experiences and their eventual career choices:

I'm sure that one of the reasons I've been interested in therapy, and in particular family therapy, is that part of what I tried to do, I think, in my youth was save my family, every way that I thought I could help things be better in the family, because it was clear that both my parents were pretty miserable people.

I don't think that I knew it at the time, but in retrospect I would say for myself and for most therapists I know, you go into this field in some part to try to understand ourselves and in some part to try to understand and heal our families or other people we loved. There's something that drives us: I need to make sense of this situation, I need to understand, I need to know what somebody might have done.

One participant reported that while his childhood was stressful enough to heighten an awareness of family dynamics, it was not so extreme as to be debilitating:

I think about all that I suffered as a child, the ways in which I felt I didn't get much that I wanted and my father didn't love me much, he loved my brother. [However] . . . there was a very solid sense that I always knew that my parents were grown-up, I didn't have to be the grown-up. I knew that I lived in a system that was basically just and fair. And I didn't have to try to fight for changing the system in that way.

In a similar way, another participant described the role that her family's involvement in music played in her development as a practitioner:

When you have things going on around you that are bad and at the same time, you have the most exquisite, beautiful music being played, it does not allow you to shut down, it does not allow you to build a fortress where you don't feel. Because you are being called to feel all the time, and in almost a noncognitive way.

Theme 2: Training Experiences Were Inadequate in Preparing the Participants for the Emotional Demands of Practice.   Participants stated that, as students, graduate school and internship training that pertained to the emotional demands of practice were hindered by a lack of awareness of this topic. In reflecting on her own training experiences, one participant stated:

Yes, I was a school teacher at the time and I was there [in counselor training] to learn how to help kids and their families. That's what I thought I was doing. So, I don't know that I would have known even if somebody was giving me something to help me. I don't think that folks knew very much about what therapists needed in those days.

While focusing specifically on her internship experience, this same participant stated:

. . . when I think about internships, I think about mostly folks trying to help us learn to work, learn skills. I don't remember any supervisor at the time ever talking about their personal journey or noticing what my struggles might be or asking me about my own struggles.

Another participant also differentiated between her training and internship experiences:

> I think that the training probably didn't have much impact one way or the other for that particular dimension. The internship, in terms of the supervisor that I had, I think that he both modeled how he handled that and in his own way probably kind of geared me toward some of it.

Finally, in reflecting on his training, one participant suggested that it is not possible to fully prepare neophyte students for the emotional demands they eventually confront in practice:

> I think they did about as well as they could do. There isn't any way that you can be prepared for the emotional demands of practice but I think under the circumstances, it was all right.

Theme 3: As Novices, Participants Searched for a Professional Niche.   Participants reported that a key task in their novice phase was finding a theoretical orientation or approach that bridged who they were personally with their emerging professional selves. In this process, participants gravitated to various theoretical orientations or approaches until they found a niche, or calling, that allowed them to smoothly integrate theory and training into actual practice in a manner that felt congruent with who they were. In reflecting on her novice phase, one participant stated:

> When I was a very young or hatching therapist . . . there was all kinds of crazy stuff going on in the world of psychotherapy and I was interested in all of it and I tried everything, and learned a little bit of every imaginable theory and then watched the places where it failed.

In another interview, this same participant discusses her efforts and commitment to be trained in an approach that felt like a match with who she was personally:

> . . . the psychiatry residency here was very much behavioral, cognitive, kind of psychopharmacology, genetics, but not psychodynamic. And I guess just something in my personality or my world view is really most interested in the psychodynamic so I joined a group in private practice here of people who did that kind of work. That's what motivated me to go to the Psychoanalytic Institute and I had to commute to Chicago to do that so that was an enormous commitment but ah, it made it possible for me to do the kind of work I wanted to do.

A different participant outlined his experience in this way:

> . . . integrating family systems into basically a psychodynamic tradition was where I started. And then I got involved in transpersonal psychology through psychosynthesis in the middle of the 1970s and incorporated Gestalt into that training. Then it wasn't until really the middle 1980s that I went underneath that and got involved in existential work and felt like I was more home.

One participant described the excitement and enthusiasm that he felt when first being introduced to family therapy, an approach that had an enormous influence on his professional life:

> That was a life-changing time. . . . The whole concept of looking at symptoms as in reframing them into positive terms, it was a brand new idea, the sense of understanding human beings in a context of the family was new . . . the rest of the world thought this was a fringe technique. I had the sense of "This is core. We are looking at some, we are seeing some truth here that nobody else sees yet."

One participant talked about her decision to leave a secure academic position in order to find a placement that was more congruent to her orientation as a practitioner:

> One of the reasons I left it is that I wanted to do more of the personal therapy work that I was having to refer people for. Once I started doing only that work, what was much more challenging for me was the use of self . . . those five years, they were exciting because it was [full of] all sorts of awe. You know, this is what I need to know, this is what I need to do, work with people to learn it.

Theme 4: Participants Learned the Role of Limits and Boundaries.   Over time, participants learned the value of establishing clear boundaries and limits in areas that included their roles as helpers, the levels of responsibility that they assumed, the structures of their practices, the makeups of their caseloads, and their relationships with clients. The establishment of these boundaries and limits enabled the practitioners to maintain a better sense of wellness and resiliency, to cope more effectively with difficult client behaviors and issues, and to manage their own continuous exposure to suffering. In discussing her role as a responsible practitioner, one participant stated:

> I'm far more wise about all the things that I don't need to know about and don't need to fix, and I think when I started out, like most of us when we start out, feeling a need to have all the answers. My job was to fix this, be helpful. I think with experience and time in the field, you learn that our job is really to relax more and sit back and listen and hear better what it is that the person is trying to sort through and discover.

Other participants discussed the establishment of limits and boundaries as a necessary ingredient in both practicing with integrity and in fostering a sense of wellness and resiliency:

> . . . I think that a very big piece of professional resiliency has to do with knowing and accepting your own limits. I feel like I give, I owe it to my clients to give them full attention and the best of my resources when I'm with them and that tires me out. So if I try to do more or operate on less than my best all the time . . . then I'm not giving my clients what I owe them. I feel like I have to practice with integrity and that means to be willing to do for myself what I expect my clients to do.

> It is up to me to do everything I can to maintain my own emotional health so that I can actually be available to my patients without needing them. I think one of the ways therapy goes awry is that the therapist starts to use the patient for their own emotional

sustenance, regulation of the therapist's self-esteem, all those sorts of things. I think that to be a good therapist you must be well fed and well loved. Basically, have a life out there that is working.

Participants noted that limits and boundaries played a key role in structuring their actual work day. In discussing the framework of their schedules, participants stated:

. . . it's important for me to keep track of the hours I'm putting in because it's very easy to start going over a 40-hour week. And I start to know that something's wrong when I wake up in the morning and I'm not rested or when I'm dreading the day, or I'll find myself sleepy or bored, and this is not boring work, and I start to make mistakes, double schedule people, or there are just certain signs I recognize as that I'm working too hard.

Well, I put very careful limits around my work day. I won't start before such and such a time, it changes depending on circumstances and won't work later than 5:30 P.M. People who require other kinds of times or accommodations, I'll refer. I will only bend so far. I create certain breaks in my days.

While reflecting on the process of implementing limits in dealing with potentially challenging client behaviors and therapeutic issues, participants stated:

I'm more sure of myself . . . I can set limits with the authority of a Dutch uncle, and it can have the subtleties of both nurturance and a stop sign.

. . . I'm pretty clear about boundary stuff . . . if I weren't, then there would be some real challenging behaviors . . . whether it's clients wanting more or calling for things or pushing my own personal boundaries. Very little of that happens for me, I think it's because . . . I send out the vibes about what's okay to do and what's not okay to do so I don't have much of that.

Another participant noted the importance of understanding her limitations as a provider:

. . . some of it is just coming to grips with that there are certain agencies that can provide certain things, and that we can't provide everything for everybody. So, part of it is accepting limitations . . .

Theme 5: Over Time, Participants Experienced Less Performance Anxiety.   With time, participants became more comfortable in their professional role. With this change, they experienced a decrease in stress and an increase in confidence and ability to handle a variety of difficult therapeutic issues and client behaviors. This shift allowed them to be more open and genuine in their role as a helper. Some participants commented:

. . . there's less of a need to prove yourself, and so you can be more open because you don't feel as much that you need to defend anything or protect anything. I think when you first start out sometimes, it feels like you're on the line. No one knows who you are, how you're doing, and so I think there's much more a sense of protection around yourself; seems like as you grow older and more experienced, there's more of a sense of "We all don't know, and we're all learning," so you can be pretty open about hearing feedback, getting information.

I laugh a lot more, a lot more. I am old. That is one thing that helps. And I am not forever wondering if I am good enough.

. . . comfort with coming to work each day and assuming that it would be okay. You know, I'd do all right somehow, or I'd be able to deal with whatever happened that day; I'm just guessing, but I'm thinking maybe ten years into my practice, I started to have that kind of sense of equilibrium about it.

. . . an accumulation of more experiences to back me up. More appreciation for . . . the shadings of the nuances where we might get hung up and more of a sense of how to avoid them, and . . . also deepened in the sense of more appreciation for the value of the differences. So I feel a lot more appreciation for the uniqueness of every individual. I feel much more sense of authority about myself as a therapist.

Oh, I think I'm much quieter and I think I feel more confident. I feel much more sure of myself when I'm working.

Theme 6: With Experience, Participants Moved from Theory to Use of Self. Participants noted that as they accumulated experience, they moved from a reliance on specific techniques and approaches to being more open and genuine. This change occurred as they became increasingly aware of the therapeutic process and how to best use self within the relationship. For these participants, the shift from a reliance on specific approaches to the use of self required an element of risk and openness. Once achieved, it felt more like a comfortable professional "fit" that was conducive in creating intimate and intense interactions with clients. Participants said:

It's almost a cliché, but it really is true: The more you learn the more you discover what you don't know . . . You have to continually approach every situation with an openness of not knowing what's going to happen.

Letting it unfold . . . and this is much more recent with me . . . toward including myself, having myself in the way, in a way that seemed purposeful in terms of what was, where this person was moving, or what seemed to be directional, what they were telling me, telling me with words and their body and their tone of voice, all of the things that we register what was directional for them.

Participants noted that the use of self in the therapeutic relationship facilitated rich interactions that enhanced their work: When focusing on the intense, intimate nature of the therapeutic relationships that they forged with clients, participants stated:

. . . you may have heard similar statements before but you've never encountered this particular person before so there is always novelty, there is always a new experience, always a new relationship.

. . . in a sense it's a joy . . . it's the fact of working with people and watching them grow and feeling that you have a part in that growth. It's fun.

I mean, honest to God, contact is very exciting. I mean, when two boundaries meet, that's where the energy is.

I think the one thing that has prevented me from burning out . . . is the fact that no two people look alike to me. The people who burn out begin to see everybody as alike; they see people as problems, and they see problems as the things they are working with.

Theme 7: Participants View Attachment and Separation as a Natural Process.
Participants discussed their belief that attachments and separations in the therapeutic relationship followed a natural course, similar to those experienced in other relationships. This belief appeared to fortify the participants through years of fostering attachments and facilitating separations with a multitude of clients. They are committed to engaging in the process of attachment and separation, even through times of difficulty. Participants have also become aware that many attachments continue. Some participants discussed their belief that the therapeutic process of separation and attachment mimics life:

> . . . it seems to me that all of life is about attachment and separation. You know, even with marriage, there are times when attachment is really important, but there's also times when separation is really important. Where you're individuals and you have different needs and different abilities to be present. So I think that's how I help myself with it, is that it feels part and parcel with just what's true in life . . . I think it's totally important that people are able to attach in order to work through some of what might not have happened for them. But I also think it's important to be able to separate and let go . . .

Another participant verbalized a similar sentiment:

> Another thing I think of is most people leave me because they're feeling so much better in their lives and they've changed so much. And there's such a tremendous satisfaction in that, it's like seeing your children leave home, you're sad but who can complain? It's a success.

Participants also discussed their experience that relationships continue beyond the separation. This continuation may exist on an internalized level or, in other cases, actually involves the client's returning to therapy. In some cases, work that began with a client eventually extended to the client's children. The enriching experience of ongoing professional relationships appeared to insulate the participants from the potential distress of repeated attachments and separations.

> And then a number of people come back over the years, so I have more and more confidence, sort of like an object constancy, in me at least, that these people remain alive in my psyche. They're out there in the world and I feel connected to them and believe that they'd return if the situation arose.

> I think in a core way, attachment is an internal phenomena rather than external. You can see people for years every day and probably not have that much attachment. So, if you stop seeing people, there is some loss, but it doesn't mean that, therefore, something got yanked out.

. . . I feel like I really do give people something, part of myself, and when they leave, I really have an investment. But these days, I almost never say a permanent good-bye to anybody. I'm always having old clients come back; I'm even having the children who were playing on the floor coming in with their spouses at this point.

Theme 8: Participants Understand Human Suffering at a Profound Level.

Through their experience, participants developed a profound understanding of suffering. This includes an awareness of the painful elements inherent in that process as well as the potential for growth. The participants' comments reflected an awareness of the suffering and healing process which is part of their role as a helper. Their hopeful outlook on how suffering can be transformed enhanced their personal lives. One participant talked specifically about his understanding of suffering and how he conceptualized his role as a practitioner:

. . . I learned to see suffering as valuable. As of value in that it is a part of a person's character and not to be denied or taken from them . . . it's two contrasting values . . . wanting to be available for somebody's life to be different in terms of having less . . . suffering on the one hand. And wanting to be absolutely respectful of their suffering as a part of their character on the other . . . I have to watch my tendency to want to take their suffering away because if I take their suffering away, I deny them their right . . .

Other participants talked about how their attitudes and perspectives had been altered due to their continual exposure to suffering:

. . . I think all in all, it leaves me with a certain kind of enthusiasm because I see people go through extraordinary pain and come out the other side. And so, it makes me patient.

It deepens me. I feel I understand pain awfully well. I think I know the issue isn't pain or suffering, the issue is not having to do it by yourself. It's really about . . . knowing that you're not alone in that core place.

. . . in visiting the intensity of the private world of several people who are clients, empathizing with the misery, it can feel like, at the end of the day, lonely to have been so intensely in all of those places and nobody had been in all of those places with me. And I couldn't tell anybody where I'd been . . . the loneliness of that is a big part of the burden, I think. But that's more like the immediate at the end of the day kind of thing. What I think I'm left with is . . . that settled sense of the humanity of it.

I think I'm a better person for it. I think I've done far more in my own regard than if I had stayed teaching math or if I had worked in finance. I don't think that I would have grown nearly as much personally as I have as a result of doing this.

. . . we end up seeing a lot of change and growth and exciting kinds of things so there's also that part that balances it . . . you develop a real optimism for life . . . And I'm really awestruck in terms of when you work with one person, the ripples . . . they'll talk about their partners feeling like they're vicariously getting therapy too because they're getting things, and I think about how they're able to parent children differently.

Category C: Creating a Positive Work Structure

Category C contains four themes that focus on how, over time, the participants created important supports that enhanced their sense of wellness in the work environment. The four positive work structure factors are: mentor and peer support, ongoing and enriching peer relationships, multiple roles (including designing their own caseloads and controlling billing), and health-promoting enviornments.

Theme 1: Mentor and Peer Support Was Critical at the Novice Phase.   Participants reported that positive mentor and peer relationships greatly impacted the novice phase of their careers. These relationships often developed during long-term first placements that were frequently described as challenging but not overwhelming. The novice setting provided enriched work environments full of learning opportunities and encouragement for responsible autonomy and risk-taking. While at these sites, a foundation was built for the participants' future practices. In reflecting on his first placement, one participant stated:

> I remember those as good years. I'm sure they were stressful because a lot was new, but I felt very supported. I had resources about me, and I was valued and also I had a tremendous amount of independence.

Another participant stated:

> [It was] a time of working intensely with colleagues in relation to having lots of feedback, lots of inspection of one's practice. All of that, by and large, was very good. I wouldn't, I certainly wouldn't trade those years.

While discussing a supervisor at her first placement following graduate training, one participant stated:

> . . . at my first job, I was fortunate enough to have a really fine supervisor who literally, I credit with the major amount of training and experience that I have. And that was totally geared to emotional self-awareness and use of self in ways in which I grew a hell of a lot, but I also learned never to ignore that part . . . it opened all the doors for me, and it also made what I was doing very vital and real, and I feel real grateful for that.

Another participant discussed her decision to join a group of seasoned clinicians who then became important mentors and teachers:

> I think that I had either the good fortune or the good judgment to join a group of senior clinicians, all people twenty years older than I, very experienced, and I brought them something they needed, which was the M.D. I could prescribe medications for their patients, and I could hospitalize their patients, which was fine. But they gave me the depth and breadth of clinical experience and an understanding of how the practice works, and it was very important to me.

Although the need for strong mentor relationships gradually diminished over time for many of the participants, the salience of these early relationships was highlighted in the reflections of one participant:

> . . . it's more in retrospect then I was aware at the time, that there were people along the way who believed in me and kind of engaged with me because they believed in me. And I really thrived on that, more than I knew, in the moment. I got so much from that in a way that if I hadn't gotten that, my life wouldn't have been—would have taken a different path.

Theme 2: Participants Have Ongoing and Enriching Peer Relationships. Participants reported that they initiated and sustained relationships with a variety of peers and coworkers beyond the novice phase. These relationships served a critical role in supporting the participants. When discussing peer relationships specific to the work environment, one participant stated:

> I think that it is actually kind of a unique and rare environment that offers a therapist that kind of support for continuing growth. One that says even if you've been in this business for a number of years, you are still allowed to not know, you're still allowed to be afraid of what's happening, you're still allowed to feel like a failure, or whatever the issue is.

Both formal and informal peer interactions were emphasized as being important components of peer relationships in the work environment. One participant described how she and her coworkers had strategically created a work environment that provided a variety of interactions:

> We've made a coffee room so that we run into each other on purpose, and we meet once a week for lunch, and that's very helpful both for relaxation and socializing and for consulting. There's always somebody I can say, "Listen to this situation, tell me what you think," and without naming names, I can describe the problem and get feedback from somebody that I respect.

In reflecting on his peer relationships, one participant highlighted the value of friendship and of sharing life events along with professional concerns:

> We sit down for our staff meeting, and before we do anything else, we just sit at the table, take a few minutes, and talk about our lives. It's sort of this is what's happening with my kids; this is what I did last weekend; by the way, I saw a great movie; and just that personal level, before we get into talking about [clients].

Often, the intimate quality of peer and coworker relationships was an enriching factor in the participants' ability to deepen their level of self-awareness and, in turn, to invest more intensely in the therapeutic process with clients. Two participants described the importance of sustained, close relationships in the actual work environment:

> Here, for example, we have a group of six, and some of us, and some of us have been together for about fourteen years, so you really have a chance to deepen the experience

with one another and, therefore, I think also be able to deepen your work with clients, because you're better able to know about yourself in relationship to the work, and other people know you well enough to say, "Hey, look at this."

So that we've been present here in this practice for going on eighteen years, and we've always done weekly consultations and the kind that really gets at what might be stopping us, what might be blocking us, what we might be struggling with.

Diverse peer relationships in the broader professional community were also highlighted as vital sources of support. Participants tended to be actively involved in numerous professional activities, organizations, and community groups. One participant discussed the value of serving on a committee with a cross section of helping professionals:

And to have all these people giving time and energy to thinking about what will make our work improve. It's just inspiring, and for me it's invigorating and energizing. Just helpful in that way.

Similarly, another participant stated:

I have a group of colleagues that are very important to me, have been for ten years now, and we meet on the West Coast every year; we spend a week together; we rent a room together for a week. They're all existentialists and they're my closest colleagues in terms of tradition, and I see them maybe two, three times a year in groups or individually . . . And that has been very, very helpful over the years.

Theme 3: Multiple Roles Are a Protective Factor.   Participants reported that they structured their practices to include multiple tasks and professional involvements. They also exhibit a measure of freedom in choosing the type of clients they worked with and how they do their billing. The ability to control the nature of their practices provided the participants with a stimulating balance of professional responsibilities while limiting the stressors they encounter. In discussing her need for task diversity versus doing only clinical work, one participant stated:

If I did only this work I would be bored out of my mind . . . it has nothing to do with the people I see; it's about having to empty yourself out so constantly and regularly to do that work. And that wouldn't be healthy; it just wouldn't be healthy.

Another participant discussed how involvement in diverse activities improved her professional and clinical work:

I think there is something really enriching about supervising and teaching. It keeps me interested in my work and feeling alive and motivated to read and to think from some point of view other than just inside my head.

Participants reported that freedom to design one's caseload and to control the billing also contributed positively to their professional experience. Regarding client-related stressors, one participant stated:

I don't think of my clients as impacting me in ways that I would consider stressors . . . there's been stuff obviously over the years . . . we'll be dealing with suicide or we'll be dealing with this or that . . . I haven't had much of that for a long time, and it's partly this practice; I mean, it's set up in a way in which I'm not dealing with crisis. I mean I'm dealing with . . . wellness probably kind of perspectives. So, I'm also not in situations at this point that would push that.

One participant discussed the way that she structured her caseload and completed billing:

I've been very fortunate in two ways. One is that I'm an old-timer, so I've developed my own reputation and my own referral. Most of my patients come referred by other patients. And many pay out of pocket, and I'm willing to make some adjustments; I'd rather give them the money than the insurance company actually in terms of discount.

Theme 4: Participants Create Health-Promoting Work Environments. Participants said their work environments were suited to meet specific needs of space, aesthetics, and personal comfort. Equally important, these environments were conducive to facilitating successful therapeutic relationships. One participant outlined the benefits of her work area:

I really like it here. I like my space. I like being here. I love being here when it's raining or snowing and it's kind of a cocoon kind of feel to it. I think about the holding environment that helps therapy to work. That is part of what's here, and I like it, and I've heard clients talk about that it's nice to be here.

Other participants also discussed the need to create a comfortable and therapeutic work area:

Space that allows for both enough distance to accommodate mine but also the other person's personal space requirements. And with clients that varies, actually. So I think sometimes I move forward or backward, depending on what I'm sensing, but also not so big that it feels like you're talking into a room rather than connecting to people. I think something that feels, that gives the sense of privacy and safety. I think it has the sense of being protected but not trapped.

You know, I'm really into friendly textures and colors and, and the light is important; the quiet is important. We went to great lengths to soundproof all these offices. The building would think that it was adequately soundproof, but I could still hear what was going on next door. We just kept putting insulation in the walls until it was soundproof. I guess I have to feel generally safe. I know people who work in clinics and kind of dangerous parts of town, and I think that's not conducive to the comfort of therapist or patient.

Category D: Protective Factors

Category D contains three themes that identify proactive strategies that participants employ to master stressors.

Theme 1: Participants Directly Engage Highly Stressful Professional Dilemmas.
Participants are skilled in their ability to handle ongoing difficult situations and to
manage crises in a proactive manner that serves to prevent future incidents. Their
strategies reflected an ability to adapt to change and to "bounce" regarding unexpected
or shifting events and issues. Participants tended to identify and frame challenges and
issues in a hopeful light and to access appropriate resources. In confronting challenges
and issues, participants discussed their need to remain receptive to possibilities and
approaches on both internal and external levels:

> And then I have to engage [the stressful issue] in myself because there's always the pos-
> sibility that there's some piece of me working here that would rather not see this, would
> rather not own the power that I have; I'd rather see that I wasn't that important, dimin-
> ish my own responsibility in that way, or minimize my responsibility to be a better atten-
> der to somebody else's experience.

> One of my most profound learning experiences was stimulated by, first of all, working
> with a couple of therapists who turned out to be highly unethical and abusing their
> patients. I also had a dear friend of mine exploited by a therapist, and I'm thinking, "I've
> got to understand this, something really went wrong here." I find myself somewhat of an
> expert on boundaries and boundary violations because it really challenged my whole self-
> concept as a therapist or challenged the whole idea of therapy as a healing process. So
> I wanted to go after that problem.

An appropriate reliance on peer consultation was a critical resource that participants relied upon in their process of exploring important issues and incidents:

> . . . I get lots of consultation, so I'm not by myself with the really hard cases. That's pri-
> mary for me. If there's anything that feels really important, it's not to be by myself in
> really hard situations, that I have colleagues with me. So that I feel that kind of a sense
> that I'm not all alone in this. It's really important to me that I'm seeing things clearly,
> and I think it's hard sometimes when you're all by yourself. And to have other eyes and
> ears looking at something with you. So that's one major way [to protect myself].

A key characteristic of the participants' reports was their willingness to remain
open and to adapt. In discussing these traits, one participant stated:

> I think sometimes it's caused me not to feel like I know what I know at times, but on the
> other hand, it also keeps me kind of fresh and open. I'm willing to entertain almost any-
> thing, and I'm willing to look at where I could be off base about almost anything.

Another participant described her daily clinical work and provided an example of
her ability to adapt from one client to another:

> I think I'm emotionally resilient in the sense of I can be with someone in their pain . . .
> but then I can in the next session be laughing with somebody about something or cel-
> ebratory with somebody. So it feels like that's a way that I get, I can move.

Theme 2: Participants Confront and Resolve Personal Issues. Participants reported that their own personal life crises and problems were challenging areas for them. They also believed that direct acknowledgment and resolution of these issues allowed for a congruence between the personal self and the professional self. One participant explained how her experience in dealing with the unexpected death of a family member challenged her at a profoundly personal level and yet allowed her to be more attuned to clients:

> Well, I think the suicide [in the family] made the work very challenging. And yet at the same time, I was fortunate in that I had a very fine therapist. And because I had that therapist, while the work was difficult, I constantly felt like I was being so tended to emotionally . . . I found myself taking from that experience and just automatically moving it into what I was doing with clients. So it's like as the therapist was willing to go with me where I needed to go and that opened up areas or that developed areas inside of me that I didn't even know were there. Then, automatically, I would hear those areas in clients. I would ask the questions because they were coming from where I'd been taken to.

Theme 3: Highly Engaged Learning Is a Powerful Source of Renewal. Participants reported that they had histories of being open to new experiences, seeking out diverse avenues of learning, and synthesizing information from multiple sources. Their lives were marked by an insatiable curiosity, a deep comfort with ambiguity, and the constant consumption of knowledge. This ongoing learning process helped them to maintain an energy level necessary to continually engage in the helper role. In discussing a draw toward learning and its effect on her, one participant stated that:

> Well, it provides constant energy for one thing, and I think what happens in our field is that we can get tired and exhausted, but I think that's one of the things that keeps me feeling high energy and a lot of interest and love for what we do, and it's exciting.

Some participants described why a tolerance for ambiguity and an openness for learning were critical ingredients in their work:

> If nothing else, you want to work with these people from all walks of life with various occupations and various interests, and if you don't sustain at least some awareness or at least openness to learn from your patients about their work, then how can you be of any use to them if you stay on the outside? So one has to have the interest and curiosity and some fondness, I think for the client. If you're not interested in joining them, then why would they trust you to come and open themselves up.

> If you can't work with the unknown and the uncertain, you can't last in this business.

Another participant discussed her efforts to bring new information into her work:

> When I read I always know what I define as active learning, which is trying to take the new information and see how I can incorporate it into what's already there, which means that I'm always modifying existing information, too. And adapting it to my needs and

integrating what I already know. It can be a negative thing if you go with the approach that everything has to fit to some rigid fixed scheme set already in existence. But I don't think I do that. I think I really constantly modify my schemes by incorporating the new stuff, but it's probably the integration and incorporation that are really important.

One participant discussed how she utilized peers to facilitate her own learning process:

I think being in a group practice has helped because it keeps you kind of interested and hungry for what's available and keeps you open, I think. I've done groups with co-therapists for years upon years. I've done co-therapy, marriage therapy. I think that also helps to stay open because you're constantly getting new information, getting new ways of thinking when working with someone. Getting input about your ways of working, so I think that also helps.

Category E: Nurturing Self through Solitude and Relationships

Participants clearly identified their need to maintain a strong sense of self. Category E contains four themes that focus on components important to the participants regarding this need. The themes reflect multiple approaches and a network of internal and external involvements that enable the participants to maintain a personal and professional congruency.

Theme 1: Participants Foster Professional Stability by Nurturing a Personal Life. Participants were aware of the importance of maintaining a balance between their personal and professional lives. They believe that their role as a helper is facilitated by a lifestyle that includes multiple involvements and connections apart from their professional life. One participant verbalized this sentiment when he stated:

What helps me do it well is to give a damn about what I'm doing, but . . . I've got to have a life out of here. This can't be everything. I can't be overinvested in it. There's an appropriate kind of investment in which I care very much about what happens here, and I'm willing to invest myself as fully as I can, and part of what helps me do that is the fact that I've got a very real existence in a lot of ways, not just this.

Another participant succinctly stated:

. . . there's some kind of larger balance. I don't think anybody could do this work just and, and not tip over in some way. The tendency to get off center is too great.

One participant reported a very similar point of view and then elaborated on the hazards of not maintaining a life outside of her professional role:

It is up to me to do everything I can to maintain my own emotional health so that I can actually be available to my patients without needing them. I think one of the ways therapy goes awry is that the therapist starts to use the patient for their own emotional sustenance, regulation of the therapist's self-esteem, all those sorts of things. I think to be a good therapist you must be well fed and well loved. Basically, have a life out there that is working.

Theme 2: Participants Invest in a Broad Array of Restorative Activities. Participants cultivate a collection of activities and leisure pursuits. While the actual involvements are varied, a shared theme that runs through them is their function of providing a diversion from work-related stressors and an avenue for reconnecting with self and others. The function of these activities and pursuits was reflected in one participant's statement:

> [Helpful is] doing things personally like physical kinds of things. When we talked about secondary post-trauma, there are some days when I just feel like I need to go out and kick something and just kind of biking real hard or walking real fast; doing things like that can be really helpful I think. I do a lot of going to plays, going to movies, getting together with friends, and just talking about plays we've seen, books we've read.

A similar draw toward multiple involvements was reflected when this participant stated:

> I love mystery stories and historical biography; that's where I learn my history, from historical novels. I like movies; I love sports; I'm an avid football fan; I knit; I do a lot of knitting and crocheting.

Other participants discussed the pull they felt to nature and other creative activities:

> I think something happens for me spiritually when I'm doing stuff with flowers and plants. I've got plants all over the place in my home, and it's kind of a ritualistic piece about tending those. I have gardens here and at a cabin up north, and there's, again, sort of a ritualistic piece with tending those. I think that takes me to a place that is real deeply nourishing, and I can get lost in it in a whole different way. I love the creative so the book that I wrote and stuff that I do for school and the papers, I really try to approach those as creative endeavors.

> I find that music is a way for me to ground myself in the larger experience of my life and life itself. I suppose that's true for a lot of people . . . but that's certainly true for me, and always has been. And one of the ways, when I find myself feeling deprived of being able to cry, it'll come through that way.

One participant discussed the critical function of travel:

> It's very helpful for perspective purposes. Very helpful. The trick is to be gone long enough . . . so you recognize fully your entire replaceability. That you are absolutely replaceable. And there, you talked about freedom and relief; there is real freedom and relief in that.

Theme 3: Participants Construct Fortifying Personal Relationships. Participants are highly skilled relationship builders. They establish nurturing and challenging connections with family, friends, and other social groups that are intimate and rich. Among

other things, their relationships with others provide consistent, ongoing support and enable a realistic perspective of self. Although these relationships are important on a day-to-day basis, they are especially critical in times of crisis. Some of the participants discussed how a network of supportive relationships fortified their lives and acted as an emotional safety net:

> If you have good friends in your life, if you have a good support system, folks will let you know that you're feeling worn out or depleted or whatever and then will support you getting some help.

> A lot of close friends and my children are best friends. And they keep me very well balanced and my perspective, don't let me get a big head. They're very good, very supportive bunch.

> Having your own family connection solid is, at least for me, is pretty important. I think I have a lot of reliance on other people in my life or friends or my wife, catching me in areas where I don't catch myself.

Some participants spoke about the encouragement and comfort they derived from a relationship with a spouse or life partner:

> I married the right lady; my wife has a master's, has a master's-level degree in child development. And so we can talk, and she understands what I do. She never worked after we got married because she started having kids right away. But we could communicate and understand each other. And she was always a nice balance when my head started getting too big. She would pop it . . . And so that was very supportive, still is.

> We met actually as classmates. And I'm sure that's probably the most important relationship personally, but also I think probably professionally in some ways. We do talk psychology with each other, have all these years. So, I'm sure that's been very important.

One participant highlighted the essential function of children and family:

> We do a lot with family celebrations. Socializing, having people over for dinner. My children, now they are out of the home, but when they were younger, I think we did some things that were really helpful. Taking time just to play some games together. Just do something completely separate from work.

Another participant also commented on the very significant role her friends played:

> What I would say is that there are a few close friends, and when I'm in trouble, when they're in trouble, the rules are we get access to each other whenever and however long we need it. And when the trouble's over, we go back to our lives. And those people are very in place, and I think I am for them too.

Participants also fostered an essential relationship with the world at large, and they usually spoke about this in terms of a spiritual awareness or in seeking a greater sense of connection with others:

I have a sense of spirit. I have a sense of reverence. I have a sense of place in the universe even though I know it's just a speck; it's a place to participate. I believe that there's benevolence in all that. I believe that warm, gentle breezes blow my way besides the cold, bitter winds.

Theme 4: Participants Value an Internal Focus.   Participants reported that they are aware of the significant role that their internal processes play in sustaining their own sense of wellness and in their ability to function effectively as practitioners. They are open to, and willingly engage in, their own personal therapy as a means of enhancing this process of introspection and self-examination. This commitment to understanding self represents an important self-care method that positively impacts their sense of resiliency and wellness in the helping role. Statements by the participants reflected the value of being continually self-aware. One said that it was important to attend to:

What's coming up in my world that needs me to understand what's going on or feel like I get it in terms of whatever's happening internally so that when I'm doing my work, I'm sort of cleared out, and it isn't that the stuff isn't in there, but I'm not obsessing about it; it's not taking me some other place then where I need to be in the room.

Another stated:

To learn something about vulnerability yourself, I don't know that anybody can really do therapy well until they know vulnerability, unless they are aware of their woundedness . . . And be able to work from there.

One participant shared her belief that staying attuned to internal processes was, in part, an ethical responsibility:

I think that's where we need to build this self-monitoring and be self-aware. If I become psychotic, then probably those around me would notice it, but outside of those extremes, if my work fluctuates on life events or whatever like physical health . . . I think to what extent one is ethical in their conduct [relates to] constantly in the kind of posture of self reflection and self monitoring and judgment.

Other participants discussed their belief that personal therapy was an important vehicle in their quest for self-awareness. One participant stated:

The other thing I would say is it's important for every therapist to know when it's time to go back for some therapy of your own; personal anxieties or problems are either getting stirred up by the work or are intruding from the outside world.

Conclusion

Several pertinent areas were highlighted in this study. Participants identified stressors connected to various therapeutic issues and client behaviors, breaches in peer relationships, and the impact of their own personal crises and life changes. The areas of stressors that were reflected in the participants' comments underscore the demanding nature of the helping role and reinforce the value of protective approaches and self-care strategies as a means of ensuring practitioner wellness and professional vitality.

Important protective factors were identified by the participants. These factors ranged from internal coping strategies to variables within the external environment. A commonality that existed among this group of participants was their commitment to self-care and their high level skill in accessing valuable resources.

These practitioners are acutely aware of their internal landscapes and maintain a watchful focus on their emotional selves. Their strong commitment to self-observation was frequently combined with a proactive style in directly confronting stressors that emerged from both their work and in their personal lives. When combined, these approaches allowed the participants to maintain a sense of personal congruence and an energy level that are critical components in professional wellness and burnout prevention.

These master therapists were nurtured through multiple avenues and relationships. The role that peers played in providing the participants with a realistic perspective and ongoing professional support was emphasized. While peer support was vital throughout the participants' careers, it played an especially key role during the participants' novice phase of development and, also, during times of unexpected crisis. In a similar way, participants also noted the importance of immersing themselves in enriching relationships and activities apart from their work environments. It appears that these diverse involvements were essential components to self-care plans that maintained a healthy sense of balance.

References

Ackerly, G. D., Burnell, J., Holder, D. C., & Kurdek, L. A. (1988). Burnout among licensed psychologists. *Professional Psychology: Research and Practice, 19*(6), 624–631.

American Psychiatric Association. (1994). *Diagnostic and statistical manual of mental disorders* (4th ed.). Washington DC: Author.

Catherall, D. R. (1995). Coping with secondary traumatic stress: The importance of the therapist's professional peer group. In B. H. Stamm (Ed.), *Secondary traumatic stress: Self-care issues for clinicians, researchers, and educators* (pp. 80–92). Lutherville, MD: Sidran Press.

Coster, J. S., & Schwebel, M. (1997). Well-functioning in professional psychologists. *Professional Psychology: Research and Practice, 28*(1), 5–13.

Deutsch, C. J. (1984). Self-reported sources of stress among psychotherapists. *Professional Psychology: Research and Practice, 15*(6), 833–845.

Dupree, P. I., & Day, H. D. (1995). Psychotherapists' job satisfaction and job burnout as a function of work setting and percentage of managed care clients. *Psychotherapy in Private Practice, 14*(2), 77–93.

Elliott, D. M., & Guy, J. D. (1993). Mental health professionals versus non-mental-health professionals: Childhood trauma and adult functioning. *Professional Psychology: Research and Practice, 24*(1), 83–90.

Farber, B. (1983a, Summer). The effects of psychotherapeutic practice upon the psychotherapists. *Psychotherapy: Theory, Research, and Practice, 20*(2), 174–182.

Farber, B. (1983b). Psychotherapists' perceptions of stressful patient behavior. *Professional Psychology, Research and Practice, 14*(5), 697–705.

Farber, B. (1990). Burnout in psychotherapists: Incidence, types, and trends. *Psychology in Private Practice, 8*(1), 35–44.

Farber, B., & Heifetz, L. J. (1981). The satisfactions and stresses of psychotherapeutic work: A factor analytic study. *Professional Psychology, 12*(5), 621–630.

Figley, C. R. (1995). Compassion fatigue: Toward a new understanding of the costs of caring. In B. H. Stamm (Ed.), *Secondary traumatic stress: Self-care issues for clinicians, researchers, and educators* (pp. 3–28). Lutherville, MD: Sidran Press.

Freudenberger, H. J. (1975). The staff burnout syndrome in alternative institutions. *Psychotherapy: Theory, Research, and Practice, 12*(1), 73–82.

Freudenberger, H. J., & Robbins, A. (1979). The hazards of being a psychoanalyst. *The Psychoanalytic Review, 66*(2), 275–295.

Grosch, W. N., & Olsen, D. C. (1994). *When helping starts to hurt: A new look at burnout among psychotherapists.* New York: W.W. Norton & Co.

Jennings, L., & Skovholt, T. M. (1999). The cognitive, emotional, and relational characteristics of master therapists. *Journal of Counseling Psychology, 46*, 3–11.

Kassam-Adams, N. (1995). The risks of treating sexual trauma: Stress and secondary trauma in psychotherapists. In B. H. Stamm (Ed.), *Secondary traumatic stress: Self-care issues for clinicians, researchers, and educators* (pp. 37–48). Lutherville, MD: Sidran Press.

Mahoney, M. J. (1997). Psychotherapists' personal problems and self-care patterns. *Professional Psychology: Research and Practice, 28*(1), 14–16.

McCann, L., & Pearlman, L. A. (1990). Vicarious traumatization: A framework for understanding the psychological effects of working with victims. *Journal of Traumatic Stress, 3*(1), 131–149.

Medeiros, M. E., & Prochaska, J. O. (1988). Coping strategies that psychotherapists use in working with stressful clients. *Professional Psychology: Research and Practice, 19*(1), 112–114.

Neumann, D. A., & Gamble, S. J. (1995). Issues in the professional development of psychotherapists: Countertransference and vicarious traumatization in the new trauma therapist. *Psychotherapy, 32*(2), 341–347.

Norcross, J. C. (1990). Personal therapy for therapists: One solution. *Psychotherapy in Private Practice, 8*(1), 45–59.

Norcross, J. C., Prochaska, J. O., & DiClemente, C. C. (1986). Self-change of psychological distress: Laypersons versus psychologists' coping strategies. *Journal of Clinical Psychology, 42*(5), 834–840.

Pearlman, L. A., & MacIan, P. S. (1995). Vicarious traumatization: An empirical study of the effects of trauma work on trauma therapists. *Professional Psychology: Research and Practice, 26*(6), 558–565.

Racusin, G. R., Abramowitz, S. I., & Winter, W. D. (1981). Becoming a therapist: Family dynamics and career choice. *Professional Psychology, 12*(2), 271–279.

Radke, J. T., & Mahoney, M. J. (2000). Comparing the personal lives of psychotherapists and research psychologists. *Professional Psychology: Research and Practice, 31*(1), 82–84.

Raquepaw, J. M., & Miller, R. S. (1989). Psychotherapist burnout: A componential analysis. *Professional Psychology: Research and Practice, 20*(1), 32–36.

Rodolfa, E. R., Kraft, W. A., & Reilley, R. R. (1988). Stressors of professionals and trainees at APA-approved counseling and VA medical center internship sites. *Professional Psychology: Research and Practice, 19*(1), 43–49.

Rosenbloom, D. J., Pratt, A. C., & Pearlman, L. A. (1995). Helpers' responses to trauma work: Understanding and intervening in an organization. In B. H. Stamm (Ed.), *Secondary traumatic stress: Self-care issues for clinicians, researchers, and educators* (pp. 65–79). Lutherville, MD: Sidran Press.

Saakvitne, K. W., & Pearlman, L. A. (1996). *Transforming the pain: A workbook on vicarious traumatization for helping professionals who work with traumatized clients.* New York: W. W. Norton & Co.

Savicki, V., & Cooley, E. (1987). The relationship of work environment and client contact to burnout in mental health professionals. *Journal of Counseling and Development, 65*, 249–252.

Skovholt, T. M. (2001). *The resilient practitioner: Burnout prevention and self-care strategies for counselors, therapists, teachers, and health professionals.* Boston: Allyn and Bacon.

Snibbe, J. R., Radcliffe, T., Weisberger, C., Richards, M., & Kelly, J. (1989). Burnout among primary care physicians and mental health professionals in a managed health care setting. *Psychological Reports, 65,* 775–780.

Sussman, M. B. (1995). Introduction. In M. B. Sussman (Ed.), *A perilous calling: The hazards of psychotherapy practice* (pp. 1–12). New York: Wiley.

6 Ethical Values of Master Therapists

LEN JENNINGS

ASHLEY SOVEREIGN

NANCY BOTTORFF

MELISSA MUSSELL

Conducting oneself ethically is a critical task of the competent therapist (*http://www.APA.org/ethics*, January, 2003). Making the best ethical decisions can be extremely challenging for most therapists due to the multitude of complex ethical situations. The goal of this study is to examine the ethical values of master therapists considered to be "the best of the best" by their professional colleagues. It is hoped that such an examination will help to illuminate what ethical values master therapists seem to draw upon in their work.

Ethics are beliefs about conduct and principles that inform rules for proper behavior (Corey, Corey, & Callanan, 1998; Knauss, 1997). In psychology, ethics codes are intended to "set out expected professional behavior and responsibility" (Eberlein, 1987, p. 354). However, studies involving ethical dilemmas have found a discrepancy between therapists' knowledge of what ought to be done and what they actually would do (Bernard & Jara, 1986; Bernard, Murphy, & Little, 1987; Smith, McGuire, Abbott, & Blau, 1991; Wilkins, McGuire, Abbott, & Blau, 1990).

Why the inconsistencies? Researchers suggest that when therapists thought the ethical infraction violated a clear professional code, they were more likely to act as they felt they should. This happened especially when the violation was bolstered by a legal precedent (Bernard et al., 1987; Smith et al., 1991). However, in situations that depended more on individual judgment, practitioners were less likely to "do the right thing." It appears that when written ethical guidelines are unclear, psychologists rely on their own individual value systems and their understanding of the ethics code (Bersoff & Koeppl, 1993; Eberlein, 1987). One possibility for the discrepancy between knowing and doing what is right is that some clinicians suffer from deficits in principles such as integrity and honesty (Smith et al., 1991). Rest (1984) theorized that a therapist who is reluctant to follow through with understood ethical behavior may lack the courage to act. To date, studies on therapist values have tended to focus on therapists' conceptualizations of what constitutes good mental health (Consoli & Williams, 1999; Haugen, Tyler, & Clark, 1991; Jensen & Bergin, 1988; Kelly, 1995; Khan & Cross, 1983; Myers & Truluck, 1998).

Kitchener (1984) believes that parts of formal organizational ethical codes are too broad, whereas others are too narrow. The fundamental ethical principles identified by Kitchener are autonomy, beneficence, nonmaleficence, justice, and fidelity. Meara, Schmidt, and Day (1996) expanded on Kitchener's work by defining principle ethics (formal, obligatory codes) as distinct from virtue ethics (focus on character traits and ideals). Virtue ethics are rooted within the traditions of a cultural group and, therefore, present a more complete account of moral life than actions based on prescribed rules. Meara et al. (1996) proposed that virtue ethics complement principle ethics by assisting helping professionals to achieve the ideals of being competent, serving the common good, and retaining professional autonomy. Given that the authors argue professional decision making is "seldom either totally absolute or completely relative and thus requires virtuous, competent individuals to exercise careful professional judgment" (p. 5), the concept of ethics should encompass issues of character as well as professional obligations. The work of Kitchener and Meara et al. supports the idea that ethical decisions in psychology are complex and rarely absolute. In order to understand ethical decision making, it seems important to know the core values of the therapist that influence each unique situation.

The majority of empirical studies that examine ethical decision making in practice have focused on therapists' responses to particular ethical dilemmas (Conte, Plutchik, Picard, & Karasu, 1989; Haas, Malouf, & Mayerson, 1988; Smith et al., 1991; Wilkins et al., 1990). A limitation of this line of research is that it tends to be about specific areas of concern, such as sexual contact with clients. Another approach has been for researchers to survey practicing clinicians in an open-ended way about their ethically challenging critical incidents. This method, as described by Pope and Vetter (1992), mirrors the original process the American Psychological Association (APA) used to create the first ethics code for psychologists. In 1952, the APA surveyed its membership in an attempt to develop guidelines for ethical conduct that reflected the concerns of practitioners. Although useful, it appears that survey research cannot capture the complexity of the nuanced thinking involved in making ethical decisions.

In a departure from survey research, Prilleltensky, Walsh-Bowers, and Rossiter (1999) conducted a qualitative study exploring the underlying core values of practitioners. When examining practitioners' professional ethics, three general principles emerge: respect for people's rights, dignity, integrity, and privacy; compassion and responsible caring; and feeling a sense of responsibility for the community. Furthermore, the practitioners described additional values they believed were fundamental in their work: encouraging clients' self-determination, advocacy for vulnerable clients, confidentiality and informed consent, strength-based empowerment, and paying attention to the best interests of the client under unique circumstances.

Thus far, little research on ethical values has focused on seasoned or expert therapists. However, studies have examined clinicians' years of experience, providing a better understanding of the growth of professional ethical judgment over the course of a career (Conte et al., 1989; Haas, Malouf, & Mayerson, 1998; Jensen & Bergin, 1988). Conte et al.'s (1989) survey of therapists found that beliefs about ethical standards varied widely. The authors concluded that certain behaviors were thought by some therapists to be inappropriate, but not necessarily unethical, whereas other therapists felt that similar behaviors were either clearly unethical or grounds for malpractice. In addition, therapists with more experience were more likely to feel that pledging to cure a client's symptoms was unethical and less likely to break confidentiality to warn a potential victim of harm.

Jensen and Bergin (1988) found that years of professional experience did not predict desirable mental health values. In addition, Haas et al. (1998) found the length of time after attaining one's professional degree to be inversely related to the psychologist's willingness to take the most ethically preferred course of action. The authors hypothesized that this surprising result may be due to burnout factors or a recent training focus for younger practitioners on specific ethical obligations.

Pope and Bajt (1988) surveyed ethically knowledgeable senior psychologists (e.g., served on boards of ethics, authors of ethics textbooks, ABPP status) and found that a majority admitted having willingly violated ethical codes. Further, 77 percent of respondents felt that formal ethical standards should be broken when necessary for client welfare "or other deeper values" (p. 828). Instead of "textbook ethics," these experienced practitioners perhaps used context-based ethics developed over years of practice.

Though the APA puts forth a set of ethical principles designed to guide psychologists to practice ethically, survey or dilemma-based research methods have yielded limited data on therapists' values in general and have, at times, painted an unfavorable portrayal of the ethical practices of experienced therapists. What appears lacking in the literature is an examination of actual values—perhaps those "deeper values" that guide therapists' ethical behavior. Even more useful may be an examination of the ethical values that expert or master therapists seem to draw upon in their work. Utilizing Consensual Qualitative Research (CQR) methods (Hill, Thompson, & Williams, 1997), the present study attempts to provide an understanding of the ethical values of master therapists. Please see Appendix A for a complete description of the study's methodology.

Results

The five most salient ethical values of master therapists identified were: (a) competence, (b) relational connection, (c) nonmaleficence, (d) autonomy, and (e) beneficence. Several quotations will be offered for each of the five ethical values. Hopefully, this will provide the reader with a better sense of the master therapists' viewpoints that comprised each ethical value.

Competence

As outlined in the 2002 APA Ethical Standards, being competent in one's work as a therapist is a hallmark of ethical practice. The master therapists in this study clearly value being exceptionally skilled in their clinical work. In fact, they are highly motivated to move beyond the minimum competency level required by ethical and practice standards and to be experts in their field. These therapists, even after years of experience and training that might have just as easily resulted in complacency, place a high value on building and maintaining their skill set. Throughout the interview data, references to becoming competent and maintaining competency as a practitioner lend support to this category. One master therapist recollects how the accumulation of experience aided in developing competence as a practitioner:

> I've got a lot more experience, and as much as I used to want to believe when I was younger that age and experience didn't count (and not just experience in the terms of being a therapist, but life experience), it counts a lot in terms of your ability to empathize and understand a wider range of things. The other part is that when I came out of school, I did not feel as though I knew much of anything. And the training and supervision and experience that I got during those years made an incredible difference.

Similarly, another master therapist also discussed the vital role of experience in building competency:

> I am really shockproof, and it took a long time not to be jarred by the stories I hear. I can't imagine how to create a graduate school program that would turn out expert seasoned therapists immediately. It's a long process.

Master therapists continually seek out formal and informal training to broaden their clinical abilities. Being perpetually open to opportunities for learning and growth in their profession seemed to be another defining characteristic of these master therapists. The drive for competency combined with an awareness of limitations inspired master therapists to be "life-long learners." It is likely that keeping current on the latest developments in the profession and exposing their work to others for feedback minimizes the potential for unethical behavior. The master therapists spoke of the importance of looking for professional growth experiences beyond didactic venues and finding other arenas for challenge and inspiration. Primarily through consultation and supervision, as well as their own therapy, master therapists seemed continually to seek out the opportunity to have others critically evaluate their work. As one master therapist stated:

> I meet with other people who are calling me on my stuff so I get a chance to look at myself on the outside over and over and over again, through personal therapy, through lots of supervision, through ongoing consultation. That helps incredibly. I think that's essential.

Amassing years of clinical practice is only one component of commitment to professional development. For master therapists, experience combined with clinical consultation, ongoing traditional academic training, and personal reflection yields a deeper level of professional growth. Again, this commitment to professional growth appears to bolsters one's competence, which in turn is an important ingredient in conducting ethical work. Challenging the idea that experience alone equals expertise, the same master therapist spoke eloquently of the importance of bolstering the accumulation of clinical experience with sustaining professional relationships to grow professionally:

> I don't think years of experience by itself does it, because I might have the same year of experience twenty times, and so I need to put that together with good consultation and a good collegial system. So that you actually are learning from what you're doing and [learning] more about how you're impacting and affecting people.

It appears that part of master therapists' becoming more competent in their work involves looking less and less for an immediate answer to clients' presenting problems because they believe tolerance for ambiguity is an important part of the therapist's role. Master therapists tend to not see easy answers in their work with clients and to conceptualize the process of staying open as a hallmark of competent practice. They seem to be searching constantly for the uniqueness and intricacy of situations. This appreciation of complexity has ethical implications in that it helps prevent premature closure (Skovholt & Rønnestad, 1995), which is a tendency of some therapists to reduce anxiety by, for example, latching onto one of the first solutions considered or to use the same techniques with virtually every situation. With a low comfort level for ambiguity and complexity, some therapists might hastily come to conclusions that primarily relieve their anxiety, yet may not be the best fit for the client. Thus, not being open to complexity and ambiguity leads to narrowing case conceptualization and treatment interventions, which can result in less than competent work. One master therapist said:

> Every person is different. Therefore, any technique that one uses, to use it each time in the same way is in some ways denying the truth of the uniqueness of every individual and the uniqueness of every interaction.

Another master therapist noted how difficult it was to train therapists who were not open:

> Having taught psychologists, they [often] grab onto an interpretation and come hell or high water, they're going to prove they're right. Instead of saying, here's an interpretation, but does it fit?

The following examples further illustrate the therapists' deep commitment to openness, which may lead to more competent, and therefore more ethical, interventions. For example, one master therapist said:

> I think you have to have a certain amount of flexibility, in that you will hear things and you won't make sudden decisions and then push them through. You sort of wait and watch until the pieces fit.

Similarly, one master therapist stated how important it is to avoid acting prematurely:

> So, I think [it is important] to be open to not knowing and to an ambiguous situation, so that you can hear what it is that is emerging, rather than laying something on the

situation . . . . When you don't know, then you can listen more curiously and have more of an openness about what all might be coming here. So, I think the ambiguity is a part of that. It helps you stay more curious about sorting it out and understanding it, finding out more.

Relational Connection

Establishing, maintaining, and honoring relationships is an extremely important ethical value for these master therapists, and an ethical value absent in the 1992 APA General Principles that we analyzed for this study. Master therapists seem to highly value the relational interaction and connection among colleagues, friends, clients, and the larger community. Developing sound professional relationships with colleagues is a core value of these therapists. They believe that in order to maintain competence and build expertise, therapists continually must be in relationship with others in the field, both for supervision or consultation and for collegial support and friendship. One therapist commented on the need to avoid professional isolation through consistent contact with other professionals:

> I have made sure to practice here with colleagues that are close by. When the leases are up and some move out, we get others in, and we meet once a week for a long lunch, to talk about cases or plants for the waiting room or whatever. That sort of collegial connect, especially on a day-in-day-out basis, is really quite important.

Similarly, master therapists spoke about the need for good relationships in their personal lives that often serve as a safeguard against burnout or impairment:

> You know, if you have good friends in your life, if you have a good support system, folks will let you know that you're feeling worn out or depleted or whatever and then will support you getting some help.

As would be expected, all of the master therapists believed that the client-therapist relationship is the key to effecting positive change in clients. One therapist stated:

> . . . [T]he core of psychotherapy to me is the development of that relationship and the connection, and so it's the development of a relationship . . . the purpose of which is to heal or help the other person. But to me, psychotherapy is the relationship, as opposed to, you know, a technique that I do or whatever else. It's really about forming and working in the "in-between."

Another master therapist also emphasized the relational aspect of effecting positive therapeutic change:

> I really believe that [psychotherapy] is a two-person operation, so that it is about us together if change happens or doesn't happen. So, I don't think about it as if something

is successful, that I did it. You know, I think it's something that we did together, and I think that if it's not working, it's something we're not doing together.

One master therapist shared:

[Psychotherapy] sort of re-establishes that kind of bridge back to humanity, it re-establishes that sense of being in the community.

Many of the master therapists interviewed seem to uphold high ethical standards when interacting with others in both their professional and personal life. In most relationships, even those in the community at large, the master therapists strive for congruence between their values and how they relate to others. One therapist captured the commitment to maintaining positive relationships in a variety of settings:

It is honoring the integrity of the relationship. Whatever relationship I have, whether it's with a friend that I'm having dinner with, or I am negotiating a price on a used car with a car dealer, or I am planning a vacation with my wife, or I'm talking with a client about his or her life, I'm going to be honest.

Nonmaleficence

Not only do master therapists value helping others, they are also aware of the tremendous potential to do damage in the context of the therapeutic relationship. They seem mindful of the ways they may potentially harm their clients and have developed measures to minimize this risk. For example, one master therapist said:

I think one of the ways therapy goes awry is that the therapist starts to use the client for their own emotional sustenance . . . regulation of the therapist's self-esteem, all those sorts of things.

Master therapists strongly believed in managing their own personal and professional stressors that can lead to harming clients. One master therapist said it this way:

Those therapists who have been in consultation with me before who were not willing to do [personal therapy] were so difficult to deal with. Any time they were stuck for a period of time, they'd make it about the client, instead of about themselves or instead of about both of them. And when you do that, you're going to be abusive to your client.

For master therapists, humility offsets the potential for grandiosity and arrogance, characteristics that may lead to harming clients. Because these master therapists realize they do not have "a corner on the truth," they seem to have a healthy perspective on their limits as practitioners and human beings. In fact, awareness of these limitations seems to inspire them to continue growing professionally and personally. This attitude is in stark contrast to those who might think they have "arrived" as a therapist and therefore do not require ongoing training and development. In addition, some master therapists expressed concern for therapists who are not fully aware of their weaknesses. For example, one master therapist said:

> One of the things that I tell people when they are looking for a therapist is to really ask them the question about what can't they do. And boy, if they don't have something they can't do, get out!

Another master therapist said:

> Bad therapists don't know what they don't know. They think they know everything, they have a "got to solve it" kind of perspective on everything. Their theory is very sound and [yet] they don't really know how little they know.

Displaying humility, one master therapist spoke of the hazard of grandiosity in considering oneself an expert:

> I think if one begins to think of oneself as a master therapist, it can lead to grandiosity. It can pave the way to all sorts of misuse of power. There is one phenomenon that has to do with the seasoned clinician who is so confident that the rules no longer apply.

Master therapists expressed a deep commitment to awareness of their own life issues. Their self-awareness seemed to center around two issues: (a) understanding and fulfilling their personal emotional and physical needs and (b) awareness of their own "unfinished business," personal conflicts, defenses, and vulnerabilities. Most importantly, the master therapists were well aware of the potential for these issues to intrude upon the therapy session and possibly do harm to the client. Awareness of personal emotional needs and fulfilling those needs through various activities—including travel, exercise, spiritual practice, psychotherapy, contacts with colleagues, friends, and family—seemed paramount to the therapists. For example, one master therapist said:

> When I think about therapists who've gotten themselves in difficulty, it's often because there hasn't been self-care, and there's been a looking either to the client to provide something for them, or else not really being available for all that the client might need or want to do as part of their therapy work.

The ability to meet clients' needs also becomes compromised when therapists do not obtain appropriate resources to meet their own personal needs. Although the therapist is (hopefully) not looking to the client to meet those needs, the client's care still can suffer. One therapist said:

> I think that self-awareness is really the key to helping you understand if you're getting in the way or not getting in the way, of facilitating, being with and not being with.

In order to be therapeutically effective, awareness of personal problems, biases, and conflicts is vital. The management and resolution of countertransference issues appears critical to these therapists in terms of providing quality care for their clients and minimizing the risk of harm to their clients. One master therapist said:

> If I'm sitting here and you're a client and I'm worried about your liking me—I'm worried about your thinking I'm competent, I'm worried about your not getting mad at me—any of those kinds of unfinished issues inside of me makes me powerless to help, makes me very self-centered, and isn't going to do much for you.

The same master therapist illustrated the connection between self-awareness and ethical behavior with the following discussion of "unfinished issues":

> Well, what I had to start looking at was the fact that I came from an alcoholic family and hadn't recognized it. So it faced me with needing to look at what it was about myself that had stopped me, I mean, what my countertransference issue was very clearly, in terms of not taking the drinking part seriously . . . It was the first real experience of running up against my own issues that were clearly getting in the way and harming my clients.

Autonomy

The right of individuals to determine the course of their own lives seemed to be another central value guiding master therapists when making ethical practice decisions. Master therapists appear to greatly respect the phenomenological worldviews of their clients and hold the belief that for change to occur, clients, for the most part, need to be allowed to determine the direction of the therapeutic process. One therapist made the point this way:

> I think you always have to give people a choice. Our basic mission is to help them see their choices, and if they want to make bad choices . . . if somebody wants to go into a bar and scream that everybody in the bar is a son-of-a-bitch and get the hell beaten out of them, that's their choice. My job is to help them see what the consequence will be if they do that.

Similarly, another master therapist emphasized the clients' need to be responsible for helping themselves:

> If you and I are a couple and I am saying "I am really wounded and it is your job to fix it," or "help me not feel the pain," we are going to be in deep, deep trouble. [Psychotherapy] is really [about] helping each of us to recognize our own woundedness and how to reparent that and how to face the disappointment that nobody else is going to do it, including your partner.

The interview data suggested that master therapists were aware of the ethical dangers of thinking they know what is best for their clients, and therefore worked to avoid imposing their own beliefs, values, and ideals on clients. Perhaps because autonomy has been such a central tenet of their own personal development, master therapists believed strongly in the ability of their clients to direct their own lives. One master therapist said:

> I mean, we really know what's best for ourselves and what the truth is about ourselves and our own direction. I think that a big part of our job as therapists is to help get all the other voices out of the way for the clients, so they can hear their own and begin to have some faith in it.

Master therapists also defined their role as assisting clients in developing personal coping and growth skills. In reference to the author Sheldon Kopp, one master therapist said:

> . . . another thing he said that impacted me was "A client comes into the room and throws himself at your feet, sort of hanging on to your ankles, hoping that you will save him. A good therapist will step back and let him fall on his face, and be there for him when he learns how to pick himself up."

The master therapists seemed to believe that encouraging the client's autonomy was a central part of ethical practice. One therapist referred to how experience and increased competence contributed to being able to better assist clients in discovering their own answers:

> The better you get, the more you know how to help the person work, instead of your trying to do the work for them.

Beneficence

Master therapists feel moved to reduce human suffering and to work toward improving the welfare of others. In the unique role of therapist, they have the opportunity to demonstrate caring by helping to transform painful experiences into sources of personal strength. One master therapist viewed the role of a therapist this way:

> Sometimes I think as therapists, we are like that second fairy godmother at the christening. I can't change what was laid down earlier, but then I can help a person soften it or make it go in ways that are more interesting.

Another master therapist described how much she cared for a particular client this way:

> There are some people who are very, very slow [to change]. I really get to care about [them] a lot. I would say to one client that I had, "You know, I could take you by the shoulders and shake you, because you won't believe in yourself at all, and you have so much reason to."

One master therapist used a metaphor that described being of help to others:

> One of the metaphors I often use with my clients is the metaphor of the Wilderness Guide, and the way I [give] back is that they can hire me as a guide, because I know a

lot about survival in the wilderness, and I've traveled through a lot of wilderness—my own, and other people's wildernesses. I've got a compass and I can start a fire in the rain. I know how to make it through.

Another master therapist shared this:

People bring in problems that are frightening and abhorrent to themselves and to most people in their lives. I try to create a situation where these problems are approachable and discussable, something that can kind of counteract the person's embarrassment or shame or whatever and be able to go on to address the problems. I think [my] empathy has the effect of helping people be empathic to themselves.

The master therapists in this sample expressed a good deal of satisfaction in helping others. However, rather than acting out of completely altruistic motives, these therapists acknowledge that they entered this field to meet their personal need to be "useful" or to accrue other personal benefits in their professional work. One master therapist succinctly shared the personal satisfaction of doing therapy:

Where else would I ever have this kind of intimate contact with such interesting people? I feel like I am doing a useful job.

Another master therapist enthusiastically described the potential of psychotherapy to be helpful this way:

It [psychotherapy] makes such a difference. Geez, does it make a difference!

Discussion

Utilizing in-depth qualitative research methods, the current study unobtrusively examined master therapists' ethical values by analyzing descriptions of their therapeutic work. Several of the study's findings seem noteworthy. To begin, three of the five most salient ethical values (beneficence, nonmaleficence, and autonomy) paralleled the foundational principles described by Kitchener (1984). Master therapists in this study seemed to be operating out of the higher order virtue ethics, as described by Meara et al. (1996). Again, virtue ethics refer to character traits of the therapist and aspirational ideals instead of "principle ethics," which focus on professional obligations of knowing specifically if a behavior is unethical. The master therapists did not appear "rule-bound" or focused on specific rules of conduct such as confidentiality, or bartering. Rather, master therapists seemed to be operating from a far more sophisticated and principled mindset when dealing with the intricacies of ethical practice.

Curiously, Kitchener's concepts of justice and fidelity did not emerge as ethical values. For example, in terms of justice, the interview data did not indicate that these master therapists worked toward equal access to psychological help for all through means such as providing pro bono work or sliding-scale fees to clients. One possible reason for this finding may be the limited demographic, cultural, and professional diversity of the participant pool. It could be hypothesized that among master therapists who served primarily disenfranchised groups, issues of fairness, equality, and justice may have been more salient, as they were for child guidance center workers studied by Prilleltensky et al. (1999). It also is possible that the absence of these concepts may be an artifact of the unobtrusive data collection method that did not allow for follow-up or probing questions that might have revealed other ethical values.

The master therapists held as extremely important the ethical value of competence. This value is explicitly addressed in the 1992 APA General Principles and the 2002 Ethical Standards. These master therapists worked hard to achieve a high level of skill as therapists and continue to hone their skills through peer consultation, continuing education, readings, self-reflection, and personal psychotherapy. The master therapists' motivation to maintain a high level of competence was a pervasive theme in the interview data. They recognized that psychotherapy is complicated, difficult work that requires a high level of skill and commitment to continually maintain one's competency. These therapists are strongly motivated to enhance their clinical work to best serve their clients. They seek out learning opportunities well beyond the minimal requirements of licensing boards. This high level of motivation to be outstanding in their work seems to be a critical trait that enables them to achieve and maintain expertise in their field. The master therapists believe that holding an attitude of "not knowing" (all of the answers) keeps them curious. Staying curious seems to serve to minimize stagnation in their work and leads to new opportunities for growth and development.

The study's most significant finding was the level of importance the master therapists placed on the ethical value of relational connection. The master therapists seemed to highly value interpersonal relationships in all areas of their lives. The interview data suggested that the therapists were very aware of their impact on others and strove for respectful, authentic interactions in professional relationships as well as casual encounters in everyday life. This finding is significant in part because the 1992 APA General Principles did not emphasize this concept as an ethical value. Gilligan's (1982) ethic of care concept seems to be closely related to the ethical value of relational connection that emerged in these interviews. Gilligan emphasized that moral decision making for women often focuses on how decisions will impact the quality of one's relationships. Whereas the 1992 APA General Principles seem to align more closely with Kohlberg's (1984) justice orientation, master therapists seem to give greater weight to how their actions impacted the quality of their working relationships with clients and colleagues.

The ethical value of nonmaleficence seemed very important to the master therapists, who appeared to work hard at not imposing their own beliefs and values onto their clients. It is their belief that if therapists impose their worldview, clients are denied the growth and personal strength inherent in discovering one's own way, thus doing the client a major disservice. In addition, if therapists do not look at how their own motives and issues may negatively impact their work, they risk harming their clients. Master therapists seemed exceptionally dedicated to the pursuit of self-knowledge in order to help them to recognize and manage countertransference issues that potentially could be harmful to clients.

Another important finding was the ethical value of autonomy. Master therapists seemed committed to encouraging clients' self-determination, while working to avoid imposing their own beliefs and values. Belief in the client's personal power may lead to a positive connection with the therapist. Clients receiving affirmation of their personal power may feel stronger in their attachment to the therapist. Respectful attitudes toward clients' self-determination may minimize the risk of harming clients.

Finally, the respectful and caring attitudes of the master therapists also are related to the ethical value of beneficence. It is clear that these master therapists care deeply about their clients' well-being, and this caring attitude most likely enhances the therapeutic relationship. In keeping with the robust literature on the efficacy of the therapeutic alliance on therapy outcomes (e.g., Lambert, 1992), master therapists acknowledge the importance of and strive towards building therapeutic alliances.

New Ethical Guidelines

The APA recently adopted a new version of the Ethical Principles of Psychologists and Code of Conduct (*http://www.APA.org/ethics*, January, 2003). Interestingly, the revisions seem to reflect a shift toward a greater understanding of the deeper character issues and values involved in the ethical practice of psychology. The new principles now are categorized as beneficence and nonmaleficence, fidelity and responsibility, integrity, justice, and respect for people's rights and dignity.

Overall, the new general ethical principles seem to reflect more fully that the practice of psychology is a value-laden endeavor and charge psychologists with the obligation to address the intrapersonal and interpersonal issues believed to affect therapeutic practice. For example, psychologists are directed to explore and manage biases, take responsible steps toward their own functional mental and physical health, and make decisions within the context of mitigating human suffering. These more directive requirements seem to mirror the self-care and self-awareness components of the nonmaleficence value that emerged in the current study. Indeed, the new APA principles appear to pay more attention to the potential harm therapists might cause their clients as a result of the therapists' powerful role and the clients' vulnerability.

Relationships are afforded more overt attention in the new code than in the 1992 code. There are many possible reasons for the change, including that this shift may indicate the increased prevalence of Gilligan's ethic of care decision-making orientation as a result of growing participation by women in the field of psychology. Regardless of the reason, the increased focus on relationships in ethical principles is a welcome modification and supported by the findings of this study.

The ethical principle category now titled justice, an apparently updated version of the 1992 social responsibility and concern for others' welfare concepts, seems to present a less directive interpretation of the appropriate role of psychologists in promoting social equality and equal access to the benefits of psychology. Although justice continues to include equal opportunity to psychological services and processes, no longer do the codes state that psychologists are "encouraged to contribute a portion of their professional time for little or no personal advantage" (APA, 1992, p. 4). This might either be interpreted as less assertive activism on the part of the APA or as a move toward broader virtue concepts and further away from directive, rule-based codes.

Limitations

A limitation of the study was the lack of a culturally diverse participant pool. Although the sampling was fairly representative of a northern, midwestern state, exploring the ethical values of only Caucasian, European American therapists limits the usefulness of the results. For example, the concept of autonomy, with its emphasis on the individual versus the group, fundamentally is representative of a Western worldview. Whether this or other ethical values from this study would emerge as primary themes for dialogues with master therapists of other cultural backgrounds remains unclear and warrants further investigation.

Another limitation of the study is that all ten master therapists were solely in private practice. Because clients seeking therapy in a private practice setting are a particular subset of psychotherapy clients, it is possible that other ethical values may have emerged in interviews with therapists working in more diverse settings. For example, the master therapists' emphasis on client autonomy with little mention of more directive approaches may be not hold for therapists working with other client populations (e.g., inpatient clients).

Another potential limitation was the use of existing interview data. Although use of this approach was elected because it is an unobtrusive, thus less reactive research method (Webb, Campbell, Schwartz, & Sechrest, 1966) and useful in identifying the values of the participants (Marshall & Rossman, 1999), it could be that other salient issues might have emerged if the researchers had interviewed these master therapists directly about ethical values. In doing so, the researchers might have been able to follow up with questions and probe to elicit a more detailed perspective of ethical values. However, with direct questioning about the ethical aspects of their work (a potentially sensitive topic), the likelihood of socially desirable responses would have increased. Despite these limitations, we found that numerous ethical values were clearly embedded in the descriptions of the master therapists' therapeutic practice.

Implications for Future Research

The current research findings outlined several ethical values of master therapists. Future research can expand upon this list and seek to support or refute these themes. To date, most research related to ethical values has utilized survey methods to assess therapists' responses to hypothetical ethical dilemmas. The logical subsequent progression for future research would be to ask expert therapists overtly about their ethical values in a qualitative study. Although this direct approach has the potential for reactivity, we believe that a dialogue with expert therapists would provide rich data on the topic. This research could be extended by contrasting the ethical values of expert therapists with novice or "typical" therapists. In an effort to move from self-report methodologies, research examining expert therapists' ethical values and decision making through simulated or live counseling sessions would provide insights into their practice behavior. Although it is useful to learn what therapists report they would do when dealing with ethical situations, to actually observe therapists handling ethical dilemmas seems to be a more robust approach. Relatedly, simulated or actual interviews with clients could be used to examine the difficulties Bernard et al. (1987) and Wilkins et al. (1990) found that practitioners have in making ethical choices when they know the preferred course of action. Finally, future researchers would do well to investigate the Smith et al. (1991) hypothesis that, in part, therapists may lack certain personal characteristics to act on their ethical beliefs. Psychotherapy research examining Rest's (1984) model of moral decision making, in which a major component of moral/ethical action is the willingness to act courageously when needed, would be a welcome contribution to the literature.

Implications for Practice

Knauss (1997) states that "[l]earning to practice ethically cannot be effective in an atmosphere that does not value or respect being ethical" (p. 292). Training programs and therapy worksites can promote ethical behavior by encouraging an open dialogue of ethical issues. In many graduate programs, evaluation in ethics courses is based upon the student's ability to memorize ethical principles and often is measured by successfully passing written tests such as state ethics exams. Training methods that are more experientially based (e.g., role plays, stimulus material for discussion, values clarification exercises, videotapes) may be more likely to encourage self-awareness on behalf of the students and, therefore, nurture the development of ethical values.

Ethics classes also may tend to focus on deficit-based training strategies, such as becoming aware of biases and stereotypes, rather than on identifying the broader values unique to the profession or to each student (Carlson & Erickson, 1999). Reframing goals of values training to include providing safe space to talk about these personal and ambiguous issues would help to develop a shared language of ethical reflection (Vachon & Agresti, 1992). Additionally, the opportunity to talk with others about the role of particular values in ethical decisions may serve to amplify students' consciousness of the importance of critical reflectiveness (Assouline, 1989) and ultimately assist them in their decision making.

Carlson and Erickson (1999) recommend that values be highlighted from the beginning as therapists-in-training construct their individual theories of the composition of psychological change. Building personal theories around stems such as "I believe" or "I value" serves to integrate personal and theoretical beliefs and invests therapists in the process of therapy. This exercise would allow students to discover values implicit in theories and would set in motion the process of bringing values to the forefront of decision making. Ultimately, it may neither be feasible nor desirable for training programs to instill a particular set of ethical values in psychologists (Mickleburgh, 1992). However, in order to achieve the goal of producing therapists who are competent to make ethical decisions in therapy, more time spent teaching therapists how to identify their own existing underlying values is essential (Assouline, 1989; Corey, 1989; Kovel, 1982).

Another helpful suggestion for both trainees and current practitioners to go deeper into the question of how values influence their work is to spend significant time reflecting on their own experiences and personality. In a traditional feminist approach that incorporates the personal with the theoretical, Bogart (1999) recommends that students answer the question: "What is it about me and my personal history that leads me to these conclusions about people and the process of change?" (pp. 46–47). Examining the ways in which therapists' backgrounds might shape the process of client assessment and conceptualization provides the opportunity to further develop self-awareness, a hallmark of competent, nonmaleficent ethical practice as highlighted by this study.

Skovholt and Rønnestad (1995) advocate the use of developmental contracts as one approach to therapist development within supervision. Constructing a formal contract that makes explicit the goal of developing awareness of particular values and their role in ethical decisions may be a useful tool, particularly because values are such an ambiguous part of therapeutic work. For example, it might be advisable to contract with one's supervisor to attend to "relational connection" for a particular time period or with a specific client population. As ethical issues then arise in supervision, both the therapist and supervisor are charged with examining how attending to relationships might be a part of finding an ethical solution to a particular dilemma. The structure of a developmental contract may increase both therapists' and supervisors' comfort level with higher-order character development because it makes value training a more overt part of the supervision process.

Conclusion

Based upon the findings of the current study, practitioners would do well not only to know their ethics code, but to continue to develop their character (i.e., virtue ethics) and find within themselves the ability to act courageously when dealing with ethically challenging situations. Due to the incomplete and fluid nature of professional ethical codes, it is important that therapists take note of the limitations of using only ethical guidelines as a guide to morally good practice (Grant, 1985).

Overall, this study reinforces the importance of several fundamental ethical principles found in the 1992 and/or 2002 APA General Principles such as doing good (beneficence), doing no harm (nonmaleficence), and respecting the self-direction of clients (autonomy). In addition, master therapists appeared to go beyond the APA guidelines to exceed the requirements to be competent, with their striving toward expertise. An important finding of the current study was the emphasis master therapists placed upon building and forming relationships and how this enhances their ability to practice ethically. The master therapists in this study demonstrated how involvement in many forms of relationships seemed to bolster their understanding of the ethical demands of their professional role.

References

American Psychological Association. (2002, December). Ethical principles of psychologists and code of conduct. *American Psychologist, 57*(12), 1060–1073.

Assouline, S. (1989). Developing moral responsibleness through professional education. *Counseling and Values, 34,* 47–49.

Bernard, J., & Jara, C. (1986). The failure of clinical psychology graduate students to apply understood ethical principles. *Professional Psychology: Research and Practice, 17,* 313–315.

Bernard, J., Murphy, M., & Little, M. (1987). The failure of clinical psychologists to apply understood ethical principles. *Professional Psychology: Research and Practice, 18,* 489–491.

Bersoff, D., & Koeppl, P. (1993). The relation between ethical codes and moral principles. *Ethics and Behavior, 3,* 345–357.

Bogart, C. J. (1999). A feminist approach to teaching theory use to counseling psychology graduate students. *Teaching of Psychology, 26*(1), 46–47.

Carlson, T., & Erickson, M. (1999). Recapturing the person in the therapist: An exploration of personal values, commitments, and beliefs. *Contemporary Family Therapy: An International Journal, 21*(1), 57–76.

Consoli, A., & Williams, L. (1999). Commonalities in values among mental health counselors. *Counseling and Values, 43,* 106–115.

Conte, H., Plutchik, R., Picard, S., & Karasu, T. (1989). Ethics in the practice of psychotherapy: A survey. *American Journal of Psychotherapy, 43,* 32–42.

Corey, G. (1989). Values in counseling and psychotherapy. *Counseling and Values, 33,* 177–178.

Corey, G., Corey, M., & Callanan, P. (1998). *Issues and ethics in the helping professions.* Pacific Grove, CA: Brooks/Cole Publishing Company.

Eberlein, L. (1987). Introducing ethics to beginning psychologists: A problem-solving approach. *Professional Psychology: Research and Practice, 18,* 353–359.

Gilligan, C. (1982). *In a different voice: Psychological theory and women's development.* Cambridge, MA: Harvard University Press.

Grant, B. (1985). The moral nature of psychotherapy. *Counseling and Values 29,* 141–150.

Haas, L., Malouf, J., & Mayerson, N. (1988). Personal and professional characteristics as factors in psychologists' ethical decision making. *Professional Psychology: Research and Practice, 19,* 35–42.

Haugen, M., Tyler, J., & Clark, J. (1991). Mental health values of psychotherapists: How psychologists, psychiatrists, psychoanalysts, and social workers conceptualize good mental health. *Counseling and Values, 36,* 24–36.

Hill, C., Thompson, B., & Williams, E. (1997). A guide to conducting consensual qualitative research. *The Counseling Psychologist, 25,* 517–572.

Jennings, L., & Skovholt, T. M. (1999). The cognitive, emotional, and relational characteristics of master therapists. *Journal of Counseling Psychology, 46*(1), 3–11.

Jensen, J., & Bergin, A. (1988). Mental health values of professional therapists: A national interdisciplinary survey. *Professional Psychology: Research and Practice, 19,* 290–297.

Kelly, E. (1995). Counselor values: A national survey. *Journal of Counseling and Development, 73,* 648–653.

Khan, J., & Cross, D. (1983). Mental health professional and client values: Similar or different? *Australian Journal of Sex, Marriage & Family, 4*(2), 71–78.

Kitchener, K. (1984). Intuition, critical evaluation and ethical principles: The foundation for ethical decisions in counseling psychology. *The Counseling Psychologist, 12*(3), 43–55.

Knauss, L. (1997). Professional training in ethics. In D. Marsh & R. Magee (Eds.), *Ethical and legal issues in professional practice with families.* New York: John Wiley & Sons.

Kohlberg, L. (1984). Essays in moral development: Vol. 2. *The psychology of moral development.* New York: Harper & Row.

Kovel, J. (1982). Values, interests, and psychotherapy. *The American Journal of Psychoanalysis, 42*(2), 109–119.

Lambert, M. J. (1992). Psychotherapy outcome: Implications for integrative and eclectic therapists. In J. C. Norcross & M. R. Goldfried (Eds.), *Handbook of psychotherapy integration.* New York: Basic Books.

Marshall, C., & Rossman, G. B. (1999). *Designing qualitative research* (3rd ed.). Thousand Oaks, CA: Sage Publications.

Meara, N. M., Schmidt, L. D., Day, J. D. (1996). Principles and virtues: A foundation for ethical decisions, policies, and character. *The Counseling Psychologist, 24*(1), 4–77.

Mickleburgh, W. E. (1992). Clarification of values in counselling and psychotherapy. *Australian and New Zealand Journal of Psychiatry, 26*(3), 391–398.

Myers, J., & Truluck, M. (1998). Health beliefs, religious values, and the counseling process: A comparison of counselors and other mental health professionals. *Counseling and Values, 42,* 106–123.

Pope, K., & Bajt, T. (1988). When laws and values conflict: A dilemma for psychologists. *American Psychologist, 43,* 828–829.

Pope, K., & Vetter, V. (1992). Ethical dilemmas encountered by members of the American Psychological Association. *American Psychologist, 47,* 397–411.

Prilleltensky, I., Walsh-Bowers, R., & Rossiter, A. (1999). Clinicians' lived experience of ethics: Values and challenges in helping children. *Journal of Educational and Psychological Consultation, 10,* 315–342.

Rest, J. (1984). Research on moral development: Implications for training counseling psychologists. *The Counseling Psychologist, 12*(3), 19–29.

Skovholt, T. M., & Rønnestad, M. H. (1995). *The evolving professional self: Stages and themes in therapist and counselor development.* New York: John Wiley & Sons.

Smith, T., McGuire, J., Abbott, D., & Blau, B. (1991). Clinical ethical decision making: An investigation of the rationales used to justify doing less than one believes one should. *Professional Psychology: Research and Practice, 22,* 235–239.

Vachon, D. O., & Agresti, A. A. (1992). A training proposal to help mental health professionals clarify and manage implicit values in the counseling process. *Professional Psychology: Research and Practice, 23,* 509–514.

Webb, E., Campbell, D. T., Schwartz, R. D., & Sechrest, L. (1966). *Unobtrusive measures: Nonreactive research in the social sciences.* Chicago: Rand McNally.

Wilkins, M., McGuire, J., Abbott, D., & Blau, B. (1990). Willingness to apply understood ethical principles. *Journal of Clinical Psychology, 46,* 539–547.

7

Portrait of the Master Therapist: Developmental Model of the Highly Functioning Self

THOMAS M. SKOVHOLT

LEN JENNINGS

MARY MULLENBACH

How can one capture the essence, the details, and the remarkable characteristics of experts performing the craft of therapy and counseling? This is an important question. Mental anguish and emotional pain form one of the most arduous variations of human suffering. A profession devoted to lessening this form of suffering is very important. And, although lessening such suffering is often very difficult in part because of the complex ambiguity of the human condition, it is still a task worthy of great effort.

Pulling us out of the thicket of darkness and multiple briers of how to really help people is the art form used by expert practitioners. Perhaps these high achievers can help us get to the light and use their methods, ideas, styles, and values. If we can copy them, learn from them, grow toward them, maybe we too can move toward performing at a high level.

Before we begin, we want to emphasize that the portrait that follows should be viewed as an ideal to strive for versus essential ingredients for any one individual. The following presentation of the data does not mean that every one of the ten master therapists possessed every characteristic at the highest level. Rather, the master therapists had varying combinations of these characteristics. What we describe in the following pages is a prototypical portrait of mastery.

To review and elaborate on the content of earlier chapters, let us first describe mastery.

Defining the Master Therapist

How should we define master therapists? We asked our expert group this question (Jennings, 1996, pp. 110–112). They gave us characteristics that have been produced by key experiences. One "recipe" or definition described the evolution of the master therapist:

> A lot of life experience, good self-esteem, openness to grow, commitment to personal growth, respect for humanity. Not having your ego tied up in it much, having a solid outside life, somebody who's not looking to have their needs met through the clients, other than financial. And a need to have an interesting, sort of fun experience. (Jennings, 1996, p. 111)

Another offered these as ingredients:

> . . . intuition, and the ability to risk going with it, being hopeful, having a positive feeling about life, in general. Knowing yourself and knowing where your buttons are. . . . Feeling free to love, not having to be so terribly protective of oneself . . . these things without theory and background aren't enough. You need the bookwork. (Jennings, 1996, p. 111)

Another looked at the question from the perspective of choosing a therapist for oneself and said:

> I'd want somebody that's accepting, somebody that's smart, somebody that's interesting, curious, stays informed, somebody who takes care of themselves, so that they have some energy to give. Somebody who has that blend of being compassionate and empathetic, but also challenging. Somebody who's available. . . . Somebody that's wise. . . . Kindness, humility is a good word. . . . Willing to listen and grow, I'm thinking, an ability to see uniqueness. . . . (Jennings, 1996, pp. 111–112)

Another depicted master therapists this way:

> They are people who are not afraid to take risks. They are people who have a deeper understanding, a more universal understanding. They are people who have a lot of integrity. They are people who are comfortable with their power, and comfortable using it. . . . I think they're people who stretch themselves and stretch other people to go beyond what they think is possible . . . give a sense of hope. . . . It's a combination of challenge and giving that other piece that helps the other person feel not alone and to feel it is possible to do or achieve. . . . (Jennings, 1996, p. 111)

Early Personal Life

What about early personal life? Were there important elements during the foundational years in the lives of the master therapists? The following developmental elements seemed evident in the early life of the sample group.

Understand Self and Others

It seems that most of these individuals were tuned in to human relationships from an early age and that understanding self and others, in a psychological sense, was important. About this, one master therapist said:

> I don't think I knew it at the time, but in retrospect I would say . . . we go into this field in some part to try to understand ourselves and in some part to try to understand and heal our families or other people we love. There is something that drives us: I need to make sense of this situation. I need to understand. I need to know what somebody might have done. (Mullenbach, 2000, p. 71)

Another person said, ". . . it's taken a ton of work to understand my family, to understand the dynamics that were back then. . . ." (Mullenbach, 2000, p. 70). These people wanted to understand the psychology of their own lives.

Significant but Not Overwhelming Stress Present in the Early Years

There may have been distress in the family or community—a disabled person, being part of a stigmatized group, a distressed marriage, an addiction, a death, one's own social isolation from peers. In some form, human suffering seems to have been a companion for many of these individuals early in life. Here is an example of some, but not an overwhelming amount, of early stress:

> I think about all that I suffered as a child, the ways in which I felt I didn't get much that I wanted [yet] there was a solid sense that I always knew that my parents were grown up, I didn't have to be the grownup. I knew that I lived in a system that was basically just and fair. (Mullenbach, 2000, p. 71)

Another example of some pain, but not too much, as ideal for early personal development, comes from this master therapist:

> I think that [if] the therapist's life is one of deprivation and isolation and pain, I don't think it would work [to become an expert therapist]. However, I think this profession wouldn't be of interest if someone didn't know about emotional pain on a very personal level. (Jennings, 1996, p. 101)

Stress during the developmental years takes a variety of forms. For example, for one person it was living in a high-conflict community where armed violence and combat was a constant reality. This master therapist said:

> [it was] . . . a real laboratory for coping with stress. . . . Those who survive, like my family and their friends, eventually actually thrive and those were probably hardier people who somehow know to see opportunities or how to look at things not always in blinders. (Mullenbach, 2000, p. 70)

Reaction to Early Stress Was to Process Rather Than Cut Off

Many of these master therapists reported complex and stressful lives during the developmental years. Yet, the level of stress was not at a level where the choice was to distance oneself from intense human relationships. Looking back, one person said about the positive aspects of the environment:

> . . . it does not allow you to shut down, it does not allow you to build a fortress where you don't feel. . . . (Mullenbach, 2000, p. 71)

Faced with severe stress, another route is to stop the processing. This has been conceptualized by Lerner (1989) as the use of emotional cutoffs. This route was not taken by these master therapists.

Also, within career psychology there is the classic distinction of being oriented to data, people, or things. Some high-tech career fields, such as engineering, enable the person to focus on manipulating objects or data. Other high-touch career fields, such as therapy and counseling, enable the person to focus on human relationships. The master therapist, of course, chooses the latter route to avoid using the cut off/shut down approach to early stress.

Taking on the Role of Helper

Members of our sample group may have been given or taken the family role of helper for others and that meant they needed to attune themselves to others. For example, one master therapist said, ". . . part of what I tried to do in my youth was save my family, every way that I thought I could help be better in the family. . . ." (Mullenbach, 2000, p. 71).

Being assigned the role of helper meant early training in seeing the world through the eyes of the other and attempting to use self-developed recipes to make things better. The practicum in helping started early. In our research, the earliest account of trying to help is this:

> . . . there are stories about me before he [the participant's father] died, I was 4 or 5, going in one day when he was in bed sick, and without saying anything pulling down the shade because the sun was shining in his eyes. So I had it [emotional sensitivity], and I don't know where that came from precisely. (Jennings, 1996, p. 100)

The master therapists may have had many years of experience by the time they started formal training. Imagine how far ahead such a person is in graduate school, compared to peers, who are just starting the helping role in their first practicum. One master therapist expressed this sentiment as follows:

> . . . I could go to school and say I don't expect to learn anything here and yet I know I'll be able to do this work because I'd already come out of that kind of environment. I already knew I could relate to a whole lot of the world.... (Mullenbach, 2000, p. 70)

Human Suffering as a Positive Part of a Deep and Meaningful Life

Personal experiences with suffering during the developmental years may have made it easier to relate to the suffering world of clients. These masters may have been less frightened than people with other developmental histories. As one master therapist said, "I learned to see suffering as valuable" (Mullenbach, 2000, p. 81). Another said about suffering:

> It deepens me. I feel I understand pain awfully well. I think I know the issue isn't pain or suffering, the issue is not having to do it by yourself. It's really about . . . knowing that you're not alone in that core place. (Mullenbach, 2000, p. 81)

About client suffering a third said:

> . . . I think all in all, it leaves me with a certain kind of enthusiasm because I see people go through extraordinary pain and come out the other side. (Mullenbach, 2000, p. 81)

Overall, the early developmental years seemed to provide a laboratory for intensive learning about human life and early therapist development. A form of significant but not overwhelming stress was present. The person took on the role of helper or at least acute observer of human behavior, and there was an approach that involved immersion in human feelings rather than distancing and cutoff. Such an early laboratory has a balance between support and challenge within the arena of understanding others and helping others. A good support/challenge balance is one way of conceptualizing optimal conditions for growth (Skovholt & Rønnestad, 1995).

Early Professional Life

What characterized their early professional development years? We do not know much about the early professional years because the interview questions did not focus on this area. Our impression is that they struggled, as do most, with early professional challenges and the "elevated stressors of the novice practitioner" (Skovholt & Rønnestad, 2001). The complex ambiguity of the human condition is the major reason why novices always struggle. It seems that these master therapists early on also felt unprepared for the realities of practice. About this period, one said:

> There isn't any way that you can be prepared for the emotional demands of practice, but I think under the circumstances, it was all right. (Mullenbach, 2000, p. 72)

Another, looking to the early professional years, said:

> It was harder to do [apologize for mistakes] when I was less secure, probably less proficient and less adept as well. (Sullivan, 2001, p. 93)

One common novice's struggle is the distressing experience that theory learned is not adequate to the task. The task is, of course, trying to find light in the thicket of the client's world and trying to go toward that light as part of reducing client distress such as anxiety or depression. Theory often does not seem to help find the light and the novice is often lost. One, commenting on theory, said:

> When I was a very young or hatching therapist . . . there was all kinds of crazy stuff going on in the world of psychotherapy and I was interested in all of it. I tried everything and learned a little bit of every imaginable theory and then watched the places where it failed. (Jennings, 1996, p. 74)

Early on, beginners need more experienced people to help them in their work. We, of course, call these people mentors, teachers, supervisors, and seniors. Sometimes it is hard to find a good one just when you need one. About this, one of the master therapists said:

> I remember those as good years. I'm sure they were stressful because a lot was new, but I felt very supported. (Mullenbach, 2000, p. 82)

Another said:

> . . . at my first job, I was fortunate enough to have a really fine supervisor who I credit with the major amount of training and experience that I have. And that was totally geared to emotional self-awareness and use of self in ways in which I grew . . . it opened all the doors for me, and it also made what I was doing very vital and real, and I feel real grateful for that. (Mullenbach, 2000, p. 83)

A third said about mentoring in the early years:

> I think that I had the good fortune or the good judgment to join a group of senior clinicians, all people twenty years older than I, very experienced. . . . they gave me the depth and breadth of clinical experience and an understanding of how practice works, and it was very important to me. (Mullenbach, 2000, p. 83)

A fourth said:

> . . . there were people along the way who believed in me and engaged with me because they believed in me. And I really thrived on that, more than I knew in the moment. I got so much from that. If I hadn't gotten that, my life . . . would have taken a different path. (Mullenbach, 2000, p. 83)

From these quotes we get some ideas about the early professional struggles of the master therapists. In general, like most they struggled with the theory-practice gulf and with the need for supervisor support.

Current Professional Life

Portrait of the Master Therapist: The Highly Functioning Self

The following portrait is a summary of the characteristics of the ten master therapists. Data used to construct this portrait was gathered over a period of seven years, (1995–2002). Interviews were conducted, as part of dissertation projects, by Len Jennings, Mary Mullenbach, and Michael Sullivan. Thomas Skovholt was the dissertation advisor for each of these projects. Combining the efforts of the three dissertation projects during this time, the sample group was interviewed for over 100 hours. Each of the ten master therapists was interviewed an average of six times. Many, many more hours were devoted to research analysis of the interviews for the three dissertation projects and for a fourth project on ethics led by Len Jennings. In total, we estimate that over 7,000 hours have been devoted to this research project.

Near the end of this long process, Thomas Skovholt conducted a taped 90-minute interview with Len Jennings, Mary Mullenbach, and Michael Sullivan. The goal of the 90-minute interview was to distill the essence of the master therapist. The taped interview was transcribed then analyzed to yield a portrait and portrait characteristics. After a draft version of the portrait was written by Tom Skovholt, further refinement of the portrait was achieved through individual and group meetings of this chapter's authors. The results of the final analysis will be presented now. Characteristics of the portrait are:

Paradox Characteristics (Figure 7.1)
- A drive to mastery, yet never a sense of having fully arrived—like traveling on an endless path.
- The ability to deeply enter the inner world of another while often preferring solitude.
- Providing an emotionally safe environment for a client and yet able to firmly challenge when necessary.
- Highly skilled at harnessing the power of therapy to help others while quite humble about oneself.
- Thorough integration of the personal and professional selves, yet with clear boundaries between these worlds.
- Voracious learner who often directs this energy to broad learning as well as specific work-related topics.
- Excellent at giving of self to others while nurturing a private self.
- Very open to feedback about oneself yet not personally destabilized by it.

Identifying Characteristics (Figure 7.2, p. 133)
- High emotional health as evidenced by self-acceptance—shadow, warts, and all.
- Understanding of the ambiguous complexity of human nature that precludes an enthusiastic acceptance of any one-dimensional view of human psychology.
- Clear rejection of simplified theories and models for use with clients.

Portrait of the Master Therapist Paradox Characteristics		
Drive to mastery	**AND**	Never a sense of having fully arrived
Able to deeply enter another's world	**AND**	Often prefers solitude
Can create a very safe client environment	**AND**	Can create a very challenging client environment
Highly skilled at harnessing the power of therapy	**AND**	Quite humble about self
Integration of the professional/personal self	**AND**	Clear boundaries between the professional/personal self
Voracious broad learner	**AND**	Focused, narrow student
Excellent at giving of self	**AND**	Great at nurturing self
Very open to feedback about self	**AND**	Not destabilized by feedback about self

FIGURE 7.1   Paradox Characteristics

- Focused motivation to develop self and the ability to be helpful to others.
- In a maximum way, used their own life experiences as food for growth.
- Deeply confident of the therapy process and their own therapy skills.
- Nondefensive acceptance of their own limitations and flaws as evidenced by knowing they are not the best therapists for some clients.
- Data from direct work with clients is highly valued.
- Drawn to paradoxical, complicated, metaphorical, and profound descriptions of the human condition.
- Feeling humility while keeping grandiosity and arrogance at bay.
- A wide spirit of empathy from their own reflected and integrated life experiences.
- Possession of an internal schema—a wisdom guide—consisting of thick webs of patterns, practices, and procedures developed over many, many hours of work.
- A close congruence between personality and demands of the work environment, a "goodness of fit."
- Having the profound ability to respectfully enter the world of another and be of assistance there.
- Reverence for the human condition.
- Living for years in a reflective, open style while searching for growth—personal and professional—has produced the Highly Functioning Self.

Portrait of the Master Therapist
Identifying Characteristics

- High emotional health — indicator is acceptance of own flaws.
- Understands the ambiguous complexity of human life.
- Rejects simplistic theories and models.
- Focused motivation to develop.
- Maximum use of personal life experiences as food for growth.
- Deeply confident of the therapy process.
- Accepts self as having professional limitations.
- Data from client work is highly valued.
- Drawn to profound views of human nature.
- Humility is present while grandiosity is kept at bay.
- Has a wide — life-generated — sense of empathy.
- The internal schema consists of thick webs of patterns, practices, and procedures.
- There is a "goodness of fit" between personality and work environment.
- Has a profound ability to enter another's world and be of assistance there.
- Feels reverence for the human condition.
- Years of living a reflective, growing life has produced the highly functioning self.

FIGURE 7.2   Identifying Characteristics

Word Characteristics (Figure 7.3, page 134).   Alive, Congruent, Committed, Determined, Intense, Open, Curious, Tolerant, Vital, Reflective, Self-Aware, Generous, Mature, Optimistic, Analytic, Fun, Discerning, Energetic, Robust, Inspiring, Passionate.

Central Characteristics.   We describe these central characteristics with the three domains of Cognitive (C), Emotional (E), and Relational (R) (see Figure 7.4 on page 135). An earlier description of this three-part (CER) model can be found in Chapter 3. As mentioned there, we propose that master therapists have developed and integrated all three domains to a very high level.

Cognitive Central Characteristics

Embraces Complex Ambiguity.   Both the known and unknown worlds have expanded. Just as answers have expanded, so have questions. Present is a comfort with not knowing everything and an ability to not have answers for everything. The simplicity of cookie-cutter answers has long ago been dismissed as not needed and not accurate for deep understanding. The master therapists are flexible and enjoy the internal remodeling process even if there is a mess during remodeling.

Guided Now by Accumulated Wisdom.   The idea of wisdom fits well here with the definition of wisdom of Bales and Staudinger (2000, p. 124) as ". . . expertise in the

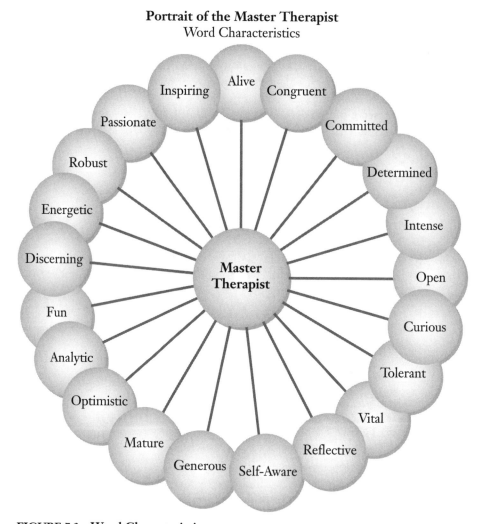

Portrait of the Master Therapist
Word Characteristics

FIGURE 7.3   **Word Characteristics**

fundamental pragmatics of life." Reflected data, book learning, and synthesized life experience have produced a smartness about human life, a deeper understanding.

There is a trust that knowledge, acquired through long effort, can be the guide. Stories are a method used to illustrate points. We will note that in other research, accumulated wisdom has been found to be a central compass for senior practitioners (Skovholt & Rønnestad, 1995).

Insatiably Curious.   A simmering hunger for seeking, knowing, and for what is around the next corner seems present; at times it bursts out as intense curiosity. Eager to learn, life-long learner, active learner are other terms. They take on learning opportunities.

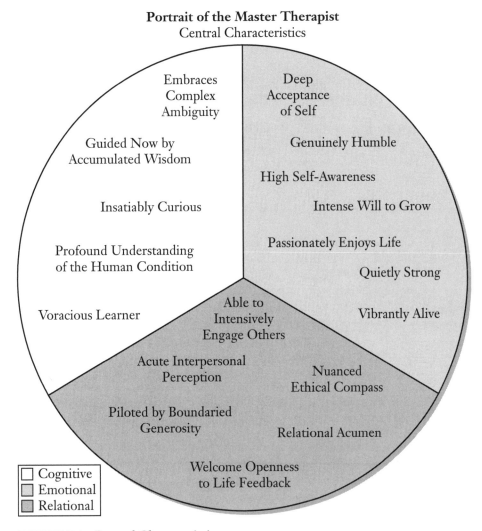

FIGURE 7.4   Central Characteristics

They appear to know a lot about a lot of things. Professionally, they appeared not to be stuck in older views of reality, although they may embrace classic theoretical ideas. A wide background of reading seems to be there. Being knowledgeable is an outcome of this stance.

Profound Understanding of the Human Condition.   Wisdom is in the center of this characteristic. Averaging 59 years of age at the time of the sampling, these are experienced people, experienced in life. They have an acceptance, understanding, and appreciation of the wide latitude of ways that children, adolescents, and adults cope, manage, and interpret human life.

Often, there is a profound religious or spiritual dimension that anchors the deeper and nuanced understanding of the human condition. This deeper dimension may have been enhanced by becoming acquainted with human suffering as expressed by numerous clients.

Voracious Learner.   Life gives a broad liberal arts education and the master therapists have taken the courses, each in his or her own way. As a magnificent renewal force, learning is enthusiastically embraced. The world—everywhere and anywhere—is a potential classroom for the intensely inquisitive master therapist as voracious learner. Much of the learning is in the professional sphere; other learning is applied to the professional sphere.

Emotional Central Characteristics

Deep Acceptance of Self.   As opposed to the proverbial wisdom that the "shoemaker has no shoes," here the shoemaker has shoes. What they offer to others—acceptance—they provide for themselves. They have done the work to get there.

Accepting the "warts of the self" takes pressure off the individual. The master therapists would talk of their failure experiences with clients with a sense that it was unfortunate but also real. For example, through experience, one master therapist learned she couldn't work with addicts. Rather than keep trying, she referred them on. Acknowledging and accepting weaknesses seemed to be a part of the picture.

Genuinely Humble.   Self-consciousness about the description by others of oneself as a "master therapist" indicates a self-perception of humility and one's own humanness. Arrogance and its first cousin, narcissism, are seen as dangerous stances for the therapist and are, therefore, actively resisted.

High Self-Awareness.   Here the sketch is of a person who is highly observant of self. It is not a self-absorbed, narcissistic quality or the stance of an "intrusive shrink." Knowing oneself is seen as an ethical duty.

Very introspective is an accurate description. This awareness of self is multidimensional, with such dimensions as physical, demeanor, verbal expression. The "observant of others" dimension involves a positive embracing of the other and the use of multiple antennas and the "listening with the third ear," to use that classic term.

Intense Will to Grow.   The central catalyst for mastery is an intense motivation to live a competent life. There have been decades of a concentrated will to grow. A parallel level of motivation is discussed in the gifted and talented literature with the term "rage to master" (Winner, 2000).

The active working on personal and professional development has brought remarkable growth and a deep integration of the self. Over the years of practice, preferred methods of growth have included participation in consultation, supervision, and personal therapy. Use of these methods parallels results found in a large international study of therapists (Orlinsky et al., 2001, 2003).

High-level functioning is the outcome of the intense will to grow that has been in operation for many years. In a larger sense, the highly functioning self is the result.

Passionately Enjoys Life.   Fun is a big word here. Zesty, pleasure, humor are other descriptors. Novel experience is sought. Sometimes wanting a position of excitement is there. Master therapists seem to be healthy, happy people.

Quietly Strong.   These individuals fight effectively against the raging power of psychopathology—the hardened categories of coping possessed by many people who seek therapy help. The master therapists possess the toughness to continue excavating pain during those times when it is necessary. In Chapter 4 by Sullivan, Skovholt, and Jennings, this strength is described within the Challenging Relationship Domain.

Vibrantly Alive.   Energetic, energetic for life, is a way of describing this characteristic. There is a deep appreciation for the entire human experience. These people really enjoy being alive. It is "in-the-moment" living. They are well rounded, alert, and animated. In the interviews, they could respond to just about anything.

Relationship Central Characteristics

Able to Intensively Engage Others.   An appetite for engaging others is present. It is an interpersonal presence. Often it functions as an open willingness to be very "in attendance" in the lives of others. A fondness for the interactive dimension of human life marks the lives of the master therapists.

Professionally, they are skilled and insightful as the therapeutic relationship is being formed, maintained, and ended. They are able to make the client feel very comfortable and very important.

Acute Interpersonal Perception.   Interpersonal perception as well as the capacity to engage others, described above, are hallmarks of the profession. Master therapists are able to quickly discern the emotional atmosphere and the interpersonal dynamics. It is these very human qualities, honed by the master therapists to a level high above the norm, that enable them to work with mastery.

Nuanced Ethical Compass.   The ethical stance is honest. The moral compass is internal and deeply embedded in higher moral principles such as those described by Kohlberg (1969) or virtue ethics (Jordan & Mears, 1990). It seems they really consider the well-being of the client and what is helpful and protective of the client's well-being.

There is not an immediate turn to ordinary rules or what others will think. If this means risk-taking, then they very seriously consider the risk. Their ethical beliefs permeated the interviews.

Piloted by Boundaried Generosity.   These are kind-hearted, compassionate people. The compassion is expressed within self-developed limits that function to keep the compassion genuine; this is not "quid pro quo" giving.

Within the professional therapy relationship, there is a commitment, generosity, and energy for the client. Yet, there is also clarity about whose work is whose work—there is work for the therapist and work for the client.

Relational Acumen.   The ability to dance with the client, using a wide variety of styles to fit with the other, marks the master practitioner. In therapy language, this is often described as an accurate use of dose and timing. They seem to be masterful at selecting relationship stances with clients. Judgment in the moment—accurate right then—is another description.

Welcomed Openness to Life Feedback.   The goal is not to take in just confirmatory feedback (Rønnestad & Skovholt, 1993). There is motivation to grow even if it is difficult. Comfort with ambiguity permits a wide net for gathering what is out there about the self. The ability to assimilate new information and constantly rebuild the cognitive framework is present versus a rigidity of structure.

Professionally, there is an ability to learn from others, both clients and peers. Master therapists are able to integrate feedback—positive and negative—into an expanded understanding of self.

What Are the Implications of This Master Therapist Portrait?

Theme 1: The Highly Functioning Self Is about Full Human Development. Qualitative research can surprise the researcher when the results emerge and reveal themselves. The researcher does not know what will emerge until the long research process nears its end. Our big surprise is that the overall summary results focus so much on human development as opposed to specific topics closely related to the occupational skills of the therapist. We did have an earlier inclination of the broader human development focus with the CER model described in Chapter 3. Yet, it was a surprise to have the broad human development focus emerge so strongly.

The portrait described here fits well with optimal models of human functioning. The October 2000 issue of the journal *American Psychologist* is devoted to "Happiness, Excellence, and Optimal Human Functioning." In this special issue, there are articles that seem to describe our master therapist sample. Some of the literature that seems most applicable to the master therapists are in these articles: "The Funds, Friends, and Faith of Happy People" (Myers, 2000); "Self-Determination Theory and the Facilitation of Intrinsic Motivation, Social Development, and Well-Being" (Ryan & Deci, 2000); "Wisdom: A Metaheuristic (Pragmatic) to Orchestrate Mind and Virtue toward Excellence" (Bales & Staudinger, 2000); "States of Excellence" (Lubinski & Benbow, 2000); "Creativity: Cognitive, Personality and Social Aspects" (Simonton, 2000), and "The Origins and Ends of Giftedness" (Winner, 2000).

In writing about gifted individuals, Winner (2000) says, "Gifted children have a deep intrinsic motivation to master the domain in which they have high ability and are almost manic in their energy level. . . . This 'rage to master' characterizes children we have traditionally labeled gifted . . ." (p. 163). We found a similar intensity of motivation in our sample group. Their "intense will to develop" served as a major catalyst for mastery in our sample group.

Winner (2000) also discusses the early signs of exceptionality as common with the gifted and talented and traces them back to roots in childhood. Earlier in this chapter we too discussed the early developmental climate in which our sample grew. Perhaps the saying "the child is the parent of the adult" is true for our sample group. In another research study, with a senior therapist group, it was striking to the authors that early developmental events were still impactful for these therapists of mean age 74 (Rønnestad & Skovholt, 2001).

Certainly the Bales and Staudinger (2000) description of wisdom and wise people seems descriptive of our sample group. They say, ". . . we define wisdom as an expertise in the conduct and meaning of life. In this vein, wisdom is a key factor in the construction of a 'good life'" (p. 124). They go on to discuss how wisdom is about the fundamental pragmatics of life and they say this relates to ". . . knowledge and judgment about the essence of the human condition and the ways and means of planning, managing, and understanding a good life" (p. 124). Such a description of wisdom fits clearly with our view of the master therapists.

In their discussion of optimal human development, Ryan and Deci (2000) ". . . postulate three innate psychological needs—competence, autonomy, and relatedness—which when satisfied yield enhanced self-motivation and mental health . . ." (p. 68). Our sample again seems represented because these three categories of competence, autonomy, and relatedness were results that arose in the qualitative research.

Overall, the point here is that our findings of optimal human development described as the highly functioning self parallels the new research in positive psychology.

Theme 2: The Results Dovetail with Earlier Descriptions from Humanistic Psychology of Ideal Human Characteristics.

In their book *Healthy Personality*, Jourard and Landsman (1980) discuss three models of the healthy personality. The most well-known model is the self-actualized person described by Maslow. Jourard and Landsman (1980, pp. 6–7) list fifteen characteristics of Maslow's self-actualized person. They are:

> a low-defensiveness in perceiving reality; high acceptance of self, others, and the realities of human nature; spontaneity and naturalness; a focus on problems outside the self; need for privacy; high degree of autonomy; continual freshness of appreciation; frequent "peak" experiences; a feeling of belonging-connecting to all humanity; a few close-loving relationships; democratic character structure; strong ethical sense; nonhostile sense of humor; creative/inventive; and a resistance to enculturation.

Reading this list, it seems remarkable that the master therapist central characteristics are so similar.

Two other models are described in this book by Jourard and Landsman (1980). One is Coan's concept of the optimal self. Coan suggests that functioning at a high level involves five characteristics: efficiency as a kind of competence, creativity, inner harmony, relatedness, and transcendence. The other model is Landsman's beautiful and noble person. Landsman says the final stage in the evolution of the beautiful and noble person (BNP) is the compassionate self—with a loving, caring orientation toward others. Two pivotal experiences for Landsman's BNP are an abundance of positive childhood experiences and the ability to turn negative, painful experiences into significant learning and growth experiences. Our master therapist portrait resonates with both of these models.

We would be remiss not to mention Rogers' (1961) model of the fully functioning person as described in his book, *On Becoming a Person*. In this classic guide to personal growth and creativity, Rogers suggests that the fully functioning person approaches life as a process not as an end point. He elaborates three parts: an increasing openness to experience, living fully in the moment (which he calls existential living), and an increased trust in oneself. Together, for Rogers, these three qualities produce the fully functioning person.

Theme 3: The Results Connect with High Functioning Descriptions in Other Places: Therapists, the Study of Political Character, and Mentoring.   Dlugos and Friedlander (2001) studied twelve therapists who received at least three peer nominations as "passionately committed." The results were described within themes and categories of (a) *Balance:* maintaining physical and psychological boundaries between work and personal life and recognition of the complementarity of personal and personal development; (b) *Adaptiveness/Openness:* obstacles as challenges and also hunger for feedback—on an openness scale, the participants were three standard deviations above the mean for the normative population; (c) *Transcendence/Humility:* prominence of the spiritual nature of the work; (d) *Intentional Learning:* personal and professional development seen as complementary and the existence of a strong orientation to continual growth.

In *The Presidential Character*, the historian Barber (1977) discusses the character of U.S. presidents. He says that presidents tend to excel in one of three dimensions: homework, rhetoric, or interpersonal relationships. Homework is a focus on detailed study and understanding of policy or theoretical issues. Rhetoric is the ability to speak to large audiences in ways that are captivating and inspiring. Interpersonal relationships describes the ability to relate extremely well to a variety of different individuals. Barber says that most presidents excel in one of the three dimensions, although the great ones are superb in all areas. And he says the superb ones can flexibly move back and forth between dimensions when necessary. His example of a president high in all three dimensions is Franklin Roosevelt. There is similarity to our notion that excellence demands high functioning across different areas.

In describing the development of mentors, Johnson (2002) says, "In essence, excellent mentors are kind, healthy, and competent" (p. 89). Here we find similarities again to the relational, emotional, and cognitive domains of our master therapist sample.

Theme 4: Becoming a Master Therapist Is Not Becoming a Technique Wizard.
Expertise is not about narrow skill development. It is becoming, over a long time, fully human. In nature, a diamond takes time to become a diamond and then more time to sparkle. Perhaps this is the most striking finding about the portrait. There is so much description of strong, broad, and deep positive human development and so little description of specific micro therapy skills. What does this mean?

It means the training of therapists in narrow, rigid schools or theories as the major aspect of therapist or counselor development is a misguided direction if the eventual goal is expertise. We do want to note, however, that the master therapists often spoke positively of their graduate training in theory and research methods within the behavioral sciences. Training of breadth and rigor seems to be key.

The current term for narrow and prescribed training is manualization and the use of manuals in therapy. Scatura (2001) modifies, expands, and complicates manualization enough so that it can be maintained as a viable part of higher-order therapist functioning.

Closely related to manualization is the work on empirically based treatments. Although such work appears right on, the research here with the master therapists suggests caution. Great artists may have started with paint-by-number, but they have moved far beyond this safe yet limited choice. Caution is also suggested by Lichtenberg and Wampold (2002) who write: ". . . it appears that 'common factors' and the individual therapist account for dramatically more of the variance in therapy outcome than do the particular treatments. . . ." (p. 310).

Let us note that beginners need structure (Rønnestad & Skovholt, 1993). So there a place for certainty for novices as in the Uncertainty/Certainty Principle of Professional Development (Skovholt & Rønnestad, 2001) where the beginner, faced with the heat of the ambiguous complexity of human life, needs help in doing therapy. But our results strongly suggest that narrow skill training, although a part of becoming an expert practitioner, is not the essence.

Theme 5: Getting to Mastery Is a Long, Hard, and Uneven Developmental Process.   Our sample group had a mean age of 59 when first nominated for this study. Perhaps that indicates the seasoning that goes along with rising to the top in quality in this profession.

The long path is described by seasoned therapists in *How Therapists Change: Personal and Professional Reflections,* an excellent and highly engaging series of fifteen first-person accounts edited by Goldfried (2001). In the book, the fifteen authors describe a wide variety of deeply engaging personal and professional events that served as channels for their development. These riveting accounts dramatically demonstrate a lesson from our master therapist sample—there is a long developmental process for therapist expertise.

Why does expertise as a therapist take time? Perhaps this is because of a variety of factors. One is that the data of therapy is the complex ambiguity of the human condition. The therapist's job is to understand one of hundreds of strains of this complex ambiguity as expressed in the life of one person at one time and then to offer assistance to that person. It takes lots of time to get good at this.

And there must be motivation to develop. In our findings we label this the "Will to Grow" and say it is the catalyst for mastery. We are reminded of the famous Thomas Edison quote about genius being 1 percent inspiration and 99 percent perspiration.

One model of therapist/counselor development (Skovholt & Rønnestad, 1995, 2001) describes much of this evolution with an eight-stage model of professional development. The stages are labeled conventional, transition to professional training, imitation of experts, conditional autonomy, exploration, integration, individuation, and integrity. Themes in this model that describe some of the struggle toward competence include

Theme 1: Professional development is growth toward professional individuation.

Theme 7: Development is impacted by multiple sources that are experienced in both common and unique ways.

Theme 8: Optimal professional development is a long, slow, and erratic process.

Theme 9: Post-training years are crucial for optimal development.

Theme 10: As the professional develops, there is a decline of pervasive anxiety.

Theme 18: There is a movement toward increased boundary clarity and responsibility differentiation.

Theme 6: Three Essential Ingredients for Growth as a Therapist: Will to Grow, Extensive Experience in the Domain, and Reflectivity.   As described above, motivation for development is a key. Second, extensive experience is important. The expertise research such as that outlined in *The Nature of Expertise* by Chi, Glaser, and Farr (1988) strongly support the idea that experience in a domain is essential for expertise in that domain.

In contrast to what academic researchers often say, experience with clients, not academic research, is the therapists' clear number one rated source of influence for growth. In a study of therapists in seven countries, the authors concluded: "The most salient positive influence on career development reported by therapists was direct clinical 'experience in therapy with patients.' Almost two-thirds of the 4,516 responding to this item gave it the highest possible rating" (Orlinsky, Botermans, & Rønnestad, 2001, p. 4).

Yet even with experience some perform poorly. For example, Vakoch and Strupp (2000) are dismayed when discussing how even highly trained and experienced practitioners performed poorly when reacting to client negativity. Another example is a study comparing two highly experienced therapists by Ricks (cited by Teyber & McClure, 2000). They wrote: "Ricks found 'staggering' differences in the long-term outcome of these two therapists" (p. 77).

Experience alone is not enough. The experience has to be used to grow. How is that done? One of the current vessels endorsed for turning experience into expertise is the use of reflection (Neufeldt, Karno, & Nelson, 1996).

A general model of development versus stagnation, with these ingredients and more, can be found in Rønnestad and Skovholt (1991) and Skovholt and Rønnestad (2001).

Theme 7: A Positive Therapy Relationship Is Central to Success.   In his interviews, Michael Sullivan concentrated on how the master therapists construct the therapy relationship. He did this in response to research suggesting that the therapy relationship accounts for a very large proportion of success (Horvath & Luborsky, 1993; Sexton & Whiston, 1994).

The master therapists endorsed this perspective with comments such as " . . . the relationship is the whole thing" (Sullivan, 2001, p. 96), "I think that [the relationship] is . . . the most central part of psychotherapy" (Sullivan, 2001, p. 96), and "I have always maintained . . . that the primary tool that I use is the relationship. I have a lot of knowledge, I have a lot of skills, but they're wasted if the relationship isn't there" (Sullivan, 2001, p. 97).

Perhaps the importance of the therapy relationship helps us see why the highly functioning self and the central characteristics described within cognitive, emotional, and relational domains are so important. These masters seem able to connect well with many people, some who may be struggling with problems such as an inability to trust or to communicate.

Theme 8: These Are Also Ordinary People.   While seeking in this book to describe the extraordinary characteristics of master therapists, we have also been pulled in another direction. We did not set out to go this way. Pursuing this direction does not seem right. It does not describe ideals for inspiration, the aspirational characteristics. It is a description of the ordinariness of the expert.

We came to these feelings when struck by the ordinariness of the offices of some of these experts. The office is often a powerful symbolic way of saying there is something special here as in special office equals special expertise. We went on pilgrimages to them to interview them for this research process. We were excited and nervous to meet these individuals nominated by their peers as the best psychotherapists. The "best psychotherapists"—how this title carries so much hope and expectation. Without knowing it, we may have thought: They will be more than mortal; they will unveil the secrets of life or at least the secrets of this profession. We were so disappointed to discover that they were also ordinary—plain, common, everyday. And with faults!

Did our idealization bring the disappointment? Did our countertransference jolt us? From a qualitative researcher's perspective, the information shouldn't stop with just our psychologizing. It is also data to communicate.

Aside from the ordinariness of the office, the disappointment of the common came through in other ways. Some of the master therapists seemed unable to be effective with certain clients. They told us so, but we also thought *Can't an expert help everyone?* A few talked too much in the interview, breaking the cardinal rule—we thought it was a cardinal rule—that therapy and counseling are about talking less and listening more. A few seemed to have personality characteristics we disliked—biased, pompous, highly anxious, morose. There were reports of relationship difficulties—*Is that a sign of intimacy inability?* Oh, how we hated to have these feelings of disappointment when we wanted so much to admire and learn. But have them we did.

We gave different meanings to the ordinary factor. Human life is so complicated; paradox is often considered a more complex form of understanding. That means a more accurate form of understanding. So the paradox is that these experts are also ordinary. Maybe the ordinary dimension is most valuable because it is a more accurate view of these expert practitioners.

A second way of thinking of the ordinary factor is captured in the book title *If You Meet the Buddha on the Road, Kill Him* (Knopp, 1976). Of course, the point here is not to criticize Buddhism. Rather, the idea is that there is danger in seeking expertise outside the self. Human life is an ambivalent search for expertise outside and inside, the going back and forth and the confusion of this search. Seeking *only* for the prophet can be dangerous. The ordinary factor is a warning to you the reader—and us—that even these acknowledged experts in human behavior—these master therapists—are fallible.

A third thought is that perhaps if people who are ordinary in some ways can also rise above and master a trade, there is hope for us. Maybe we too can become experts.

Returning to the office as a symbol, perhaps the simple workspace reflects the security of some of these practitioners. They did not need the trappings of expertise to feel secure, successful, and highly competent. This is another interpretation for the ordinariness of the offices of some.

Let us add, as we have in other places in this chapter, that in the interviews these experts did communicate many wonderful qualities such as humility, caring, respect. An example of the many statements of humility included the comment that one should take a long enough vacation so that, after returning, it is clear that the world functioned just fine without you. The exact quote is:

> . . . the trick is to be gone long enough . . . so you recognize your entire replaceability. That you are absolutely replaceable. (Mullenbach, 2000, p. 100)

For us, the lesson here is the simple, and difficult, idea that expert practitioners are complicated. They have many wonderful qualities and some not so good ones. Another can teach each of us . . . sometimes. Perhaps knowing they are both ordinary and extraordinary can help us mortals keep trying and keep us from giving up, in our own quest to become more skilled practitioners.

Theme 8: Caution—the Bias of Western Psychology Is Its Euro-American Worldview.   The overwhelming percentage of the world's six billion people do not live in Europe or North America. Hence, we must be cautious when using models such as those described in Themes 1 and 2 above to describe optimal human life for all. A Eurocentric view is limited. Gilbert Wrenn, a professor in our graduate program at Minnesota, first warned us back in 1962 of this bias in his now classic article, "The Culturally Encapsulated Counselor."

The caution should also be extended to our study of master therapists. We have studied expertise in a large North American metropolitan area where most of the experienced practitioners are white. As a result, all of our ten master therapists, chosen by peer nomination, are white. However, we should note that the majority—seven of ten—are female. Yet, the biases of culture, class, ethnicity, and nationality wrap around us as researchers. We suggest caution in applying our results as universal principles.

Summary

Our hope in this chapter and in this book has been to describe the high functioning of a group of exceptional performers in the illusive but important skill of therapy and counseling. In an attempt to learn the essential characteristics of these masters and to avoid guru glamorization, we have not identified them. The point of this qualitative research is to look for broad principles and deeper understanding.

Learning the art and science of helping others cope with life's challenges is an important calling. As recent research has suggested, the highly skilled therapist can make a big difference in outcome (Teyber & McClure, 2000; Wampold, 2001). Learning how to lessen human suffering and increase human competence, even in small margins, is worthy of great effort. We hope in these pages the reader has gleaned some useful information for that quest.

We end with words from an expert therapist whose premature death left her out of our master therapist research process. In another context, at age 68, she described the pleasure and effectiveness of the work at the expert level. The quote is from Skovholt and Rønnestad (2001, p. 96):

> With diminished anxiety, I became less and less afraid of my clients and with that came an ease for me in using my own wide repertoire of skills and procedures. They became more available to me when I needed them. And during those moments it became remarkable to me that someone would have the willingness to share their private world with me and that my work with them would bring very positive results for them. This brought a sense of immense pleasure to me.

We hope the impact of our research on master therapists will lead more practitioners to such a positive stance.

References

Bales, P. B., & Staudinger, U. M. (2000). Wisdom: A metaheuristic (pragmatic) to orchestrate mind and virtue toward excellence. *American Psychologist, 55*, 122–136.

Barber, J. D. (1977). *The presidential character: Predicting performance in the White House.* Englewood Cliffs, NJ: Prentice-Hall.

Chi, M. T. H., Glaser, R., & Farr, M. J. (Eds.). (1988). *The nature of expertise.* Hillsdale, NJ: Lawrence Erlbaum Associates.

Dlugos, R. F., & Friedlander, M. L. (2001). Passionately committed therapists: A qualitative study of their experiences. *Professional Psychology: Research and Practice, 32*, 298–394.

Goldfried, M. (Ed.). (2001). *How therapists change: Personal and professional reflections.* Washington, DC: American Psychological Association.

Horvath, A. O., & Luborsky, L. (1993). The role of the therapeutic alliance in psychotherapy. *Journal of Consulting and Clinical Psychology, 61*, 561–573.

Jennings, L. (1996). *The personal characteristics of master therapists.* Unpublished doctoral dissertation. University of Minnesota.

Johnson, W. B. (2002). The intentional mentor: Strategies and guidelines for the practice of mentoring. *Professional Psychology: Research and Practice, 33*, 88–96.

Jordan, A. E., & Mears, N. M. (1990). Ethics and the professional practice of psychologists: The role of virtues and principles. *Professional Psychology: Research and Practice, 21*, 107–114.

Jourard, S. M., & Landsman, T. (1980). *Healthy personality.* New York: Macmillan.

Kohlberg, L. (1969). Stage and sequence: The cognitive-developmental approach to socialization. In D. A. Goslin (Ed.), *Handbook of socialization theory and research.* Chicago: Rand McNally.

Knopp, S. B. (1976). *If you meet the Buddha on the road, kill him: The pilgrimage of psychotherapy patients.* Toronto: Bantam Books.

Lerner, H. (1989). *The dance of intimacy: A woman's guide to courageous acts of change in key relationships.* New York: Harper Perennial.

Lichtenberg, J. W., & Wampold, B. E. (2002). Closing comments on counseling psychology's principles of empirically supported interventions. *The Counseling Psychologist, 30,* 309–313.

Lubinski, D., & Benbow, C. P. (2000). States of excellence. *American Psychologist, 55,* 137–150.

Mullenbach, M. A. (2000). *Master therapists: A study of professional resiliency and emotional wellness.* Unpublished doctoral dissertation, University of Minnesota.

Myers, D. G. (2000). The funds, friends, and faith of happy people. *American Psychologist, 55,* 56–67.

Neufeldt, S. A., Karno, M. P., & Nelson, M. L. (1996). A qualitative study of experts' conceptualization of supervisee reflectivity. *Journal of Counseling Psychology, 43,* 3–9.

Orlinsky, D., Rønnestad, M. H., Ambuehl, H., Willutzki, U., Botersman, J., Cierpka, M., Davis J., & Davis, M. (1999). Psychotherapists' assessments of their development at different career levels. *Psychotherapy, 36*(3), 203–215.

Orlinsky, D. E., Botermans, J. F., Rønnestad, M. H., and the SPR Collaborative Research Network. (2001). Toward an empirically grounded model of psychotherapy training: Four thousand therapists rate influences on their development. *Australian Psychologist, 36,* 1–10.

Orlinsky, D. E., Rønnestad, M. H., Willutzki, U., Wiseman, H., Botermans, J. F., and the SPR Collaborative Network. (2003). The prevalence, parameters and purpose of personal therapy: An international perspective. In J. D. Geller, J. C. Norcross, & D. E. Orlinsky (Eds.), *The psychotherapist's own psychotherapy: Patient and clinician perspectives.* New York: Oxford University Press.

Rogers, C. (1961). *On becoming a person.* Boston: Houghton Mifflin.

Rønnestad, M. H., & Skovholt, T. M. (1991). A model of the professional development and stagnation of therapists and counselors. *Journal of the Norwegian Psychological Association, 28,* 555–567.

Rønnestad, M. H., & Skovholt, T. M. (1993). Supervision of beginning and advanced graduate students in counseling and psychotherapy. *Journal of Counseling and Development, 71,* 396–405.

Rønnestad, M. H., & Skovholt, T. M. (2001). Learning arenas for professional development: Retrospective accounts of senior psychotherapists. *Professional Psychology: Research and Practice, 32,* 181–187.

Ryan, R. M., & Deci, E. L. (2000). Self-determination theory and the facilitation of intrinsic motivation, social development, and well-being. *American Psychologist, 55,* 68–78.

Scatura, D. J. (2001). The evolution of psychotherapy and the concept of manualization: An integrative perspective. *Professional Psychology: Research and Practice, 32,* 522–530.

Sexton, T. C., & Whiston, S. C. (1994). The status of the counseling relationship: An empirical review, theoretical implications and research directions. *The Counseling Psychologist, 22,* (1), 6–78.

Simonton, D. K. (2000). Creativity: Cognitive, personal, developmental, and social aspects. *American Psychologist, 55,* 151–158.

Skovholt, T. M. (2001). *The resilient practitioner: Burnout prevention and self-care strategies for counselors, therapists, teachers, and health professionals.* Boston: Allyn and Bacon.

Skovholt, T. M., & Rønnestad, M. H. (2001). The long, textured path from novice to senior practitioner. In T. M. Skovholt (Ed.), *The resilient practitioner: Burnout prevention and self-care strategies for counselors, therapists, teachers and health professionals* (pp. 25–54). Boston: Allyn and Bacon.

Skovholt, T. M., & Rønnestad, M. H. (1995). *The evolving professional self: Stages and themes in counselor and therapist development.* New York: Wiley.

Sullivan, M. (2001). *Master therapists' construction of the therapeutic relationship.* Unpublished doctoral dissertation, University of Minnesota.

Spitz, B. (1989). *Dylan: A biography.* New York: McGraw-Hill.

Teyber, E., & McClure, F. (2000). Therapist variables. In C. R. Snyder & R. E. Ingram (Eds.), *Handbook of psychological change* (pp. 62–87). New York: Wiley.

Vakoch, D. A., & Strupp, H. H. (2000). Psychodynamic approaches to psychotherapy: Philosophical and theoretical foundations of effective practice. In C. R. Snyder & R. E. Ingram (Eds.), *Handbook of psychological change* (pp. 200–216). New York: Wiley.

Wampold, B. (2001). *The great psychotherapy debate: Models, methods, findings.* Mahwah, NJ: Lawrence Erlbaum Associates.

Winner, E. (2000). The origins and ends of giftedness. *American Psychologist, 55,* 159–169.

Wrenn, C. G. (1962). The culturally encapsulated counselor. *Harvard Educational Review, 32,* 444–449.

APPENDIX A

Methodology

Introduction: Rationale for Qualitative Research Methodology

Researchers in the field of counseling psychology have begun to recognize the importance of methodologies traditionally used in allied fields such as anthropology, education, and sociology and in European psychology more than in American psychology (Hoshmand, 1989; Patton, 1990). Recently, these qualitative methodologies have become very popular in American psychology as evidenced by Patton's book going through fourteen printings since publication in 1990. Hoshmand (1989) states that with qualitative research, the emphasis is on understanding meanings or illuminating them. In contrast to the tradition of experimentation with its emphasis on hypothesis testing and empirical verification, qualitative research allows for description, discovery, and theory-building. According to Whitt (1991), the goal of quantitative research is generalization, whereas the aim of qualitative research is understanding. Morrow and Smith (2000) suggest that researchers' desire for alternative methodologies represents their understanding of the "growing pluralism in the theories and practices of counseling psychology as a whole" (p. 199).

Other differences between the research paradigms exist as well. For example, traditional experimentation utilizes methodologies that seek to simplify and reduce complex phenomena to a single score or set of scores, whereas qualitative research seeks to build understanding and knowledge by studying complex, living systems and interrelationships in a holistic versus reductionistic form (Hoshmand, 1989). Traditional quantitative methods are directed by a predetermined hypothesis that uses standardized measures to fit the reports of a large sample into a limited number of responses (Patton, 1990). In contrast, the researcher who utilizes a qualitative approach is able to engage in an in-depth study that draws a store of rich information from a small sample of respondents or cases (Patton, 1990). Qualitative methods are arguably superior than quantitative methods for understanding complex human phenomena. For example, Bertaux (1981) described the value of tapping the respondent's wisdom through qualitative interviews:

> . . . those who urge educational researchers to imitate the natural sciences seem to ignore one basic difference between the subjects of inquiry in the natural sciences and those in the social sciences: The subjects of inquiry in the social sciences can talk and think. Unlike

a star, or a chemical, or a lever, if given a chance to talk freely, people appear to know a lot about what is going on (as cited in Seidman, 1991, p. 2).

Qualitative studies differ from quantitative methodologies in another important way. With its emphasis on discovery and theory building, qualitative research is emergent and allows for "unplanned backlooping and decisions to change course" as opposed to the preplanned, linear nature of quantitative methods (Hoshmand, 1989, p. 14). Qualitative analysis is considered to be "guided not by hypotheses but by questions, issues, and a search for patterns" (Patton, 1990, p. 15). In addition, subjects (called respondents, participants, or informants in qualitative research) are viewed as collaborators or co-investigators in a nonexploitive relationship assisting the researcher in elucidating meaning and understanding. Finally, qualitative designs are considered by many methodologists as the most effective means for the exploratory phase of an investigation (Hoshmand, 1989; Patton, 1990). Because of the exploratory nature of the current research studies and the desire to gain a better understanding of complex human constructs, qualitative research methods were selected.

Respondents: Sample Selection

A combination of purposeful sampling strategies were used to identify the ten master therapists investigated in the four qualitative research studies presented in this book. With purposeful sampling, exemplars of the concept being studied are identified (Patton, 1990). Unlike experimental methodology, which allows for generalizability to a larger population based on the use of a random and representative sample, Patton (1990) states that "the logic and power of purposeful sampling lies in selecting information-rich cases for study in-depth. Information-rich cases are those from which one can learn a great deal about issues of central importance to the purpose of the research" (p. 169).

In the present studies, well-regarded psychotherapists in a major midwestern metropolitan area were approached and then asked to nominate colleagues they considered to be master therapists. This type of purposeful sampling method is called "snowball sampling." With snowball sampling, "well-situated" people are asked to identify information-rich key informants (Patton, 1990, p. 176). Typically with this method, in time a number of key names are repeatedly mentioned. The individuals who are repeatedly named by a variety of informants constitute the core participant pool (Patton, 1990).

Inherent in the snowball sampling method is a reliance on the judgment of peers or colleagues regarding the construct under study. Peer nomination techniques have been found to accurately assess personal and interpersonal characteristics for a wide variety of subject groups including psychotherapists (Cole & White, 1993; Hillerbrand & Claiborn, 1990; Luborsky et al., 1985; Serbin et al., 1987). Based on research focused on determinants of therapist success, Luborsky et al. (1985) assert that "therapists are able to identify other potentially effective therapists and to discriminate them from those who are less effective" (p. 609). Peer nomination procedures have been given psychometric support by Anastasi and Urbina (1997). They conclude that peer nomination is a reliable technique that has been used in a variety of settings and state, "When checked against a variety of practical criteria dependent on interpersonal relations, such ratings usually have been found to have good concurrent and predictive validity" (p. 468).

The snowball sampling peer nomination method used in this study was extended and intensified. The psychotherapists ultimately chosen for interviews were distinguished from a larger pool of individuals who were named occasionally. This modification led to what Patton calls "extreme case sampling" (Patton, 1990, p. 169), which focuses on cases that provide rich information because the cases are outstanding or special in some regard.

An example of this method (i.e., snowball sampling, extreme case sampling, and peer nominations in combination) was used in the classic Peters and Waterman (1982) study, *In Search of Excellence*, in which characteristics of the best-run U.S. companies were described. The authors utilized a sampling method in which an informed group of observers of U.S. businesses were asked to identify companies considered innovative and excellent (Peters & Waterman, 1982). Similarly, the present study invited well-regarded practicing psychotherapists to nominate colleagues they considered to be master therapists.

To begin the nomination procedure, three well-regarded practicing psychologists (two male, one female) with a mean of thirty-one years of therapy experience were chosen as key informants. These three initial key informants were chosen because of their: (a) involvement in the training of therapists, (b) long-standing involvement with the local mental health community, and (c) reputation for being well-regarded therapists. Two of the key informants worked at a major university counseling center and one worked in private practice.

Each key informant was asked to nominate three master therapists within the large metropolitan area of the sample group. Nomination of master therapists was based on the following criteria: (a) This person is considered to be a "master therapist," (b) this person is most frequently thought of when referring a close family member or a dear friend to a therapist because the person is considered to be the "best of the best," and (c) one would have full confidence in seeing this therapist for one's own personal therapy. Therefore, this therapist might be considered a "therapist's therapist."

Len Jennings telephoned each person nominated as a master therapist by one of the key informants. In the next step of sample selection, the nominated master therapist was asked to nominate three master therapists using the same criteria. Master therapists were not allowed to nominate themselves.

Patton (1990) recommends that the investigator conclude this sample-gathering method when a point of redundancy and saturation occurs, that is, when certain individuals are repeatedly nominated and few new names emerge. In determining the present master therapist participant pool, eight repetitions of the nomination procedure were needed to reach a point of redundancy/saturation. When the nomination process was concluded, a total of 103 different therapists had been nominated as master therapists. Of the 103 therapists nominated, 66 therapists received one nomination, 12 received two nominations, 15 received three nominations, 3 received four nominations, 2 received six nominations, 2 received seven nominations, and the remaining three therapists received 10, 12, and 17 nominations.

A minimum of four nominations was chosen as the cutoff point for the sample group. This breakpoint was chosen so that not too many or too few master therapists were interviewed. In choosing between breadth (brief interviews with many subjects) and depth (in-depth interviews with few subjects) the authors chose what they considered a sufficient number of participants to obtain an adequate balance between breadth and depth. The mean number of nominations for the $N = 10$ sample group was 8, with the range of nominations between 4 and 17. Overall, the ten master therapists from the pool of 103 accounted for 36 percent of the total nominations (77 of 212).

The ten psychotherapists with four or more nominations were sent an invitation to participate in the study. All ten agreed to participate. Of the ten master therapists (seven women and three men) interviewed, there were six Ph.D. psychologists, three masters-level social workers, and one psychiatrist. All held licenses in their respected fields, with some holding more than one license. At the time of the sampling (i.e., fall, 1995), the master therapists ranged in age from 50 to 72 ($M = 59.00$, $SD = 7.89$). Their level of experience practicing psychotherapy ranged from 21 to 41 years ($M = 29.50$, $SD = 6.62$). The theoretical orientations of the master therapists were divided into four major camps: four psychodynamic therapists, two family systems therapists, two integrative therapists, and two existential-humanistic therapists. All of the master therapists were European American. All worked full-time in private practice. Overall, their therapy practices included short-term and long-term work, with both managed care and "out-of-pocket" clients who paid fees within the fee structure of the community.

Trends evident in the therapists' descriptions of their clients indicate these therapists are able to be selective in their clientele. However, early in their careers these therapists worked with a wider range of clients. It appears that some clients are other practicing therapists. These therapists see clients who are functioning well in some areas of life, but perhaps not so well in other areas. Diagnostically, depression and anxiety are most frequently mentioned. This group of therapists generally does not see clients who have an active addiction or who are psychotic.

Methodology for the Jennings and Skovholt Study

Procedure

An interview/follow-up design (a first interview set and a follow-up interview set) was selected in an attempt to achieve "validity through dialogue" (Skovholt & Rønnestad, 1995, p. 147). Guba (1978) says this methodological approach enhances validity: "Who is in a better position to judge whether the categories appropriately reflect their issues and concerns than the people themselves?" (pp. 56–57).

The principal investigating method was a semi-structured interview questionnaire consisting of 16 open-ended questions used as an interview guide, a method of interviewing that is flexible and conversational, while seeking to capture the essence of the research questions (Patton, 1990). Patton defines an interview guide as "a list of questions or issues that are to be explored in the course of the interview" (p. 283). While the focus of the interview has been determined in advance, the interviewer remains "free to build a conversation within a particular subject area, to word the questions spontaneously, and to establish a conversational style" (p. 283). Patton goes on to outline the strengths of an interview guide approach:

> The outline increases the comprehensiveness of the data and makes data collection somewhat systematic for each respondent. Logical gaps in data can be anticipated and closed. Interviews remain fairly conversational and situational. (p. 288)

Initially, a list of questions was generated partly by the first author drawn from topics illuminated by a literature review on therapist effectiveness and partly from a list of questions produced by a survey of cohorts from the first author's counseling psychology program. The questionnaire was designed to elicit information concerning the characteristics of master therapists. The counseling psychology students were instructed to think of questions that they would like to have answered by a master therapist. After an initial rating process for clarity and salience by three doctoral interns in counseling psychology, the questionnaire was revised. Next, the first author conducted two pilot interviews with experienced therapists using the questionnaire. Then, the interview questionnaire was modified once more by the researchers (see Table A.1).

The first set of interviews were audiotaped and conducted at the respondent's practice site. Before each interview, the first author explained the purpose of the study

TABLE A.1 Interview Questions for Master Therapists (Jennings & Skovholt)

1. How are you different from when you started your career?
2. What distinguishes a good therapist from a great therapist?
3. What do you think are the characteristics of a master therapist?
4. To become a master therapist, does one need years of experience? Explain.
5. Given two equally experienced therapists, why does one become an expert whereas the other remains mediocre?
6. What is particularly "therapeutic" about you?
7. Is there one distinguishing aspect of your expertise?
8. How does your emotional health impact the therapy you do?
9. How does the person you are impact the therapy you do?
10. How do you know when you are doing a good job with a client?
11. Are you helpful with some clients and not others? Explain.
12. Can you estimate what percentage of your clients you have helped?
13. What is psychotherapy?
14. How does psychotherapy heal?
15. How much of psychotherapy is an art versus a science?
16. If there were a recipe for making a master therapist, what ingredients would you include?

and each respondent signed an informed consent form. Each interview averaged approximately 90 minutes in duration.

A necessary step before data analysis was verbatim transcription of the audio-taped interviews. Due to an equipment malfunction, one of the audiotapes from the first round of interviews was deemed inaudible. The respondent agreed to be interviewed again, and another interview covering the same questions was conducted. After the transcripts were completed, the first author listened to each interview while reading the typed transcriptions to ensure the accuracy of the transcriptions.

Analysis of the data was based on inductive analysis (Patton, 1990). With inductive analysis, theories about what is happening are grounded in direct experience rather than imposed a priori through hypotheses or deductive constructions. As Patton (1990) states:

> The strategy of inductive designs is to allow the important analysis dimensions to emerge from patterns found in the cases under study without presupposing in advance what the important dimensions will be. The qualitative methodologist attempts to understand the multiple interrelationships among dimensions that emerge from the data without making prior assumptions or specifying hypotheses about the linear or correlative relationships among narrowly defined, operationalized variables. (p. 44)

Inductive analysis starts with specific observations and builds toward general patterns. The data analysis consisted of organizing the smallest units of data (concepts) into meaningful and progressively broader themes, categories, and domains. The inductive analysis procedure utilized in this study was a collaborative process in which the researchers, a research assistant, and the master therapists themselves contributed to the analysis of the data. In the beginning stages of the analysis, the researchers and the research assistant identified the concepts and themes. The latter stages of analysis involved the master therapists and the researchers identifying themes and categories.

To begin the data analysis, the first author and the research assistant analyzed each paragraph and wrote one or two words that best represented the concept for that paragraph. A concept is defined by Strauss and Corbin (1990, p. 61) as "conceptual labels placed on discrete happenings, events, and other instances of phenomena." Borrowing from grounded theory analytic procedures (Strauss & Corbin, 1990, p. 63), the researchers suggest creating names of concepts by asking questions of the data such as: "What is this? What does it represent? What is the major idea brought out in this sentence or paragraph?"

Next, each concept was written on one side of a notecard with the corresponding supporting data, which was a quote from the respondent on the opposite side. A total of 1,043 concepts were generated from a paragraph by paragraph analysis of the ten written transcripts. At this stage of analysis, Patton (1990) emphasizes identification of important examples, themes, patterns, and natural variation in the data. The 1,043 concepts were then sorted by the first author and the research assistant into many different groupings until themes and categories emerged. From this process, forty preliminary themes were identified by the researchers and organized under four major categories.

Approximately two months after the first interviews were analyzed, a 60-minute follow-up interview was conducted with each respondent. The follow-up interview focused on validating and refining preliminary results derived from an analysis of the first interview data. The follow-up interviews were also audiotaped. During this interview, respondents were asked to evaluate the accuracy of the preliminary data by indicating which themes and categories seemed to fit with their individual experience. Respondents were invited to comment regarding how the results did or did not reflect their experience. Finally, respondents were asked to add any information not yet addressed that they considered relevant in defining the term "master therapist." Quotes that best represented each theme were later transcribed.

Based on feedback obtained from respondents during the follow-up interviews, themes and categories were again modified. Only themes in which the majority of respondents (i.e., 8 out of 10) agreed accurately represented their individual experiences, perceptions, and beliefs were included in the results. Domains as the major organizer were then selected based on themes and categories. Twenty-six themes within eight categories were organized under the following three broad domains: cognitive, emotional, and relational. These domains represent major attribute areas of a master therapist. In the final data analysis by the researchers, the themes were incorporated within the text to describe the categories and another category was identified. The results of the Jennings and Skovholt study have nine categories under three domains.

Methodology for the Sullivan, Skovholt, and Jennings Study

A qualitative interview study is an appropriate method for investigating therapist contributions to the therapy relationship because in-depth interviews with practicing therapists may provide data for variables that have yet to be identified in the research literature. When the purpose of a study is to describe clinically relevant therapist modes of perceiving and acting, a discovery-oriented approach is deemed most suitable (Marshall & Rossman, 1999). The authors of the present study are interested in what master therapists can tell us about their construction and use of the therapy relationship. In the pursuit of this research question, information-rich informants provide the kind of data this investigation seeks.

Instrument

Questionnaire Development. The first author developed an initial set of questions after a review of the literature on therapy relationships, particularly the therapy alliance (Bachelor, 1991; Bordin, 1979, 1994; Gaston & Marmar, 1994; Henry & Strupp, 1994; Horvath, 1994, Horvath & Greenberg, 1994; Luborsky, 1994; Marziali, 1984). The initial set of questions were reviewed and amended by the second author. The first author then further refined the questions by conducting two pilot studies. The first of these was comprised of two sessions discussing the questions with a focus group of practitioners, and the second was an in-depth interview with a practicing psychotherapist. The questions received a final revision, including question wording and order of questions, from the second author.

The content of the questions reflects concern with clinical relevance while also incorporating aspects of alliance theory. Table A.2 shows the correspondence of interview questions with alliance concepts.

Procedure and Data Analysis

The interviews occurred over a two-month period. The audiotaped interviews averaged one and one-half hours. At the beginning of the interview, the purpose of the study was explained and an informed consent form was obtained from each respondent. One of the respondents had to be reinterviewed because of an audiotape error. The verbatim transcriptions were checked by the interviewer for accuracy.

Inductive Analysis. An inductive analysis procedure described by Patton (1990) and Jennings and Skovholt (1999) was utilized in this study. The data analysis proceeded inductively from the smallest unit, concepts, to themes then to categories then to the largest unit, domains. A concept comes from analysis of a small part of the transcript,

TABLE A.2 Correspondence of Interview Questions with Alliance Concepts (Sullivan, Skovholt, & Jennings)

Alliance Concept	Interview Question
Therapist/client agreement on the tasks of therapy (Bordin, 1979, 1994; Horvath & Greenberg, 1994).	How do you establish agreement with clients as to the tasks of therapy?
	How do you work with clients when they are not following through on their therapy tasks?
	Do you have a set way of establishing the respective roles of therapist and client and how do you go about doing this?
Therapist agreement as to the goals of therapy (Bordin, 1979, 1994; Horvath & Greenberg, 1994).	How do you proceed to work with clients when their goals for therapy do not match the needs they seem to have?
	Describe in what ways you acknowledge client's success in reaching their goals.
	How do you establish an alliance with clients as to the goals of therapy when a third party. . . ?
Therapist/client emotional bonds (Bordin, 1979, 1994, Horvath & Greenberg, 1994).	Describe the importance in your work with clients of establishing a positive therapy relationship.
	Describe how a novice therapist might acquire the skills necessary to establishing a good therapy relationship.
	How do you go about repairing a therapy relationship that has become problematic?

such as a sentence or a paragraph answer supplied by a respondent. All the concepts are then examined and ordered for the purpose of identifying themes. Themes are identified by organizing a variety of concepts to make a coherent whole. Next, themes are examined for the purpose of identifying categories. Categories organize a variety of themes. Finally, the categories are examined for the purpose of identifying domains. Domains, the largest organizing unit, house similar categories. The analysis involves a time- and labor-intensive back-and-forth process where:

> . . . both the meaning of parts of the text and global meaning of the text are continually modified through an analysis of both. One arrives at a better understanding of the parts through analysis of the global meaning, and one arrives at a better analysis of the global meaning through analysis of parts. (Skovholt & Rønnestad, 1995, p. 148)

The third author, an experienced qualitative researcher, served as the auditor. As a validity check, the auditor and first author separately coded portions of three transcripts from the study for concepts. Concepts derived from the two analyses were compared and discussed until substantial agreement was obtained. The first author then completed the identification of concepts resulting in 567 concepts. Each concept was then written on one side of a card with the corresponding quote put on the other side.

As another data source and using the same procedure described above, transcripts from Jennings and Skovholt's (1999) study of the same master therapists were analyzed for concepts. Only portions of the Jennings and Skovholt's (1999) transcripts in which the respondents were specifically discussing aspects of the therapy relationship were analyzed. This analysis resulted in 185 concepts; the total number of concepts from both analyses was 752.

The concepts were then grouped into themes. As emphasized by Patton (1990) and described in Jennings and Skovholt (1999): "At this stage of the analysis . . . important examples, themes, patterns, and natural variation in the data" (p. 5) are sought out and uncovered for the purpose of identifying themes and categories (composites of themes) from the data. The preliminary grouping of concepts resulted in 44 themes within four general categories.

Follow-up interviews were conducted approximately six months after the last initial interview was completed. The follow-up interview focused on respondents giving their reactions to the initial formulation of the themes. Nine out of ten of the respondents were interviewed in the follow-up interviews. Sadly, one of the therapists died before the follow-up interviews were completed. Themes and categories from the preliminary analyses were presented to the respondents during a 60-minute interview. This interview was also audiotaped and focused on (a) respondents' agreement or disagreement with the themes and categories as formulated, (b) respondents' comments about the results as reflective of their therapy experience, and (c) respondents' comments about aspects of the therapy relationship that were not reflected in the results.

After a second analysis of the data was conducted incorporating the master therapists' feedback and in consultation with the auditor, the number of themes was reduced from 44 to 18. This reduction focused on retaining the strongest themes as endorsed by the respondents and then consolidating them. Only themes that seven out of nine respondents agreed with (78%) were retained. The themes were organized to create categories. With the categories created, the themes disappeared as a separate organizing structure. Six categories within two domains constitute the final formulation.

Methodology for the Mullenbach and Skovholt Study

Qualitative analysis of the data relies on an inductive approach that allows for in-depth exploration without the restraints of preconceived expectations. According to Patton (1990):

> The strategy of inductive designs is to allow the important analysis dimensions to emerge from patterns found in the cases under study without presupposing in advance what the important dimensions will be. The qualitative methodologist attempts to understand the multiple interrelationships among dimensions that emerge from the data without making prior assumptions or specifying hypothesis about the linear or correlative relationships among narrowly defined, operationalized variables. (p. 44)

This process begins with the identification of specific observations and, from there, works toward the goal of highlighting and building an understanding of more general themes and patterns (Patton, 1990).

Approaches that ensure the credibility, or rigor, of data analysis have emerged directly from qualitative paradigms (Morrow & Smith, 2000). Researchers (Creswell, 1994; Hill, Thompson, & Williams, 1997; Patton, 1990) suggest that triangulation strategies are an important component in building a solid qualitative design. The current study used three types of triangulation to strengthen internal validity: (a) triangulation of qualitative data sources (Patton, 1990, p. 467), (b) triangulation through the use of an auditor (Creswell, 1994), and (c), triangulation through multiple analysts (Patton, 1990, p. 467).

Patton (1990) suggests that "triangulation of qualitative data sources" (p. 467) is achieved by the investigator's use of a secondary data source. In this current study, two sources of data were analyzed. In addition to data obtained from the most recent interviews, relevant transcribed statements from interviews previously conducted by Jennings and Skovholt (1999) were re-analyzed for this group of master therapists.

In his discussion of internal validity, Creswell (1994) discusses triangulation through the use of an audit. This occurs when the data analysis approach includes another researcher who serves in the role of an auditor. Creswell states that this individual "might provide an 'audit' trail of the key decisions made during the research process and validate that they were good decisions" (p. 158). In this study, a research auditor reviewed uncoded transcripts and randomly coded individual paragraphs. A comparison of the coding was then completed. The auditor was a masters-level practitioner with experience in qualitative research.

Patton suggests that "triangulation through multiple analysts" (p. 468) assists in preventing the potential bias that results when one individual assumes complete responsibility for analyzing data. A key approach to this type of triangulation is to have the respondents serve as reviewers for the findings:

Evaluators can learn a great deal about the accuracy, fairness, and validity of their data analysis by having the people described in that data analysis react to what is described. To the extent that participants in the study are unable to relate to the description and analysis in a qualitative evaluation report, it is appropriate to question the credibility of the report. (Patton, 1990, pp. 468–469)

According to Morrow and Smith (2000), involving the respondents in this way "is a powerful tool for enhancing the rigor of a qualitative study" (p. 220). Similarly, in his discussion of validity, Creswell (1994) stresses the importance of working collabo- ratively with respondents throughout the investigation. He specifically recommends that the researcher "take the categories or themes back to the informants and ask whether the conclusions are accurate" (p. 158). Hill, Thompson, and Williams (1997) use the term *testimonial validity* when referring to this process. This study included a second round of interviews with the respondents. The primary purpose of these inter- views was to obtain feedback and consensus regarding the results of the data analysis.

Terms

In this study the term *professional resiliency* refers to a dynamic pattern that, over time, is marked by positive adaptation to an array of normal stress factors as well as other non-normative incidents or experiences that are acute in nature. The term *emotional wellness* is focused more specifically on the internal landscape of the practitioner and the maintenance of emotional health. It is the day-to-day process of sustaining a stable state of emotional equilibrium.

Data Collection

Instrument. A semi-structured interview consisting of 22 open-ended questions was employed (see Table A.3, pp. 158–159). These questions were cultivated from existing research, (Coster & Schwebel, 1997; Farber, 1990; Jennings & Skovholt, 1999; Savicki & Cooley, 1987) focused on work-related stressors among mental health practitioners as well as from studies that looked at expertise among practitioners. A pilot study was completed to further refine the questions. The pilot interviews were conducted with two practitioners who reflected many of the same characteristics as the sample. Each interview lasted one and one-half hours. Following the interviews, the practitioners were invited to provide feedback regarding their impressions of the order and content of the questions. Additional refinement of the interview questions was completed based on their feedback.

Procedure. All of the practitioners from the original master therapist respondent group ($N = 10$) were contacted by letter and invited to participate in a follow-up qual- itative study that would explore emotional wellness and professional resiliency. An article by Skovholt, Rønnestad, and Jennings (1997) was included with the letter to provide a clearer description of ideas on professional mastery. Practitioners were also offered a recent literature review completed by the investigator. The letter requested

TABLE A.3 Interview Questions for Master Therapists (Mullenbach & Skovholt)

Demographics

- Age
- Degree(s)
- Licenses
- Years of experience
- Theoretical orientation

Professional Development

- How do you define emotional wellness?
- How do you define professional resiliency?
- How well did your graduate training and/or internship experience prepare you for the emotional demands of practice?
- Research in the area of career development for helpers suggests that the early, novice stage of practice (e.g., the first five years) is particularly difficult. Please reflect on your own career and comment on this.
- Reflect on your professional career and talk about the most challenging phase(s) in regard to your emotional wellness and professional resiliency.
- Reflect on your professional career and talk about the issues that have been the most challenging.
- Talk about how childhood experiences influenced you in your professional development.

Work Environment

- What factors in the work environment promote emotional wellness and professional resiliency?

Difficult Issues and Client Behaviors

- What therapeutic issues are the most challenging to your own emotional wellness and professional resiliency?
- What client behaviors are the most challenging to your own emotional wellness and professional resiliency?

Professional Experience

- Discuss a critical incident that occurred in your professional career and talk about how it impacted you.
- What factors enable you as a therapist to constantly engage in a process of attachment and separation with many clients over time?
- What impact has continuous exposure to the suffering of others had on you?
- What has enabled you to practice for this long and yet remain vital in the profession?

Social Support

- What role have supervisors and mentors played in your emotional wellness and resiliency as a professional?
- Other than supervisors and mentors, what role have your relationships with other professionals played in your emotional wellness and professional resiliency?

TABLE A.3   **Continued**

Social Support

- What role have your relationships with family and friends played in your emotional wellness and professional resiliency?

Personal Experience/Self-Care

- What factors promote emotional wellness and professional resiliency?
- What methods do you use to maintain your own emotional wellness and professional resiliency?
- What characteristics are especially resilient about you?
- Who or what do you turn to for help?

Conclusion

- Is there anything that we haven't covered that you feel would be important to add?

approximately two hours of time from each practitioner. It also stated that each would receive a follow-up call from this investigator within two weeks to confirm his or her participation and to respond to any questions or concerns. Each respondent was contacted by phone, and for those nine who agreed to participate, interviews were scheduled.

At the beginning of each interview, the study was explained and the consent form was reviewed. Respondents were interviewed at their work sites. The interviews were semi-structured and utilized an interview guide (Patton, 1990). The interview guide consisted of 22 open-ended questions that were designed to access information related to emotional wellness and professional resiliency in six areas identified through an extensive literature review (Ackerly, Burnell, Holder, & Kurdek, 1988; Rodolfa, Kraft, & Reilley, 1988; Savicki & Cooley, 1987): (a) professional development, (b) work environment, (c) difficult issues and client behaviors, (d) professional experience, (e) social support, (f) personal experience. A final question elicited any other relevant comments that the respondents might want to offer.

The initial interviews averaged one and one-half hours. All of the interviews were audiotaped. The purpose of the second interview was to elicit feedback from the respondents in regard to themes derived from the data analysis of the first interviews and the secondary data source obtained from the initial study by Jennings and Skovholt (1999). In this process, the respondents listened to a review of each theme, and their feedback was invited regarding the relevance of the theme in their own experience.

Data Analysis

Audiotaped recordings from each initial interview were transcribed verbatim by a professional secretary. One of the transcripts was inaudible due to background noise in the recording environment. The respondent agreed to be reinterviewed and a second interview was completed and transcribed. After the transcriptions were completed, the investigator listened to the audiotaped interviews from each of the respondents to guarantee the accuracy of the transcripts. Transcripts being used as a secondary data source had previously been checked for accuracy by Jennings and Skovholt (1999), who followed this same procedure. Following this review, four copies were made of each transcript from both the recent interviews, as well as those that were being utilized as a secondary data source. One of these copies was considered a master copy and it was stored in an alternative site for safe keeping; the remainder of the copies were used in the data analysis process.

Data obtained from all of the open-ended questions was inductively analyzed by the investigator and interpreted according to Patton's (1990) content analysis procedure. "Inductive analysis means that the patterns, themes, and categories of analysis come from the data; they emerge out of the data rather than being imposed on them prior to data collection and analysis" (p. 390). Each transcript from the initial interviews was read individually by the investigator and each paragraph coded with one or two words that best captured the content of that paragraph. Relevant paragraphs from the secondary data source were also read individually and coded with one or two words that best captured the content of that paragraph. These small units of information are referred to as concepts (Patton, 1990). The investigator read each paragraph a minimum of three times in order to enhance the reliability of the findings. In an effort to insure internal validity, the research auditor also reviewed three uncoded transcripts and randomly coded a minimum of six single paragraphs per interview. A comparison of coding was then completed to discern any discrepancies. If discrepancies were noted, further discussion and random coding were completed.

In keeping with the procedure established by Jennings and Skovholt (1999), each concept was written on one side of a notecard with the appropriate quote attached to the opposite side. Following this, the concepts were analyzed and used to develop larger patterns, themes, and categories that eventually led to interpretations (Whitt, 1991). The second step of the analysis consisted of identifying themes that illuminated the findings (Patton, 1990). In the third step, these themes were grouped to form more general categories. At this point in the analysis, the investigator was involved in weekly consultation with the research auditor. The auditor reviewed the themes and general theme categories, discussing them with the investigator until consensus was reached.

Follow-up interviews were conducted with eight of the nine the respondents and their feedback was invited in regard to the accuracy of these themes. Due to health issues, one respondent was unavailable for the second interview. The purpose of the follow-up interviews was to check the validity of the data analysis by reviewing the themes and inviting feedback in regard to their accuracy. There was consensus among the respondents regarding the accuracy of the themes.

The final analysis yielded twenty-three themes within five categories. The five categories are: (a) emergence of the expert practitioner, (b) creating a positive work structure, (c) professional stressors, (d) protective factors, and (e) nurturing self through a balance of solitude and relationships. The results of this study were presented by using description and direct quotes from the transcribed interviews.

Methodology for the Jennings, Sovereign, Bottorff, and Mussell Study

Procedure

This study utilized data derived from transcripts from the Jennings and Skovholt (1999) study in which master therapists were asked questions about their personal characteristics and therapy practices (see Table A.1). Using archival data enabled the current researchers to unobtrusively assess the ethical values of master therapists. The possibility of socially desirable responses is stronger if the master therapists were asked directly about their ethical values. For purposes of this study, ethical values were defined as strongly held beliefs that inform moral judgment and professional conduct. To begin the data analysis, we chose the CQR method (Hill et al., 1997) to code the transcripts. The steps of the CQR method, requiring the use of rigorous scientific procedures for qualitative research, have been explicated by Hill et al. (1997). One major advantage of CQR is that the use of multiple researchers, decision making by consensus, and systematic examination of the data across cases can greatly reduce the biases of a sole investigator.

The primary research team consisted of a psychologist and two doctoral-level graduate students. Another psychologist served as auditor, a role recommended by Hill et al. (1997) to enhance the trustworthiness of the results. The auditor reviewed the research process and provided analysis feedback to the research team. For example, we discussed the possible implications of unequal power dynamics between the students and psychologists on the research team. We decided to address this concern at the outset and to readdress it throughout the coding process so as to minimize the potential of the students' deferring to the psychologists during the coding and auditing process.

Data analysis began by choosing a preliminary ethical framework for analysis of the transcripts. Our research team elected to create a set of sensitizing concepts as a "start list" (Hill et al., 1997, p. 543) to identify, classify, and categorize the qualitative data. These sensitizing concepts, preliminary ideas derived from the relevant existing research or theoretical literature, were used to structure the initial analysis. We first considered the basic moral principles described by Kitchener (1984) and Meara, Schmidt, and Day (1996) that Corey, Corey, and Callanan (1998) stated "form the foundation of functioning at the highest ethical level as a professional: autonomy, nonmaleficence, beneficence, justice, fidelity, and veracity" (p. 12). However, after discussion by the research team and a conclusion that these principles might be too broad in scope, we chose as our preliminary sensitizing concepts the values embedded within the six General Principles of the Ethical Principles of Psychologists and Code of Conduct (APA, 1992): competence, integrity, professional and scientific responsibility, respect for people's rights and dignity, concern for others' welfare, and social responsibility.

We began by consensually analyzing the explanatory text of the six APA General Principles, line by line, coding the ethical values embedded within. From the original six APA General Principles, we identified 24 ethical values. Then in a pilot analysis, each of the researchers individually coded a copy of the same transcript using the list of 24 ethical values. After coding the first transcript, the research team met and together examined each line of text, consensually determining which ethical value seemed to best represent each quotation or unit of meaning. Differences in coding among the researchers were resolved through the process of discussion and debate until there was consensus. After using this process with the transcripts of three master therapists, the researcher team met with the auditor for feedback on the pilot analysis.

Based upon the auditor's suggestion, we revisited the writings of Gilligan (1982), Kitchener (1984), Kohlberg (1984), and Meara et al. (1996), to ensure that we had not overlooked other important ethical concepts. From this search, two ethical values (i.e., the ethic of relational connection from Gilligan's work and fidelity from Kitchener's work) were added to our ethical value list. In addition, six new ethical values (i.e., faith, courage, openness, resiliency, self-actualization, and cultural competence) were added based upon ethical values we identified during our pilot analysis. As a next step, all of the transcripts were analyzed with the final list of thirty-two ethical values. That is, each researcher first individually analyzed a transcript by assigning an ethical value to each quotation in the transcript. Then the researchers met as a team and consensually decided on how to the best code the ethical value for each quotation from that transcript. This process concluded after all ten transcripts had been analyzed, resulting in over 1,300 quotations coded with one of the thirty-two ethical values. Next, each of the 1,300 quotations was cut and pasted onto notecards to facilitate the manipulation and organization of the data.

The 1,300 quotations comprising thirty-two ethical values were reexamined by the researchers. At this point, quotations that were deemed by consensus as only minimally related to ethical issues were excluded from the analysis. Next, the researchers tallied the number of quotations representing each ethical value as well as the number of therapists holding that particular ethical value. Of the thirty-two ethical values, nine (confidentiality, professional responsibility, equality, justice, truth, integrity, philanthropy, resilience, and fidelity) were eliminated because they were associated with a low number of quotations by a few therapists or because they logically could not be consolidated with another ethical value. The remaining twenty-three ethical values and corresponding supporting data were consensually reexamined for internal consistency. At this point, some data (i.e., notecards) were reassigned to a more appropriate code by the research team. During this stage of the analysis, we determined that the remaining twenty-three ethical values logically could be consolidated into nine themes of ethical values. Obtaining additional feedback from the auditor regarding overlap in themes, we were able to combine values once more bringing the final total to five primary themes representing ethical values.

Quotations then were analyzed within each of the five values. Those quotations that seemed to be excellent illustrative representatives of the ethical values were identified, a subset of which are presented in the results section of Chapter 6.

Special Note

Please note that in all of the studies, minor grammatical corrections and editing were completed to add clarity to the quotes. In addition, the terms psychotherapist, therapist, counselor, and practitioner were utilized interchangeably throughout the book.

References

Ackerly, G. D., Burnell, J., Holder, D. C., & Kurdek, L. A. (1988). Burnout among licensed psychologists. *Professional Psychology: Research and Practice, 19*(6), 624–631.

American Psychological Association. (1992). Ethical principles of psychologists and code of conduct. *American Psychologist, 47*, 1597–1611.

Anastasi, A., & Urbina, S. (1997). *Psychological testing* (7th ed.). Englewood Cliffs, NJ: Prentice-Hall.

Bachelor, A. (1991). Comparison and relation to outcome of diverse measures of the helping alliance as seen by client and therapist. *Psychotherapy: Theory, Research, and Practice, 28*, 534–549.

Bordin, E. S. (1979). The generalizability of the psychoanalytic concept of the working alliance. *Psychotherapy: Theory, Research, and Practice, 16*, 252–260.

Bordin, E. S. (1994). Theory and research on the therapeutic working alliance: New directions. In A. O. Horvath & L. S. Greenberg (Eds.), *The working alliance: Theory, research, and practice.* New York: John Wiley & Sons.

Cole, D. A., & White, K. (1993). Structure of peer impressions of children's competence: Validation of the peer nomination of multiple competencies. *Psychological Assessment, 5*, 449–456.

Corey, G., Corey, M., & Callanan, P. (1998). *Issues and ethics in the helping professions.* Pacific Grove, CA: Brooks/Cole Publishing.

Coster, J. S., & Schwebel, M. (1997). Well-functioning in professional psychologists. *Professional Psychology: Research and Practice, 28*(1), 5–13.

Creswell, J. W. (1994). *Research design: Qualitative and quantitative approaches.* Newbury Park, CA: Sage Publications.

Farber, B. (1990). Burnout in psychotherapists: Incidence, types, and trends. *Psychology in Private Practice, 8*(1), 35–44.

Gaston, L., & Marmar, C. R. (1994). The California psychotherapy alliance scales. In A. O. Horvath & L. S. Greenberg (Eds.), *The working alliance: Theory, research, and practice.* New York: Wiley.

Gilligan, C. (1982). *In a different voice: Psychological theory and women's development.* Cambridge, MA: Harvard University Press.

Guba, E. G. (1978). *Toward a methodology of naturalistic inquiry in educational evaluation. CSE Monograph Series in Evaluation No. 8.* Los Angeles: Center for the Study of Evaluation, University of California.

Henry, W. P., & Strupp, H. H. (1994). The therapeutic alliance as interpersonal process. In A. Horvath & L. S. Greenberg (Eds.), *The working alliance: Theory, research, and practice.* New York: Wiley.

Hill, C. E., Thompson, B. J., & Williams, E. N. (1997). A guide to conducting consensual qualitative research. *The Counseling Psychologist, 25*(4), 517–572.

Hillerbrand, E. T., & Clairborn, C. D. (1990). Examining reasoning skill differences between expert and novice counselors. *Journal of Counseling and Development, 68*, 684–691.

Horvath, A. O. (1994). Research on the alliance. In A. O. Horvath & L. S. Greenberg (Eds.), *The working alliance: Theory, research, and practice* (pp. 259–286). New York: Wiley.

Horvath, A. O., & Greenberg, L. S. (1994). Introduction. In A. O. Horvath & L. S. Greenberg (Eds.), *The working alliance: Theory, research, and practice* (pp. 1–9). New York: Wiley.

Hoshmand, L. L. S. T. (1989). Alternate research paradigms: A review and teaching proposal. *Counseling Psychologist, 17*, 3–79.

Jennings, L., & Skovholt, T. M. (1999). The cognitive, emotional, and relational characteristics of master therapists. *Journal of Counseling Psychology, 46*, 3–11.

Kitchener, K. (1984). Intuition, critical evaluation and ethical principles: The foundation for ethical decisions in counseling psychology. *The Counseling Psychologist, 12*(3), 43–55.

Kohlberg, L. (1984). Essays in moral development: Vol. 2. *The psychology of moral development.* New York: Harper & Row.

Luborsky, L. (1994). Therapeutic alliances as predictors of psychotherapy outcomes: Factors explaining the predictive success. In A. O. Horvath & L .S. Greenberg (Eds.), *The working alliance: Theory, research, and practice.* New York: Wiley.

Luborsky, L., McLellan, T. A., Woody, G. E., O'Brien, C. P., & Auerbach, A. (1985). Therapist success and its determinants. *Archive of General Psychiatry, 42*, 602–611.

Marshall, C., & Rossman, G. B. (1999). *Designing qualitative research* (3rd ed.). Thousand Oaks, CA: Sage Publications.

Marziali, E. (1984). Three viewpoints on the therapeutic alliance: Similarities, differences and associations with psychotherapy outcome. *Journal of Nervous and Mental Disease, 172*, 417–423.

Meara, N. M., Schmidt, L. D., & Day, J. D. (1996). Principles and virtues: A foundation for ethical decisions, policies, and character. *The Counseling Psychologist, 24*(1), p. 4–77.

Morrow, S. L., & Smith, M. L. (2000). Qualitative research for counseling psychology. In S. D. Brown, & R. W. Lent (Eds.), *Handbook of counseling psychology* (3rd ed.; pp. 199–230). New York: Wiley.

Patton, M. Q. (1990). *Qualitative evaluation and research methods* (2nd ed.) Newbury Park, CA: Sage Publications.

Peters, T. J., & Waterman, R. H. (1982). *In search of excellence: Lessons from America's best-run companies.* New York: Harper & Row.

Rodolfa, E. R., Kraft, W. A., & Reilley, R. R. (1988). Stressors of professionals and trainees at APA-approved counseling and VA medical center internship sites. *Professional Psychology: Research and Practice, 19*(1), 43–49.

Savicki, V., & Cooley, E. (1987, January). The relationship of work environment and client contact to burnout in mental health professionals. *Journal of Counseling and Development, 65*, 249–252.

Seidman, I. E. (1991). *Interviewing as qualitative research.* New York: Teachers College Press.

Serbin, L. A., Lyons, J. A., Marchessault, K., Schartzman, A. E., & Ledingham, J. E. (1987). Observational validation of a peer nomination technique for identifying aggressive, withdrawn, and aggressive/withdrawn children. *Journal of Consulting and Clinical Psychology, 55*, 109–110.

Skovholt, T. M., & Rønnestad, M. H. (1995). *The evolving professional self: Stages and themes in therapist and counselor development.* Chichester, UK: Wiley.

Skovholt, T. M., Rønnestad, M. H., & Jennings, L. (1997). Searching for expertise in counseling, psychotherapy, and professional psychology. *Educational Psychology Review, 9*(4), 361–369.

Strauss, A., & Corbin, J. (1990). *Basics of qualitative research: Grounded theory procedures and techniques.* Newbury Park, CA: Sage Publications.

Whitt, E. J. (1991). Artful science: A primer on qualitative research methods. *Journal of College Student Development, 32*, 406–415.

Interviews with Master Therapists

Introduction

The following are three full-length interviews that were completed with the master therapists. The transcripts were jointly edited by the researchers and the master therapist participants with a focus on creating clarity and protecting confidentiality. The letter "R" denotes research interviewer. The letter "P" denotes therapist participant.

Master Therapist #1 (Len Jennings, Interviewer)

The following is a full transcript of Len Jennings' interview with one of the master therapists:

R: What do you think about being nominated a "master therapist"?

P: I am a Midwest female and I am supposed to be modest . . . I just got around to telling my kids and my son had a most wonderful response. He said, ". . . that is going to trip you into going back and looking at your own stages of development."

R: How are you different now from when you began?

P: I laugh a lot more. I am old. That is one thing that helps and I am not forever wondering if I am good enough.

R: How did you get to that point?

P: I don't know. I still question periodically, "Have I made a therapeutic error?" and I make them but I am not as anxious going into it . . . It is an odd piece of humility . . . it is like saying, "I am not that important" . . . What goes on here is important, but we are both experts and if I make a mistake the client can also do some things to make it better. I am not that responsible . . . I don't feel totally responsible for an end result.

R: Did you feel that way when you started?

P: I think so. I started out as a nurse so my job was to cure people or to ease pain. I have moved through that more.

R: As you moved through it what did you notice as different philosophically?

P: In the corner of my office I have my teachers and expect them to be judging my performance. There are times when I look up and see Carl Rogers and I say, "I am sorry, Carl, I am not that patient."

R: Did you work with Carl?

P: Yes, and I was truly impressed but I am not that patient. I still compare myself to my mentors but I am not as caught up in it.

R: You are more accepting of your of your own style . . . compared to earlier on?

P: Oh sure. I tried on styles just like kids try on clothes. I tried on roles. Some of them worked and others worked a little bit.

R: Now you have found something that fits?

P: Fits better and if people don't like it they go away. They find the therapist who fits for them.

R: It's a complex interaction . . . we are talking about the combination of therapist-client variables and client readiness . . . I am going to focus on the therapist. What is it about you that . . . facilitates therapy?

P: A lot . . . my nursing background. I attend to bodies. I would not consider seeing a new person with depression without referring them back to their doctor to get a physical. I bring my age. I am going to be 71 this week. I have seen a lot happen and I think that is a gift to people. I have been exposed to a lot of different therapies . . . so I have a variety of techniques. I go with the old joke: A man wants a blue suit, turn on the blue light. Have you read Prochaska? . . . This guy is talking about different therapies working for different times in a client's life . . . I think that this is true. I am glad that they are beginning to document it.

R: Where do you fit on that spectrum? Where are you most effective?

P: I am in private practice and mainly see therapists. I don't see many people who are just thinking about change. I am dealing more with people who are in pain or wanting to change. I collude with them in making a plan for change. I work to heighten their awareness of their patterns. It opens options for them to find other ways. I get into trouble when I think I have the way, and occasionally I do that. I saw a new woman today who has young children and is in the process of divorce . . . I said, "We are going to have to be careful because I had young kids and went through a divorce. If you hear me giving you prescriptions that were fitting for me forty years ago, tell me." I bring experience and I work not to project on the client.

R: You have a sense of your own countertransference?

P: Yes, and I heighten it so that my client knows it is a danger too.

R: Is it harder to work primarily with therapists?

P: There are funny things about it. I work with new graduates and they are forever critiquing my style . . . The older therapists may be more prone to think and not act so then the question is, "What is your plan and which part of it are you going to do between now and next week?"

R: Do you find they are in their heads a lot and not applying . . .

P: Yes. Once in a while I get cynical and say, "What we are having here is the Academy Award for pain" . . . People kind of treasure their pain and think that their pain is more exquisite than anyone else's pain. I work not to get impressed, but to acknowledge pain and pay attention to it and then to ask "What's next?"

R: . . . with your experience you have come to see pain in a variety of ways and are not . . .

P: . . . seduced by it. First you do no harm, but second, you don't get so impressed with their pain that you don't do anything . . . That is a mistake that I have made a lot. I get so impressed with someone's horrendous stories. I had a client who brought in pictures of the holocaust. I said, "Would you rather be a person who didn't feel this pain?" She went right back into realizing that it made her a deeper person.

R: You gave her permission to normalize that it was a human experience to go through something like that?

P: Yes.

R: Do you think that to be a master therapist you need years and years of experience?

P: No. I think most of us therapists got started when we were 2 . . . I got labeled as a nosy kid. I was forever curious about people, what made them tick, and what would make them feel better. Being a Midwestern female, I was into making them feel better. I do think there are people who get started as therapists very young . . . they were trained by their families.

R: Let's say there are two therapists with similar experiences. One goes on to be a master therapist while the other one doesn't grow as a therapist. Why does one benefit from experience and another does not?

P: One of the things for me is that I have a great need for novelty. I can't stay content in what I know. I get embarrassed at how much I seek out learning experiences. My family is forever teasing me about it.

R: The perpetual adult learner . . . are you looking at other areas of knowledge beyond psychology?

P: Not as much and I fault myself for that. Margaret Mead said we are the first generation to learn from our kids and I think that is true. I have a daughter who is studying collage . . . That is a visual way of doing therapy. I wish I would do more of it . . . I took autoharp lessons . . . It was great fun and it really deepened my sense of tradition. I sang in gospel choir until my knees gave out . . . that made me a minority and I got in touch with myself in that culture.

R: Seeking out new experiences feeds . . .

P: . . . the more pejorative way of saying it is that I am easily bored.

R: Let's return to the emotional well-being of the therapist. How do good therapists figure out their stuff and not let it get in the way of the work that they do with clients?

P: Everyone of us goes through that in our early training . . . We are forever diagnosing our friends and relatives . . . I think that we grow through it. There is a piece of us that still labels people with terrible psychiatric diagnosis whenever we get mad at them. I think it is there for every one of us.

R: How does your emotional health impact the therapy that you do?

P: That is a wonderful question. I have been through a hard five years during which time I sold my house, moved into another place, had my last surviving sibling die, my mother die, and an aunt. I was picking myself up and kind of holding on to myself for a while. The interesting part is that, when I was in the most pain, I was a very good therapist. It was like the bank robbers who sandpaper their skin so that they can be really sensitive to the movements of the machine they are trying to break open. In one sense, it was such a relief to come here and to be outside my own struggle, but also to have my nerves just sandpapered down to the loss and the pain. I was trying to get away from it and I was more sensitive to what my clients were doing.

R: Was that surprising?

P: Yes, because I would have expected that I would have been more incapacitated . . . Do you know about Harry Stack Sullivan? He was this wonderful black Irishman who went through depressions several times and it made him more sensitive to what his patients were doing. I think that having pain both sensitizes me to it and makes me want to get away from my own so I am willing to invest out there.

R: What about as a child growing up . . . is pain an important ingredient in creating that compassion?

P: I don't know. I grew up in a very small town, population 3,000, and was in the public eye because my father was a school principal . . . Then my father died when I was 6 so I had that sense of loss; however, there are stories about me before he died. I am 4 or 5, and go in to his room when he was in bed sick, and without saying anything, I pull down the shade because the sun was shining in his eyes. So I had it, and I don't know where that came from precisely.

R: How does the person you are impact the therapy you do?

P: I am really grounded. I worked hard to get grounded physically and psychologically. That had an impact on people . . . literally, my weight is evenly distributed in my body . . . I also think that being a big woman is useful because people project power into that.

R: Tell me more about the power piece and how that might impact what goes on here . . .

P: A piece of it is getting old enough not to be seen as sexy so the energy does not get confused.

R: How did you use that confusion piece in therapy before?

P: I mainly used it to confuse myself . . . As I got older it seemed to calm down I have a number of middle-aged male clients who are comfortable with me and I think that is a piece of it.

R: Are master therapists experts at working with those pieces of information and dealing with them more effectively?

P: That is a funny question because I consider myself a good therapist but, until I got your letter, I didn't consider myself a master therapist. It is a funny kind of humility to say I am good but I am not that good, or I am good but not in this arena.

R: Does that serve a function for you?

P: Sure, because if I am not working well with a client I can refer them on, which I do.

R: What clients do you work the best with?

P: Everybody dreams of the literate, articulate, wanting to change, therapist . . . I am very lucky that I have gotten this caseload. Once I realized that I had it, I started to publicize it so that I could get more of them. Now I have literally stopped taking clients who are not either spiritual directors or psychologists.

R: You have gotten to the point where you pick the people you work with the best to set up success?

P: Yes . . . I can't pick out the ones I am going to work well with right away . . . It takes two or three times before I feel a physiological piece in me that says this is not working. My main way of experiencing life is kinesthetic so that if I start to feel queasy, that is when my brain finally gets the signal.

R: . . . You have developed a keen sense of your signals.

P: We try to teach that in terms of shuttling. To pay attention to client and to pay attention to what's in here . . . back and forth . . . we are our best instrument.

R: As you have gained more experience you've become more refined in doing that?

P: Yes. Still not swell.

R: It takes two or three sessions now, what about when you first started out?

P: Oh, I could go ten, twelve . . . and if a client is like a part of me that I don't like, then I want to get in there and fix it up quickly.

R: Very earnest.

P: Yeah. Oh, I do get very earnest. I have to laugh at myself sometimes.

R: Again it shows a step back . . . a lot of new therapists are so overwhelmed that they are not seeing the humor, or their role, the client's role, or the relationship part of it. Where does that ability to distinguish come from?

P: I struggled to learn . . . I am not a good historian about that. I know I have taught it. I don't remember a time that I didn't have it at all.

R: . . . the literature about expertise talks about master chess players. They just see the pattern, they can't really tell you any more where it came from or how to develop it. Sometimes the greatest chess players or therapists aren't that good at teaching the neophyte because they are so far away from it . . . One therapist said that he wishes he could recall all those clients he saw in the first five years and say, "Look, I know a lot more now and I will give you a break, free sessions for a while."

P: I feel that way about early classes that I taught. I want to go back and say, "I know we believed it then, but . . ." . . . don't think that I did bad therapy, I just didn't do really good therapy.

R: . . . you've worked hard to become grounded. What have you done to facilitate that?

P: I have done my own therapy. I spent a spell of time looking at body language, paying attention to my own and others' so that I could literally think about whether or not I was centered . . .

R: . . . when you are working with a client, do you use that as a gauge. . . ?

P: If I am off-centered, I have this kind of checklist that says, "Is it me, my client, or is it us?" It could be any one of the three . . . It could be just be just me . . . I am part of a psychologist forum and one of the women last week said she has a client she likes but she is tired of doing therapy. She just feels it in her body. . . . I also had a client and I would feel slimy every time he left. As it turns out he was my idea of what is really evil. When I finally caught on to that, I referred him on. Sometimes if a client brings in a slightly different version of my issue, I need to be careful . . . if a client is like the part of me that I like, then I tend to get blinded to what else needs to be done.

R: . . . a master therapist could be defined as one who gives therapists therapy because you know that process.

P: I assume the danger then is to think that I know the territory. There may be some places I don't know and I could get complacent . . .

R: Maybe some of the therapists who continue to learn and develop are open to the experiences of life.

P: I think so . . . For a long time my daughter was a reference librarian and I would take any speaking engagement. I would go anywhere and talk about anything. I would get an assignment and then I would call her up and say, "Amy, for God's sake, I said I would talk about X, what can you find me about it?" I would work hard to become at least mildly expert at whatever it was that I was talking about. It was like letting the world bring me a new area that I had to learn.

R: You had the sense that you could pull it off . . . a sense of self-efficacy.

P: Yeah, I could pull it off and I would put the work into learning.

R: It pushed you?

P: Yeah, in directions that I was kind of open to.

R: An adventure seeker?

P: Oh yeah.

R: How do you know when you are doing a good job with a client?

P: . . . do you know the book *Flow?* . . . You know you are in the flow when enough challenge is coming up but it is not overwhelming. People are doing their work and they are having difficulties, but it isn't overwhelming. That is when I know that the time people spend here is useful.

R: Again, it sounds like you have learned to trust that . . .

P: Yeah, it is a sense of we are both doing our work and I am not working too hard. When I catch on that I am working too hard, then I have to step back again and say, "What's going on here?"

R: I was thinking about just letting things happen, it sounds like there is a letting go of what should be . . .

P: At least it is a willingness to be amazed . . . I don't know if I let it go because I do have control needs. It is more like within this container, let's see what happens.

R: . . . with the factors that are there, you, the client, the relationship.

P: Yeah, like the former client who was in this morning with this immense pain, but not being able to make the world better. I know her well enough so I just said, "Now would you want to be the kind of person who didn't feel that pain?" It rocked her back and she got this smile on her face . . . So it is sort of like attending to what goes on within the container.

R: How did you know that was the right thing to say?

P: Oh, I didn't. . . . I think you have a number of options of what to say and most of them will not be wrong. You are just suggesting. If she had gotten mad at me, then I would have pulled back and done something else. Part of it is a gestalt concept of dosage. You have to put out the right level . . . if it isn't enough it is not going to get the adrenaline going and if it is too much they get overwhelmed. It is a matter of trial and error.

R: Are master therapists willing to take those risks and make mistakes?

P: I think so. They are not as focused on being absolutely correct because they know that there is no such thing as being absolutely correct.

R: This is all an experiment . . .

P: Yeah . . . and if you do it out of a decent motivation you're probably not going to hurt them.

R: Therapeutic intention . . . It seems like a complex skill . . . it seems challenging to know when to make those decisions . . . My question is, what's your view of human nature in regard to client's durability and ability to handle mistakes?

P: They are adults . . . They come in here for an hour. They are competent and what they want is to have less pain. . . . Any little piece I can do will help . . . I basically trust my own motivation to not hurt them. I am really clear about that. Once in a while, when I get with someone I want to knock flat, I do them a huge favor and send them on.

R: How did you develop that sense of safety?

P: Carl Rogers threw one of my best friends out of therapy and I just loved it . . . He said, "I watch you struggle. I can't be helpful to you until you can more honest with me". . . . It had a huge impact on him . . . and most of it useful. One of the mottoes in my family is to tell the truth in love. It is hard to go wrong with that and I think that is what Carl did.

R: Did you say "truth". . . ?

P: I think the truth by itself can be a terrible weapon but he was literally telling the truth in love.

R: Tell me about how love plays a part in your work?

P: It has to do with being open-hearted. Caring what goes on with a person but not fussing over them. A disciplined, intelligent love. It is not gushy. It can be warmly sympathetic when that feels appropriate. At other times it can be stand-offish. It is interacting with the client's best interests at heart. . . . I am not sure where I got it but I have been the recipient of it from therapists, teachers, friends, and family.

R: Is there an element of spirituality in what you do?

P: Oh sure. That is something that therapists have such trouble admitting to . . . Most of us want to do good. Some of us translate that into seeing God in the other person or showing God's love . . . I had one woman who prayed for every one of her clients every day. Now I don't carry it to that extent but I do not want to damage a person. I have also been involved with a group of psychics and took a class in psychic development. . . . One interesting thing that it has done for me is that several of the psychics refer clients to me because I am not put off by that view and I feel trustworthy for that reason. I don't buy it all but I don't disparage it either.

R: You talk about openness . . . you are not just carving out a narrow slice of what could possibly be.

P: Yeah, and I really believe that a client could see me twenty times, go away, and I will not know what our interaction has been. That is humbling . . . and amusing.

R: So someone who has a need to know would probably find this a very frustrating field?

P: I think it is. Sometimes I see a client three or four times and then they drop off the scope and my concern is, "Was I the least bit useful?" Then a year or two later they start referring clients to me.

R: What percentage of clients do you think you have helped?

P: I don't have a clue. . . . I would like to think everybody in some way but maybe it was something they didn't want or I didn't plan to give . . . I think I help people hold life a little more lightly. That would be one of my aims.

R: How did you develop . . . to see the "lightness" of life?

P: In the last ten years I have been talking more about cosmic jokes. That comes out of my own spiritual development of having gone through different Protestant divisions of life and then settling into one that is not necessarily satisfying but it will do as well as any. It is holding the universe more lightly.

R: Some people may have taken a more cynical turn with all the losses you talked about . . . Why does one person choose a path and another get stuck?

P: I got a lot of support . . . family support and community support. . . . I think support helps me not be cynical. Or, maybe my cynicism comes out in looking at cosmic jokes.

R: . . . a cosmic joke, just what do you mean by that?

P: . . . you and I know how the world is but suddenly, in God's wisdom, we've been sent this totally bizarre happening that doesn't fit in anybody's parameters. It is here so what are you going to do with it? I will tell you a cosmic joke . . . my church is as poor as a church mouse . . . the true cosmic joke is that we have just gotten a million dollars. That is going to be one of the trials of the century for that church. To have longed all this time to have enough money and then, plop!

R: . . . again, an openness to whatever is happening . . .

P: Yeah, my joke is that when I die they ought to put on my epitaph, "Now her question is answered". . . curiosity has been a big thing all of my life.

R: It must be infectious . . . one of the reasons people seek you out.

P: I invite them to examine what is going on without getting so caught up in the drama.

R: There is something soothing about that, I imagine.

P: It is irritating for some people.

R: What do you think is therapy?

P: It is an opportunity to pay attention . . . it is a grace or gift to be able to look at where I am in my life. What contributes to where I am? What are my options now? . . . It is an opportunity to step outside of time into a place that is safe to lay out this stuff and look at it.

R: Quite a gift.

P: I think it is. When people come in we make jokes about putting it on the white table and just sorting through it. . . . Sometimes I say, "What do you want to put out today?" and I make a list. Which one is most important?

R: How does psychotherapy heal?

P: I don't know that it does . . . one of my teachers has a new book out that I read the first ten pages of and what I like is that he puts his values out first. He says that we teach people how to live beautifully . . . I think that fits nicer than how do we "heal." We teach people . . . how to live beautifully . . . it is how to be more artistic with our lives.

R: Do you see the artist in a person?

P: I think so.

R: How do you tap that?

P: Margaret Mead's daughter wrote a book on creating our lives and occasionally I invite people to that book . . . Having a focus or a vision. Who do you want to be in the next two or three years?

R: Are you working with that versus the past?

P: Yeah . . . I do a lot of stuff around the past but then given that . . . in Snow White, the Disney version, there is a fairy godmother who is all bumbly and she doesn't get to the christening on time so the original curse has been laid on Snow White that she will die. This fairy godmother cannot take that original curse away but she can soften it so that Snow White doesn't die, she just falls into a sleep. As a therapist, I am like that second fairy Godmother at the christening. I can't change what was laid down early but I can pay attention to it. Then I can help a person soften it or make it go in ways that are more interesting.

R: It sounds like Frankl . . . we cannot choose our conditions but we can choose how we respond to them . . . and acknowledging that the conditions are painful.

P: Yeah . . . there are terrible things in childhood and you learn really destructive patterns . . . one of the things that Earl Polster walks about is "the nextness" and it is, given that, what so you want to do with it . . . You can be impressed with it, but that would be a hell of a place to live your life.

R: One of the therapists I talked to said that people come in wanting to change, and yet they don't want to change. . . . The job of the therapist is to ask the hard questions and get them moving. What do you think of that notion?

P: What I like to say is, "Of course there is a part of you that doesn't want to change. Let's honor that part. Talk to me out of that part. Now there is a part of you that wants to change. Let's hear what that part has to say." It is not my question to answer. My question is to just say, "Let's see what is going on here."

R: That makes sense if you are having some conflict.

P: Yeah . . . now let's have a debate between these two parts. Let's just listen to this dialogue . . . It is out of the gestalt concept that awareness is curative.

R: Would you call it your theoretical orientation?

P: Gestalt? I am an impatient client-centered, gestalt therapist. My value system is rooted in client-centered therapy.

R: Why does that speak to you?

P: Because it is Midwest. . . . Roger's father was a county agent and I was once a public health nurse I know what that means in terms of being scientific and being helpful and caring about people but it doesn't have enough action for me. I added gestalt as a technique that goes on top of that.

R: I think of a client-centered approach as being the foundation to forming the therapeutic alliance . . . but maybe it doesn't get you to the action stage as well as gestalt does?

P: That is my experience.

R: . . . Gestalt does a good job of opening up issues quickly . . .

P: Yeah, usually. For example: You said you wanted this change and you tried that. How was it for you? What needs to be adapted? There is not much shame in it. And, it is forever interesting. You just have to give it that because it is hard to know how a person is going to try out something and how they will sort that through.

R: How much of psychotherapy do you see as an art versus a science?

P: Oh, about 95 percent to the art . . . There are people who do it more towards the science but that is not my cup of tea. I wouldn't say you don't have to learn theory and technique. A lot of those, but after that I think it is an art.

R: So you get the technique, you get the training, and then use those rules in an artistic way.

P: Yeah. I think you have to learn your trade . . .

R: I notice that you are doing a lot of reading. Do you keep active with that?

P: . . . They had the first international gestalt conference in New Orleans and I put in to do a proposal on introjects and age . . . I presented and while I was there, I bought the Gestalt Institute Press because I got a 40 percent discount . . . so I had my reading for the next year laid out. It is wonderful because a lot of the writers are my former teachers so I can pick up on what they are doing now . . . it is exciting.

R: . . . it has taken a lot of reading, experiences, and learning to be at this stage of practice.

P: I am not really out of whack but I also don't feel like I am a truly well-balanced human being because I hardly ever read novels. I really enjoy reading this other stuff.

R: Do you love what you do?

P: Oh yeah.

R: How much of a factor is that for therapists who become very good?

P: I don't know . . . I just went to my financial planner . . . and it is so strange because I can't tell myself I have to go to work to make a living. I have to be more honest and say that I enjoy it, I like the guys I work with, I like the people I see mainly. I have gotten smarter so I don't work as much. Where else would I ever have this kind of intimate contact with such interesting people? I feel like I am doing a useful job.

R: That has got to be infectious . . . positive energy created by doing what we love.

P: Yes. It is an amazing gift.

R: Did you find that it took courage to become open or was this natural for you?

P: I never experienced it as requiring courage. I backed into this career. I did not set forth purposely to be a therapist. I took advantage of what came my way and what interested me. It was more like I got seduced into new and interesting places. So it was not a matter of saying, "By God, I am going to learn this." I don't experience it as taking courage.

R: What was it that got you interested initially?

P: l don't know. Carl Rogers was the first therapist I ever had any close contact with. I was not important to him but he was important to me. That way of being is seductive; to be able to be on earth and be honest and useful.

R: A mission?

P: I would not have thought that . . . My mission at that point was to survive. To make a living for my kids and get on with things.

R: Do you have a formulated mission statement for yourself?

P: I work on it every year about this time. My mission next year is to deepen my spiritual life because I have one but it is mildly proforma, and to enhance my relationships. . . . I am purposely setting forth to strengthen the relationships that I have because I had so many losses. Every year I literally write a mission statement and I go back to see what happened to it.

R: You are taking time to be introspective and to see where you are headed.

P: Yeah. Of course the big one that I am avoiding is retirement. I am just playing with knowing that is there someplace . . .

R: We have one or two more questions. If there were a recipe for making a master therapist, what ingredients would you include?

P: Getting grounded in any theory, practicing, and then being open for the embroidering that goes around it.

R: The art?

P: Yes.

R: What questions would you want to ask of a master therapist?

P: I would be curious about what they learned, what piece they got from each of their mentors.

R: Mentors, it sounds like they were important to you.

P: Yeah. We get different things from different people. We are attracted to people because of what they have and then we incorporate it more.

R: Do you have a mentor now?

P: Joseph Zinker is a person whose thought pattern I follow but he is not a mentor. I think that I am older than he is actually, but his thought pattern is fascinating.

End of interview.

Master Therapist #2 (Michael Sullivan, Interviewer)

The following is a full transcript of Michael Sullivan's interview with one of the master therapists:

R: How do you introduce your clients to the therapy experience?

P: I begin introducing them to it on the phone as soon as I call them back in terms of what they are wanting. When I am talking to friends about picking a therapist, what I say to them is that even on the phone they should feel understood, at a minimum, and possibly feel a little connected in terms of who they are talking to. My goal when I talk to people on the phone is to get a sense of what they are looking for and to let them know I have heard them. Then I also let them know what fee I am going to charge and the amount of time I'll be seeing them. I give them the parameters of what they are signing up for and ask them if they have any questions. Right from the beginning it's getting a sense of them, helping them feel understood minimally with whatever they are telling me and make sure they know what they are walking into. I try to do that in a very respectful way

R: Do you have a formal aspect of that that comes later?

P: Yes, I let them know on the phone call what they can expect from the first session and that I will take a look at whether I think I can be helpful to them. I'll let them know that, by the end of the first session. They should be looking at whether they feel understood and whether they can work with me. We will be taking a look at each other in the first session and that, at a minimum, they should hear from me whether I think I can be helpful and what I think the issues are. That is right from the beginning, as they are signing up on the phone. Then when they come here, I'll have that session because we have already talked about what is going to happen. If, at the end of it, we are all in agreement and I am feeling I can help them and they feel understood and hopeful, we go on to four more sessions. We will then evaluate at the end of that time. There is an evaluation at the end of the first session and then there's an evaluation at the end of four. It's pretty specific and the feedback I have gotten from them is that it feels reassuring. They aren't signing up forever and they have a chance to renegotiate whether they want to be with me.

R: How do you establish agreement with clients as to the tasks of therapy?

P: The main thing is you ask . . . often when people come in what they are really asking for is different than what they are saying at the beginning. It's fleshing that out and determining how I can be helpful in a realistic way. We come to some agreement about that . . . I do a lot of couples work and it is so important . . . that I get what the goals of each one are and to not make assumptions in any way. I might see a couple and he is already in love with somebody else and he is here as a last ditch effort to see if he wants to be in the marriage. That's a very different thing than the wife who is sitting there and saying? "I really want to save the marriage." I have to really work with them about the differences before we can come to something that is a common agreement.

R: Do you have a set way of establishing the respective roles in therapy of therapist and client and how do you go about doing this?

P: I'm sure I do. One of the roles for me is of helper and being in charge in some ways but letting the clients be in charge of themselves. I do that mostly experientially and I do a tiny bit of educating . . . when people come into therapy I certainly ask them what they are expecting of therapy and what they are expecting of me. One of the questions that I always ask is how they heard about me, because how they heard about me brings them in with certain expectations. Sometimes the expectations are that I am going to be an advice giver and that I have answers that they don't have. I find out what the expectations are and then clarify that I am here to help them find their own path . . . I am here to help them find what's right for them and I am not going to be doing a lot of advice giving unless they are in crisis. That sets it.

R: How do you work with clients when they are not following through on their therapy tasks?

P: Let me use examples with that. I do the same thing actually with couples or individuals. One of the things I ask people to do sometimes is left-handed, nondominant handwriting, to get past the intellect and into the feelings. If they have gone home and not done that and come back and say they haven't, I suggest that we take a look at what goes into not doing it. You simply respect and look at the resistance. You don't shame them. . . . It's the same with couples when they're supposed to be working on something. I want to know what went into their not working on it, not in a shaming way but in a loving, curious way. What it says to me is a part of you doesn't want to do this and you have good reasons why you don't want to, so let's just understand the reasons.

R: Describe the importance in your work with clients of establishing a positive therapy relationship.

P: If you don't have a working alliance, you don't have much. It's not always positive but there has to be a working alliance . . . a feeling that they can work with you and that they can get somewhere. If you don't have that they shouldn't be trusting you; you haven't, as a therapist, done your job about helping them get through whatever they are not trusting you about or whatever they are resistant about. Let me give you one example: A client may come in who really wanted to look at his life but he was very afraid that if he came in here and started looking at himself it would mean that I was going to recommend he leave his partner. What I had to do is let him know that he was totally in charge of that. I was not here in any way to influence him about what he was going to do in his marriage. I was simply here for him to find out what was right for him. You work through as much as you can or you're going to be in a power struggle. If you're in a power struggle over a long period of time you won't get anywhere. There's another part of this. You don't have a positive relationship all the time. If my client is coming in and I'm reminding them of some abusive mother, they're going to have a lot of angry, distrustful transference with me. My job is then to work through that with them even though at the time there is not a positive alliance. It's important to know you don't need that positive alliance all of the time. In fact, if you do, you're never dealing with anger or disappointment or negative transference.

R: Describe how a novice therapist might acquire the skills or ability necessary to establish and maintain a good therapy relationship.

P: At the beginning you need a lot of experiential time and then some help from somebody who knows how to unravel it and work with it. A lot of new therapists are a little bit scared about whether they are doing things right and that can certainly interfere. Consult your supervisor. Don't do it on your own.

There are some questions at the beginning to help you get into that alliance . . . very basic questions like, "How do you feel about being here? What is it you don't want to have happen here? What is it you're hoping will happen? What are some of your fears?" At the end of the first session I think this is critical for any of us to say, "How have you felt about this hour with me? Are there things that you have liked? Are there things that have been particularly helpful to you?" They know they have the freedom to talk with you about what they like and don't like, which means they feel safer with you. Those are the kinds of things that I work with therapists about.

R: Describe how you go about repairing a positive therapy relationship that has become problematic . . . repairing a rupture in the therapy relationship.

P: Putting it in terms of a rupture is good. Let me give an example: A client may feel misunderstood because I have misinterpreted something very important to her right at the end of the session. She may come back looking different. She may be more reserved and sort of tight looking in her face. You pay attention to that. It's not just what they look like, some of them come back and say, "I'm madder than hell at you." Go to what it is. . . . You let them talk about what the rupture is. How you disappointed them and what they're mad about. You give them the experience that so many people don't have in their families of being able to talk honestly about their disappointment and you be empathic. That will usually help heal it.

R: Do you plan for and discuss termination with clients and, if so, would you describe how you might typically do this?

P: I plan for and we discuss it. You're not asking how I know when it's time to terminate, you're asking how do we approach termination.

R: Both parts of that sound interesting. How do you do it and how do you recognize it's time?

P: This is what I talk with them about when I am reviewing what's happened in their therapy. The way you recognize it's time is that when people first come in they are feeling pretty helpless about things or are in crisis, and they don't know what to do or how to deal with themselves. In the middle phase they are beginning to gain some awareness of what part they play in whatever the issues were and, by the last third, they are coming in having dealt with most things and simply tell me what a good job they have done. When I start recognizing that, I do a summary and we decide what, if anything, we still have to do in therapy. That's how I get to the termination and let people know it's time to end. Then I'll set a time with the client, like a couple of months down the road, depending on who much of this we have done before. I want the client to have time to deal with ending with me in a positive way. Usually what I find happening is that they do a lot of regressing. I'll sometimes take six months to end. I name the time, like January 12th, so that they have a specific time they can relate to because it pushes them to deal with their ending issues. Most of them have never had a positive ending before so they are going to get a chance to review what was good. They're going to get a chance to look at what they wish would have been different with me. They're going to get a chance to do some regressing back to some old issues that we dealt with at the beginning. They're going to get a chance to say good-bye.

R: Do you typically set a date and, if so, can it be renegotiated?

P: It can be renegotiated. If you don't set a date and you simply say, "We will end sometime soon," it doesn't have the same impact in terms of what it brings up for them. . . . Both of us can renegotiate the date if it looks like it's really not time, but naming the date is very helpful. It gives them a chance to work toward an ending and just not fade.

R: Does level of client motivation for therapy affect the therapy relationship and, if so, how?

P: Sure it affects the therapy. If you have someone who's very motivated, the therapy is easy to do. There is not much resistance to taking a look at themselves, or at the past, and how the past is affecting the present. It you've got someone resistant . . . I can give you an example: A client may be returning to therapy for a second time. The first time was to please his wife. It was much more superficial. The therapist couldn't get him to go back and examine what was going on inside of him. He was wanting to deal more with what was going on between him and his spouse and how he was being pushed around, rather than looking at himself. He is now back, understanding that there is something going on inside of him. He is going right into looking at himself and the impact that his parents have had on him and what he is doing in the relationship instead of what she's doing. There's an incredible difference. The therapy is much easier, deeper, and more effective with someone who is motivated.

R: How do you proceed to work with clients when their goals for therapy are not sufficient for the needs they seem to have?

P: . . . I reflect with them what their goals are. I'll name with them what the goals are. We talk about what their needs are and then I'll say, "I'm really confused about this, let's think about what's going on here for you. The goals aren't meeting what your needs seem to be. Let's start there." So I get them to do the work around it.

R: Using the material they brought to point out the discrepancy, perhaps?

P: It is part of any ending. It is not just the endings. I help them see what progress they have made. It means helping them look at where they started, where they are right now, how they feel about those changes, and helping them feel a sense of mastery. I may have a client ending with me and we talk about what she could do that would best show her the changes she's made. What she may do is go back home and write what it was like when she was first here, what she was like, all of the things that she has changed for herself, and where she is now. She may come in here and read it. We talk about it. I do it in many different ways but I make sure that they know what they have done . . . that they can see it and take credit for it.

R: It seems like you make an emphasis on their working there, reflecting their own progress.

P: Yes, what they have done so that they walk out with a feeling of mastery.

R: How do you establish an alliance with clients as to the goals for therapy when a third party (i.e., a parent, a spouse, the courts, perhaps a HMO requirement) has provided a goal for therapy that clients are not committed toward working on?

P: I don't get any of the court-ordered clients like I used to. . . . The only ones I see now are when, for example, I may have a couple in and the husband or wife has an agenda for the other person. I do a lot of reflecting back to . . . Then I'll go to her and talk about what she wants and what it is like to have someone else wanting something different for you. I untangle it and help her take responsibility for what she wants and help him deal with the fact that the only person he can change is himself. When I used to work in the court system and I had people on probation, basically I would talk about the fact that I know . . . they would absolutely not be here unless they had the order to be here. I'd say that I wasn't any happier about that than they were and how are we going to make the best use out of it? That's to see if I could get a working alliance with them. Otherwise it's an elephant sitting in the middle of the room. . . . It's no fun for me to be in the room with somebody who doesn't want to be sitting across from me.

R: Do you ever discover that there is a third party of whatever stripe somewhere down the line in therapy? That you have worked with someone for a while and they say, "Well, it's really my wife that wants me to be here."

P: Sure. What I'll do with that is say "I'm going to find out if it's just because your wife is saying that you should be in therapy that you're here." Then what I go to is that "You know I'm not going to be as disrespectful of your feelings as you are . . . I will not step over your feelings the way you're stepping over them to be here because you're doing it to please someone else. I won't treat you that way." That's very powerful . . . I won't do it if they don't find a reason for why they want to be here themselves. It's very stunning to most people to say, "I won't do what you're doing to yourself, it's too disrespectful. I want you to think about that and I'll see you one more time so we can talk about it again but if that's where it continues to stay, I won't do it. You deserve more."

R: How do you make use of the client/therapist relationship as part of your technique of doing therapy?

P: I use that a lot. I work with transference and I work with it in terms of the present. If there are things that they don't like about me we talk about that. I use myself a lot. If I say something very confrontative, I will ask them how they feel about my saying that. If they're hurt about it or have a reaction to it, we deal with it. So on that present level very much and on the level of transference. If I am reminding you of your mother and you're having some reactions, then I will work the transference, "How am I like your mother?" They might say, "You know you're judging me like my mother," I'd be asking, "How am I judging you? What kind of judgments are coming out?" Then they start telling you how they used to feel about their mom. I use myself over the present and in all the transference.

R: Are there phases to the relationship and could you describe them?

P: Yes. At the beginning if there is a positive connection, there is often some idolizing that goes on by a client as they would do with their parents. For the first period of time the positive idolizing is okay because it helps you get into what's going on and they trust you a lot. But, you have to be prepared to help them look at the idolizing and look at who else they've idolized in their life. To look at what it is they're wanting from the idolizing because often they are looking for somebody to take care of them. As you do the therapy you move to a more equal place. By the time you end the therapy they are seeing you more as an equal. . . . You talk about it all the way through.

R: The objective of talking about the transference overall is to . . .

P: The objective of using the transference is to help the client sort out what beliefs she/he is putting on themselves and living by with little or no awareness. Without that awareness the choices they make are often determined by projections or beliefs they have projected unconsciously or created from the past (e.g., the client's parents).

Dealing with the transference helps the client see and integrate the past, use the past and not be the past. Through the transference you can help the client see themselves as separate from how they may have been seen in their family. They can begin to see how they behave in ways that can recreate the struggles they had in their family of origin.

The patterns of feeling and behavior that were creative defenses in the past are now barriers to living in the present. By the time they feel separate and equal (with parents and therapist) the therapy is nearly over.

R: Would you briefly describe the range of clients that you see? . . . are your answers only in reference to current clients?

P: I'm in the position right now of basically seeing people who are bright, most of them very motivated, a lot of them having seen therapists before.

R: How would your responses be different or would they be significantly different if you were talking about prior clients?

P: If I'm dealing with people in crisis that's a very different story . . . and that may be the case, for example, a divorce, death, suicide or some other life crisis. Then you become directive, structured, or whatever is needed to provide a feeling of safety and containment. At a time of crisis helping them function is the focus. Once the client feels safe and contained, you can help them understand their feelings and what the crisis means to them. Clear structure, boundaries, and predictability are important characteristics of all therapy.

R: Do differences between you and your client in factors such as class, age, religion, gender, or culture affect how you establish a client/therapy relationship and, if so, how?

P: Where there are real differences and people are concerned about my being able to understand that, I acknowledge that I have not walked in their shoes and there is a way that I cannot understand but that I will do my best. I acknowledge when I don't know. I acknowledge the differences. For example: I have a 20-year-old I'm working with and I'm as old as her mother and she is concerned whether I will be able to understand. What I am saying to her is, "Test me out and let's talk about it when you feel that you're not being understood". . . Whatever the covert differences are that may be a concern need to be talked about.

R: Is it tricky to raise that question and is it presupposed that there is an issue?

P: As long as you say "How do you feel about my asking a question," you can deal with the response. I would rather err on asking too much than to let something go because I'm walking lightly. Carefulness in therapy can abort the therapy. Make the observation, make the comment, ask the question, and ask them how they feel about it so that you know how they are reacting and how they're using it, don't be careful.

R: If you were in the position where you were talking to different master therapists, what would you ask them if you could ask them about the therapy relationship?

P: I guess some questions I would ask are: What do you consider the most important approach or intervention that therapists have to make in terms of forming the alliance right on the phone? It is truly listening, being interested, and feeding back what you are hearing from the very beginning. I have heard more clients say that they felt hurt, or disrespected, or people are too curt with them.

      Some of the questions are: What do you consider the most important approach or intervention that therapists have to make in terms of forming a therapeutic alliance throughout the therapy? How do you use yourself in the relationship? How do you process the relationship?

R: Often relationships develop over time, you're empathizing that right from the get go. How are you able to do that?

P: The relationship needs to be respectful, boundaried, and talked about from the beginning. This is what you can expect from me and this is what I expect from you. At the end of the first session you ask how he/she experienced the hour with me, how is he/she feeling, and do they have any questions. We are a team in developing the client's self awareness, and develop a sense of empowerment over self. The client needs to know that therapy is not something we do to them, they are ultimately the experts on themselves. We just help them find that self.

End of interview.

Master Therapist #3 (Mary Mullenbach, Interviewer)

The following is a full transcript of Mary Mullenbach's interview with one of the master therapists:

R: . . . what is your definition of emotional wellness?

P: . . . I think about one's ability to take care of oneself so that one has all of, or as much of, one's personal resources to bring to the therapy experience. I often think that we are our tools in terms of our work . . . So, for me, it's how to help oneself stay alert, alive, well, fully present.

R: Being able to keep a reserve of resources to draw from?

P: Being able to replenish myself.

R: How would you define professional resiliency?

P: I've never thought of it in terms of my professionalism. I think about it with clients who talk about how is it that they survived when their siblings are hospitalized or someone else committed suicide I often think about resiliency in that respect . . . but you're absolutely right, we have to be resilient, particularly when we hear so many stories that drain us. . . . Sometimes we have heard so many abuse stories that we feel like we have secondary post-trauma. . . . How do we come back from that experience rather than continue going in the direction of feeling that we can't do this ever again. What are some of the characteristics that help with that? . . . How do we not get burnt out? . . . resiliency is such that we can come back rather than get so burned out we can't come back. Tell me your definition again.

R: Okay. My definition of professional resiliency is simply a positive adaptation to normative and non-normative stressors that we encounter as professionals. My definition of emotional wellness was much like yours . . . keeping our resources at a level that enables us to be helpful.

P: Resiliency is more about the ability to adapt in a way that's helpful.

R: In a way that we're able to face stressors, especially when we're in a crisis. When you think about your graduate training or your internship experience, how well do you think it prepared you for the emotional demands of practice?

P: Not at all. I don't know whether that's a function of the kind of training we were getting in those days because now I've been working with some interns and it just feels so much different than our (training) was. It also may be that I was in a whole different place back in those days. I didn't have any idea what therapy was about, I had never been in therapy. I don't think I knew anyone who was in a therapy.

R: It was foreign?

P: Yes. I was a school teacher at the time and I was in graduate school to learn to help kids and their families. . . . I don't know that I would have recognized if somebody was giving me something I needed. It also felt, when I think back about it and when I talk with others about it, that folks didn't know much about what therapists needed . . . this was back in 1971.

R: Are you speaking specifically about the curriculum that was offered in the graduate department or the courses?

P: . . . I was just talking about the educational piece. For example, one of the things that drew me to the university was Don B.'s developmental counseling text that we had used where I was taking some graduate classes. I was interested in that whole aspect but no one ever talked about that as a model in terms of our development as therapists. Whereas now, Tom Skovholt does a lot of thinking and talking about the development of a therapist . . . that's kind of an example where it feels like graduate training is now thinking about how some of those concepts apply to us.

R: Looking specifically where the graduate student is at and where they're going?

P: As far as I remember. As I said, I may not have been aware or open to it either because I was so new to all of it. In terms of internships, when I think about internships I think mostly about supervisors trying to help us learn to work, learn skills. I don't remember any supervisor at the time ever talking about the personal journey, or noticing what my own struggles might be, or asking me about my own struggles. I think it was after I graduated and I sought out supervisors to help me with some of the work that I experienced more of that. . . . I really feel that's where my learning came from.

R: You've had a lot of contact with experienced therapists?

P: I think once you get out and start working you realize where some of the holes are, and what some of your needs are, and then where to get those met.

R: . . . that's a good lead-in for my next question. In looking at the early novice stage of your practice . . . those first five years, what were they like for you?

P: You know? I'd have to ask you to differentiate because the first six years after I got my masters, I worked in a community college counseling center. That was a much different experience than the first five years after I got my Ph.D. and I worked in a private practice clinic setting.

R: . . . Could you say a little bit about both of them?

P: Sure. The post-masters job was much less challenging in terms of doing therapy work because a lot of what was expected of us was more career counseling and advising. There were some opportunities for personal therapy but for the most part things were on a quarter system. Students would go; we were expected to refer people at that point in time. So much less challenging personally for me. One of the reasons I left it is I wanted to do more of the personal therapy work that I was having to refer people for. Once I started doing only therapy, what was much more challenging for me was the use of self. There was much less down time. Down time meaning doing whatever . . . the meetings for the college, career classes, and things of that sort . . . Those first five years of doing only therapy work were exciting because it was all sorts of . . . this is what I need to know, this is what I need to do, and working with people to learn it. It was being in supervision groups with people for the first time where it felt like people were willing to be vulnerable and talk about what they were struggling with and, not only was that okay, but it was expected, welcomed. That was very freeing.

R: . . . did you do peer consultation or was there a supervisor. . . ?

P: It was mostly group consultation . . . what I remember most is the group consultations . . . the group was really helpful . . . in terms of hearing other people's cases. We did some of that in the graduate program but not nearly as much.

R: It sounds like it normalized your experience . . . as a professional and then created a whole professional support.

P: Then there were two of us who began practice here and we were soon joined by a third. It wasn't much later that we were joined by two others. We've always met weekly here for case consultations . . . we've been in this practice for going on eighteen years and we've always done weekly case consultations . . . the kind that really get at what might be stopping us, what might be blocking us, what we might be struggling with. It's been really helpful.

R: When you think about your professional career, the whole span, what were the most challenging phases in regard to your own emotional wellness and professional resiliency?

P: Boy, when you ask the question I think every phase is challenging. Mostly because of the clients. What I'm really struck by is everyone has a different story and every year of my practice I've been challenged by some in terms of where they get stuck, how to be more useful in terms of helping them understand themselves better, and continually examining what is it that we really do as therapists . . . with the managed care piece coming in, the whole emphasis on goals and objectives, whereas before that time it was more a sense of just helping people learn about who they are, what their choices are, and helping that to unfold. It seems to me that there's a kind of constant challenge in terms of what is it that we do, and how is it that we do what we do . . . how is it helpful and how is it not? I can't think of a time that that hasn't been . . . helpful but also, part of the struggle. I come from a math science perspective where you did this, you arrived at this answer, and it was concrete and specific and . . .

R: Linear?

P: . . . linear, right. This feels so much more creative, much more that the answers will make themselves known. If someone struggles and has a process you need to have a sense of how to help someone be on that journey. I can't think of any particular time that was more challenging than another. It just feels like it's always been challenging. I think it's also why I stayed interested.

R: . . . you've changed throughout your career . . . you've met new challenges all along the way?

P: I can remember, for example, when I first started working with PTSD clients. We never talked in graduate school about PTSD, even some of the statistics we were getting said it was rare. So to have that whole area of mental health come to the foreground and there weren't any rules for how to work with PTSD, they were all evolving. We were learning along with everyone else.

R: You've touched on a couple of things. One is that a new diagnosis that can come to the fore and the other is . . . the demands of the environment. Managed care is an example.

P: Yeah . . . it feels to me like each stage of my career there have been many advances and challenges that I have to think about, integrate, process.

R: . . . When you think about your professional career, what issues have been the most challenging?

P: One that personally is most challenging is to move away from the position where I thought that I needed to have all the answers and worked really hard to know as much as I could. . . . Recognizing that our work isn't really about having all the answers. It's about having the information to inform our work . . . to really be more present with clients, to help them, and to really listen to what it is that they're struggling with.

R: . . . moving to a place where you use yourself as a tool?

P: And still needing to be informed . . . Not to stop reading, or to stop knowing, or to stop understanding but to use that more as background rather than foreground. That's been challenging to me, particularly coming from a math and chemistry background where knowing and being the expert was really important.

R: That's what you needed to do . . .

P: If you weren't going to blow up the chemistry lab, by golly, you needed to know a lot about what you mix together and how.

R: . . . you taught students so it was about delivery of information . . .

P: I taught at a high school in math and chemistry. You have people coming in who knew nothing about chemistry, about algebra or trig, and they needed to go out of there with a good grasp to move on to the next step. It was really different.

R: Very much so. How did you do it?

P: I think it's a long process and I'm probably still evolving. A lot of it had to do with getting help with supervision to challenge me. A lot of it was doing my own therapy work which was extremely valuable to me in terms of getting a grip on what's really important. Listening to clients, also, in terms of what's been useful to them and helpful for them. Rarely is it that someone gave me this wonderful piece of expert advice. It's more that I finally found someone who could listen or someone who would really help me think about some things I hadn't considered before . . . I'd say clients have been a big impact, getting feedback from clients.

R: . . . your therapy, clients, and supervision, maybe an underlying commonality between those three is that you're open to it?

P: Yes, I think that's really been helpful . . . clients pick that up and so they give you that kind of information too. I really think that's important. Being in a group practice has helped because it keeps you interested and hungry for what's available and it keeps you open. I've also done a lot of co-therapy. I've done groups, . . . I've done conjoint marriage therapy. That also helps me stay open because I'm constantly getting new information, getting new ways of thinking when working with someone. Getting input about different ways of working.

R: Can you describe the supervision that you've had for these group meetings?

P: The one here I'd describe as open, challenging, supportive, and thoughtful. We have five people who are all curious, hungry for new information, willing to share, interested in having others do well, competitive in the sense of always wanting to know what somebody else knows, not wanting to be left behind. . . . But also cooperative in the sense of sharing. I have this, do you know about it? I went to this workshop, would you like these handouts? That kind of sharing . . . then there's been the consistency over a lot of years.

R: I would imagine that they can serve as a check in point at times . . .

P: Yeah, "You've been saying the same thing for five years, when are you going to give it up? You never think that you're good enough, here it is again." Or ". . . every time you bring in something where it feels like you're just going nowhere, the next session . . . you see something differently or the client comes in and they're in a whole different spot." So . . . being able to watch themes, watch patterns. There's a lot of trust here which helps.

R: It's very nurturing?

P: Yeah. You can count on folks treating you respectfully, with confidence.

R: Could you talk about how childhood experiences might have influenced you in your professional choice and development?

P: I'm sure that one of the reasons I've been interested in therapy, and in particular family therapy, is that part of what I tried to do in my youth was save my family in every way that I thought I could . . . it was clear that both my parents were pretty miserable people. I hear that so often from other therapists . . . why they got interested in the field was in trying to make sense of what they were experiencing themselves.

R: It started very young?

P: Yes.

R: . . . did you have other siblings in your family?

P: I have four other sisters . . . all of us are in helping professions, which I think was quite common for women in our day. One became a secretary or worked in nursing or teaching . . .

R: . . . your childhood experience of trying to save the family, how did that impact you in moving from teaching to counseling?

P: I was always trying to make sense of the family. When I started teaching, a lot of parents would come to me trying to make sense of what was happening with their kids. What I was aware of is I didn't understand it myself and that's why I got interested, even as a teacher, in taking some classes to understand what's happening in relationships, particularly between parents and kids . . . So, just trying to understand that . . . the curiosity about my own family might have always been there too. I have several uncles and aunts who have suffered with mental illness. I never could quite understand what that was all about. I've always been interested in knowing more, wishing that there had been somebody there to help them, thinking that they would have a different life if somebody had been available to them. That was more in retrospect, I didn't know that growing up as a child. . . . I'd never heard of a psychologist, we didn't have counselors in our schools. I didn't know anybody who went into therapy. I didn't know anyone who saw a counselor. That wasn't part of my milieu.

R: You didn't have the model so it makes sense that you started in teaching and then gravitated. My next question focuses on work environment. What factors in the work environment help promote emotional wellness and professional resiliency?

P: What works is having other colleagues who are willing to share. Other colleagues who are interested in the profession. I've been really fortunate wherever I've been, there's been folks like that. People who are just excited by what they're doing, interested in learning more, wanting to try new things, looking for what are the needs of the population that we're working with. Those are really pluses. One of the reasons I got out of the community college is that being part of a big system was problematic for me because you had to be part of a bigger system serving on committees, being part of the nuts and bolts of the organization. I've always been involved in professional organizations. I've served on Minnesota Psychologists in Private Practice board, I've served on Minnesota Women Psychologists board, I've served on committees for MPA and for MAMFT. I've always been involved but that's different. That feels like it's more being involved in what we do as therapists as opposed to . . . being part of a structure. I prefer that, which is why I'm in the setting that I'm in. Working in the managed care environment has been both helpful and not so helpful. It's been helpful in that it's caused all of us to look at what we do and how we do it. Sometimes it doesn't feel so helpful because you have people who review your work but don't know very much about it or the client. It's all based on written pieces of information.

R: How do you deal with that?

P: Part of it has been to really advocate for clients where it feels important. Part of it has been to make alternatives available like sliding fees for people. Some of it is just coming to grips with . . . we can't provide everything for everybody . . . accepting limitations. I did some work for walk-in counseling for a while as a volunteer because it felt like there needs to be places like that where people who can't afford ongoing therapy can have still some assistance. Some of it is trying to look at what's here, what lessons are here for us to learn from so we continue to impact what's happening. We do that through some of our professional organizations. Then, even with all that, accepting our limitations. There are some policies that won't cover our services and clients just can't afford to pay so it means encouraging them to use the resources that are available to them.

R: . . . based on what you said, then, the primary factor in the work environment is having peer support?

P: That includes support to care for oneself.

R: So an attitude among your peers where it's okay not to work a 60-hour week?

P: Yes. We happen to be all women with children and that makes a difference in terms of thinking about career and supporting one another. Even if someone were here who didn't have that . . . we'd really support their recreational and life there . . . And supporting people in following what's important to them. We try to do for one another what we encourage our clients to do about themselves. Follow their dreams . . . Setting the limits, all those things. Being assertive, saying no.

R: The next couple of questions deal with difficult client issues and client behaviors. What therapeutic issues are the most challenging to your own emotional wellness and professional resiliency?

P: I think you touched on folks who were suicidal . . . that's just one that we live with all the time. The post-trauma also . . . it's impossible not to feel secondary trauma after a while. Those are two big ones that stand out. It's hard when families are falling apart. They've looked at everything they can . . . and it's not going to work. Even though everyone involved may see that this is what needs to happen, it's still painful. Part of it is also getting used to being with pain . . . That it needs to happen. It's still hard.

R: How do you resolve working with a suicidal client?

P: What's going to be a common theme is that I get lots of consultation so I'm not by myself with really hard cases. That's primary . . . It's important that I'm seeing things clearly and it's hard sometimes when you're by yourself. To have other eyes and ears looking at something with you . . . that's one major way. I've always had consultation outside of the consultation at my office here with my colleagues and that's been really helpful because they're people that have been in the profession longer than myself. They're people I can call on who have had more experience . . . That's been important for me. Recognizing what's important for people's healing . . . Like when you take your child to get shots, it's not something that you look forward to, it's not something that you particularly enjoy, but yet you know that it's an important part of child rearing . . . some of the hard things just need to happen. Not that somebody needs to suicide but sometimes people do go through periods where it feels like they can't survive. They need to talk about the despair . . . it feels important to be a person who is willing to hear and to not hold back or, if you are, to notice that and to be able to talk about it. All that helps me.

R: Understanding that it's a natural process, that is your work?

P: Having a spiritual sense also. That sense of being present in the current moment. I'm much more interested in an Eastern kind of spirituality in the sense of being present in the moment, not being able to perceive the future, not to see so many things in black and white, to respect the questions rather than the answers. All that's been important too.

R: How did you become involved in Eastern philosophy?

P: Mostly it's been just curiosity, reading; there are waves that sweep across the community and being aware of the workshops, a lot of thinking, sharing, reading. A lot of times through books that clients are reading that they recommend. I try to read some of those and to see what's speaking to them, what's helpful to them.

R: That's another way that clients can act as teachers?

P: Yes. No doubt about it.

R: Different life experiences can result in post-traumatic stress. Are there any particular life experiences that you found more difficult to work with?

P: It has more to do with when there's been a lot. For example, there are some weeks where it feels like you always thought you heard the worst that you could possibly hear and then someone comes in with something worse about what people are able to do to others that causes pain and distress. It's more the quantity that you don't have control over. . . . Now this winter, for example, because we've had longer periods of gray days than we've had for years . . . a lot of people were feeling like they were slogging through molasses. When spring broke, a lot of folks broke through that molasses . . . some of that had to do with what was going on in the environment. Again, it was more the weightiness of so many people who ordinarily felt like they would be moving along in their therapy work . . . That feels more problematic to me than any particular or kind of experience. . . . If I have five marital cases and four of them are moving along . . . and one of them is struggling . . . That's easier than if you have three out of the five of them who are struggling. Sometimes you have waves of that. That's what I find really, really difficult.

R: . . . you said something a few minutes back about what people can do to each other . . .

P: Yes. Some of it also has to do with how damaged the person is . . . and that goes back to . . . resiliency. It feels like some kids had more resiliency and were able to cope differently than others. When you don't have that resiliency and you had extensive abuse, everything is a struggle in the present. That's been hard.

R: What client behaviors are the most challenging to your own emotional wellness and resiliency?

P: . . . depression that doesn't lift. After all kinds of interventions . . . some people have had therapy for years before they get to me. Some of them have had shock treatment, some of them have had medication, and nothing seems to be helpful . . . there are some people for whom it feels like we don't have what's needed yet. Not just that I don't have it because there are also some clients who do therapy with a support group and they really work hard . . .

R: They've done it all?

P: It feels like it and some folks still are entrenched in the depression. That's difficult.

R: And when you're faced with those clients, what's your response?

P: Again, getting lots of consultation. Trying to get lots of folks thinking about this with me. Taking a piece of what we might be able to work on, bringing some relief in some areas.

R: Breaking it down and finding an area to focus on?

P: Right. That's been helpful. Looking at what other alternatives there are that might also be helpful . . . I've had some psychoanalytic psychotherapy training. Sometimes I think if these people could be in four-times-a-week analysis over a long period it would be helpful, but there's not the resources to do that.

R: Knowing that might be helpful and that you can't provide it . . .

P: What I've been looking at is more alternatives. In the analytic community we talk about having an institute where there would be people in training . . . to take a few cases that they do as part of their training to be an analyst . . . Sometimes I think that there might be some possibilities and I've been a real supporter . . . because that could be helpful . . . one of the difficult pieces is not knowing what would be helpful . . . But I also subscribe to the belief that each time the person comes away with something they didn't have before.

R: How do you keep the belief?

P: . . . you hear from clients . . . "Now I can have relationships with my family and that's been helpful to me even though I still don't feel a lot of joy."

R: . . . the next group of questions will focus on professional experience. The first: Can you describe a critical incident that occurred at some point in your professional career and just talk about how that impacted you?

P: A critical incident? Well, the first thing that came to my mind was my client . . . She got my name out of a phone book, she was extremely paranoid . . . she couldn't trust anybody. She knew that this was totally out of her realm to come to me. She was more paranoid than anyone I had ever worked with or experienced. It felt out of my realm. It meant trying to think about who could be helpful to her. I thought that she needed to see a psychiatrist . . . but she was also really scared to do that and trust again. I ended up asking the psychiatrist if we could do the appointment together as kind of a transition. It was a real opportunity for me in terms of the psychiatrist who had a lot of experience and was very comfortable with having me be part of it. This was early on in my private practice . . . his approach and attitude helped me with that whole sense of this is how our work needs to be. Where we're willing to share, we're willing to teach what we know, we're willing to be available, there's something that we can offer. He was available for consultation afterwards to talk about what he experienced. That was really helpful to me . . . to that part of me that knew I didn't know. It was helpful to know there were people that you could seek out. That was a early, early lesson that was extremely valuable to me. I'm appreciative of that experience because it could have been very different, it could have sent me down a whole different path . . . It might seem small to not know what to do when you're presented with this paranoid client but when you come from the perspective of you ought to know . . . to face that part of yourself that says, "Well maybe I ought to know but I don't know and who can I go to that might know."

R: . . . taking that risk and it worked out positively. One thing I heard when you were talking about that as a critical incident was how many times you have mentioned the importance of peer support . . . that happened at a very early time in your practice years. It seems like it reinforced so much of what was to follow.

P: That has been my experience with colleagues. If I picked another critical incident, it was a person who attempted suicide, didn't complete it, but could have if someone hadn't found her . . . again, the support from the community of people who were willing to work with me . . . The psychiatrist who's working with her medication, the hospital where she went for treatment, the previous colleagues who had had contact with this person, or people who had worked with suicide and were experts in that field I could talk to. My experience has been pretty positive in terms of reaching out for help and expertise in my community.

R: You take the risk to do it and you have an eye for people?

P: I hope that's true . . . it certainly has been a good experience for me.

R: . . . that's the message that I'm getting. What factors enable you to constantly engage in this process of attachment and then separation with so many clients over a period of time?

P: What happens in therapy is similar to parenting . . . where attachment is extremely important but so is the ability to separate and to follow a client's pacing because some folks need more attachment or they need to talk about how scary it is because of earlier experiences. One of the things we struggle with is pacing. Being willing to follow the client's cues without also getting stuck if they're stuck because of being scared; being able to talk about the scaredness too. It seems to me that all of life is about attachment and separation. Even with marriage there are times when attachment is important but there's also times when separation is important . . . where you're individuals and you have different needs and different abilities to be present. So that's how I help myself with it. It feels part and parcel with what's true in life. I think coming to grips with death is really important, being able to think about and talk about death which is the ultimate separation in some respects. It's an extremely important process. It's important that people are able to attach in order to work through some of what might not have happened for them . . . it's also important to be able to separate, let go, and recognize that that needs to happen . . . it's exciting in lots of respects.

R: . . . if I'm hearing correctly, you see it as part of life . . . this is what you do in general, it's what you do as a mother, it's what you do as a partner . . .

P: It's what we do as friends.

R: And, if I'm hearing you correctly, your job is to help client through that and to learn that process.

P: Without a doubt. I think that is what helps people . . . being with the separation which often includes being angry and being disappointed. Very similar to what happens with our children as they grow up. They realize you don't know everything and they passed you by in certain respects. That happens with clients too.

R: They get angry at you, get disappointed with you?

P: I think that can be part of it, the separation process. To be able to be present for that in the same way you were present for the attachment. That's where we as women, particularly, are challenged. Sometimes the attachment phase is easier than the separation phase . . . as much as you might honor and respect it, it still has a life of its own that is pretty rocky sometimes.

R: And clumsy?

P: Yes, "clumsy's" a good word, thank you . . . have someone who I'm in the middle of that right now. Yes, "clumsy's', a great word for it. As much as we know and think we know and been through it before . . . It's a unique experience each time.

R: It really is . . . what can you do to assist that separation?

P: One thing is . . . when it starts happening and somebody doesn't want to be here as much as they used to, not to see that as terrible, awful, bad, pathological . . . but what does that say about what's different about you now then before. . . . Sometimes folks could hardly wait to get here because it was so important, so needed. Now they have other places and things in their life that are offering that and to help the client articulate that, not be threatened by it ourselves . . . Not avoid it.

R: What impact has the constant exposure to the suffering of others had?

P: . . . Sometimes I question whether we even know what the impact is because we're still in it. It's like when I wrote my dissertation. I couldn't believe after I was finished with it what a weight I was under when I was doing it, I wasn't even aware of it until later. I wonder if we're really aware of what the impact is sometimes. I try to find places in life where I can laugh a lot, but I still think that spending day after day for so many years dealing with what's problematic can produce . . . a seriousness. And yet, seriousness isn't quite it. I know a lot of therapists who are a lot of fun; we laugh a lot here. I get teased by my colleagues who hear me laughing through the walls but still, there is a way that it's different than if you were spending your life singing or umpiring games. I just wonder what the difference is . . . also, we end up seeing a lot of change, growth, and exciting kinds of things, so there's that part that balances it . . . we develop a real optimism for life too because we can see what people do and things they're able change. I'm awestruck in terms of when I work with one person, the ripples . . . that sometimes they'll talk about their partners feeling like they're vicariously getting therapy too . . . I think about how they're able to parent children differently.

R: And that feels good?

P: Yeah, sometimes I think the feeling good part balances the heavy-duty listening part . . . I just think it has a pull in a different way when working in this field. But then we have nurses, we have doctors, we have oncologists, we have so many people in our culture who are also doing that, so, I don't know the answer for sure.

R: . . . what you're saying is that it gives you a different way of looking at life?

P: I think I'm a better person for it. I've done far more in my own regard than if I had stayed teaching or if I had worked in finance, for example. I don't think that I would have grown nearly as much personally as I have as a result of doing this. I've looked at myself more than I would have.

R: You spoke of the commitment you had to staying healthy so that exposure to the suffering doesn't wear on you.

P: We have a lot of fun here. We go on retreats together, we do outrageous sorts of fun things, we laugh a lot, and we go out to lunch together. I do a lot of physical kinds of things. I think that's really important.

R: What has enabled you to practice for this long and yet remain vital in the profession?

P: Doing a lot of continuing education . . . doing a lot of work with colleagues, not being by myself . . . doing things personally like physical kinds of things. When we talked about secondary post-trauma, there are some days when I feel like I just need to go out and kick something . . . biking real hard or walking real fast, doing things like that can be helpful . . . going to plays, going to movies, getting together with friends and just talking about plays we've seen, books we've read.

R: What kind of continuing education have you gone to, is it traditional courses through a university or is it workshops?

P: It's been more workshops than courses and it reflects what I've shared about myself so far. If you looked at what I turn in for continuing eds, there's a wide range. So, for example, I took training in ENDR because I was interested in knowing if it was going to be helpful to some clients who get stuck. I've been interested and have continued to try and stay with the hypnosis training. I'm interested in crisis kinds of therapy. I'm interested in relationship. I did the program in psychoanalytic psychotherapy where we did coursework over a three-year period every Friday afternoon and we did supervision along with it. I'm getting ready for something that looks more at the mind-body connection. . . . I'd like to know more about that . . . I'm just interested in some of those interrelationships. Mostly it's what's happening with the clients and then I get interested in what we know about that . . .

R: And then to work with colleagues doing co-therapy. . . ?

P: Oh, right. Like doing groups with colleagues. I've done groups with a number of different people. You do get a chance to talk about treatments, clients, and the work. That's been revitalizing for me too.

R: How much of your practice consists of groups and doing co-therapy?

P: Less now than earlier on. For a while I was doing five groups, that was with maybe four different therapists. As I've grown older what I've found is that I can't keep up with that many.

R: It's a lot.

P: It is a lot. That's forty people a week just in groups. When I was younger and had lots more energy that wasn't an issue. Now I find that it's too hard to do it and now I just do two different groups with two different colleagues. A lot of it depends upon my age and stage. I've always been a high-energy person; it's been kind of a humbling experience to find out that my energy isn't what it used to be. I thought it would always be the same. There's always the person held up who's climbed Mt. Everest when they're 80, or they're swimming, or they're doing marathons. I always thought that was going to be me. I'm coming to grips with maybe it's not going to be.

R: Is it just the energy or is part of it the level that you're working at?

P: I don't know . . . I think it could be both. Certainly, the longer that you work, your work goes deeper and you work with people in a whole different way than you knew how to before.

R: It takes a different sort of mind and energy?

P: Energy. That could be true but I also just know that I have what I call "fatigue flashes." I never used to feel that, but it could still be a result of the kind of work. I think it's also physical. I used to be able to do all kinds of physical activities and not get tired but not now.

R: What is your schedule like?

P: It varies a lot depending upon what's happening. I taught a class at the U. so I had a lighter load. If I'm getting ready to go on vacation, I might not take new clients prior to going. If I'm going to be gone a couple weeks I don't want to have started with someone who's right in the middle of some heavy-duty work and then be gone.

R: What role have supervisors and mentors played in your emotional wellness and resiliency as a professional?

P: They've helped me develop my confidence. They have been challenging but I always was harder on myself than any supervisor had been on me. They challenged me not to be so hard on myself, that's been useful to me. They've been willing to share some of their own struggles which also helps.

R: Modeling?

P: Yes. I remember a time when we were talking about the fear of having two people show up at one time for an appointment and the supervisor saying she had, that very week, three people show up at the same time and that was a clue to her that she was on overload and she needed to cut back. That was really helpful . . . those pieces of shared information.

R: Who were your mentors?

P: I don't think that I've ever had just one. Some people had one person that they feel really took them under their wing and mentored them. I never felt like I had that. Sometimes I wish I had but I've been fortunate to have a lot of folks who were willing to be there. I had two psychiatrists as part of an analytic training program. They were both very helpful, very good. To stay with the same case for three years with the same person. That was helpful . . . always folks who were willing to be there, available, and never felt like any request was outrageous . . . I've been struck by how committed people are in our field . . . you go to a workshop and there's 700 people all there wanting to learn, struggling to get better, doing research. It's a fantastic thing when you look at the commitment in people's hearts and their willingness to work hard.

R: Other than supervisors and mentors . . . what role have your relationships with other professionals played in your emotional wellness and professional resiliency? You have answered this . . .

P: The part of that I haven't talked about as much is being on the professional organization committees. Those would be more colleagues than mentors or supervisors and they were different than the folks here, but have also been helpful. For example, I've really benefited from being part of Minnesota Women Psychologists. I've served in a number of capacities for that organization and have always worked with other people who have been very good. Marriage and Family Therapy . . . the same way. I was on a supervision task force for Marriage and Family Therapy and it was hard-working, committed, interesting, challenging folks who were always a part of those kinds of committees. If I were talking to somebody who was wanting to know what was helpful, that would be something I would really encourage people to do.

R: How is that helpful for you specifically?

P: To be with people who are really committed to what they're doing. To be with people who are really interested in what we're doing. To be with people who are interested in brainstorming an idea. I served on a committee for impaired psychologists with a group of other psychologists who came from different areas. It's an opportunity to be involved with people from a cross section . . . other therapists in private practice whose paths I wouldn't ordinarily cross . . . to have all these people giving time and energy to thinking about what will make our work improve. It's just inspiring and, for me, it's invigorating and energizing. Just helpful in that way.

R: What role have your relationships with family and friends played in your own emotional wellness and resiliency?

P: I get a lot of support from both family and friends, a lot of encouragement, a lot of affirmation, a lot of recreation, a lot of opportunities to do some of what we were talking about, which is just to have fun, be physical.

R: For you personally, what factors promote emotional wellness and resiliency?

P: Reading does for me. I try to do some daily reading, it's a sort of meditation. If you asked me if I meditate, I wouldn't say I do, but it has that quality of reflection. Talking with other colleagues about things that I've been reading and what they're thinking about it. Taking time to go completely away like movies . . . I use movies a lot in my work too because so many people see their storylines and then they're valuable . . . with my colleagues I have a walking group that meets every Thursday. We walk and we go out to eat together. Things like that that I'm pretty consistent about and are ongoing, personal. We do a lot with family celebrations. Socializing. Having people over for dinner. My children . . . when they were younger we did some things that were helpful. Taking time to just play some games together. Doing something completely separate from work. I . . . got used to how valuable it was and how much I liked it. That's why I find ways to do that now.

R: So . . . having other areas in your life that provide nurturance or simple entertainment or release . . .

P: "Release" is a good word. Having time by myself is also very important to me because we spend so much of our time with others. I'm an extrovert but I find if I don't have some time every day just by myself it's really hard, I feel deprived. Right now I probably have about three hours a day. I get up early and my spouse stays up late . . . he has the evening time for himself and I have early morning time for myself. This morning I was up at five and I didn't have to be here until eight. I had a wonderful time . . . if I don't do that, then I feel wound up, too anxious . . .

R: There's lots of methods to ensure you've got the support . . . it's probably important to have variety and not rely on one main solution . . .

P: For me that's true. It's like what I was saying about all the various theories that I draw from, all the places that I go . . . I mean, that is who I am.

R: I picture you with a tool belt with all these tools . . .

P: I used to envy and long to be able to focus in on just one thing and it always felt like life would be simpler but, as I've grown older, I've really come to accept this is who I am and that has value too.

R: When you were at the point where you were just looking for one focus, why was that?

P: I felt like I could really hone in on just one thing to be an expert at it.

R: Then life would be easier?

P: That's right.

R: Part of becoming a seasoned professional has been to get comfortable with how ambiguous the work is and then really being able to appreciate that you like to have lots to draw from?

P: More accepting of who I am rather than trying to move myself to being something else.

R: What characteristics are especially resilient about you?

P: Characteristics? Probably energy level, even though I was talking about how I have these fatigue flashes . . . I bounce back though. I might have one and then the next moment I'm going to have something that sparks my interest and I'm there again. So, that would be one. I'm emotionally resilient in the sense that I can be with someone in their pain and suffering but then I can in the next session be laughing with somebody or celebratory . . . I can move . . . I could be struggling with a knotty issue and can be chewing on it but then have the ability to let it go and step back from it and know when to do that.

R: That's important.

P: Yeah, very important. I don't think I could do that as well earlier. What else? I have a capacity to roll with the punches. I don't get bogged down . . . I have an openness . . . sometimes it's caused me to not feel like I know what I know but it also keeps me fresh and open. I'm willing to entertain almost anything and I'm willing to look at where I could be based on anything.

R: So, you might question yourself and, though well that could be a drawback, it's also necessary.

P: I think so.

R: People come in the door and it's best not to think you know what they're talking about?

P: Right. Plus things do change, things that we thought we knew ten years ago, we don't know any more . . . I think about all the folks who thought schizo-phrenia was about mothers . . . and now I think, "Geez, look at all mothers who were faulted . . . And maybe some of them were fluctuating but how much of that was because of what they were dealing with. . . " There's so much that we don't know . . . It's scary sometimes to think about what we're going to find out . . . I just hold onto Maya Angelou's words about ". . . we knew then what we knew how to do and when we knew better, we did better."

R: Exactly. Who or what do you turn to for help?

P: Colleagues. I go back to the team . . . the first place I go is peers. It's nice when you present something and all four will say, "Huh?!?" and you have universal consensus. But, if everybody says, "Well, I can see it this way and I can see it that way," then you have more of a sense of this is what we're struggling with and need to stay open to. It's really helpful.

R: Are there ever disagreements in the group?

P: Hardly . . . they're not disagreements as such . . . More the sense of . . . someone saying I think about it differently or I'd go in this direction. Somebody recently was giving an example of something that she was thinking about it and several of us said, "Geez, we think about it entirely differently," and she said, "That's helpful because it feels like the only way I had to think about it was the way I was thinking about it and that wasn't working." It is an opportunity to challenge yourself. Those are disagreements but they're not hostile disagreements, they're not adversarial . . . still disagreements.

R: . . . how you would kind of summarize your professional changes from when you started eighteen years ago?

P: I listen more, talk less. I know what I don't know as well as what I do know . . . I've walked the trail with a lot of folks but each time I walk the trail it's different. Yet, it's different having walked the trail a lot of times than if you're just walking it for the first time. I feel less anxious. If I'd stayed the same I wonder if I would have this much enthusiasm and interest? I have more diplomas and clients now. More of a sense of it's okay to share . . . more acceptance . . .

R: Where do you see yourself going?

P: I don't know. I was talking to a 76-year-old who's still doing therapy and says she does about 12 hours a week. Someone asked her when she'll know it's time to stop and she said, "When I wake up in the morning and I don't want to go to work." So sometimes I think, I'm 55, people retire at 55, what do I want for myself? I still have a lot of interest in what I do, I feel a great sense of satisfaction for what I do. In terms of myself personally, I can see myself continuing but maybe a little less of it. My husband's going to retire in August, which changes a lot for us . . . I don't know what that's going to mean to me in terms of wanting to spend more time with him. Professionally, I mentioned wanting to know more about the mind-body connection. I can see myself professionally continuing to want to learn more about what's developing. I can see myself continuing to do more of what I do already in terms of couples work, individual work, group work, consultation, and teaching. I think I'll probably keep doing all that because I like the variety I get. I can't imagine . . . cutting all that out. Sometimes I think if my husband wants to travel more and I want to be gone more, I might cut out some kinds of things that I do to accommodate . . . I do a lot of long-term work and a lot of intense work, maybe I might not to be able to do as much of that if I'm gone more . . . I don't know if that will mean that my practice will shift. I'm hoping to do all that and I don't know what's going to happen . . . I just need to be open to it unfolding.

End of interview.

Master Therapists

AUTHOR INDEX

SUBJECT INDEX

DATE DUE
Fecha Para Retornar
